IMAGES of America

ASHE COUNTY *Revisited*

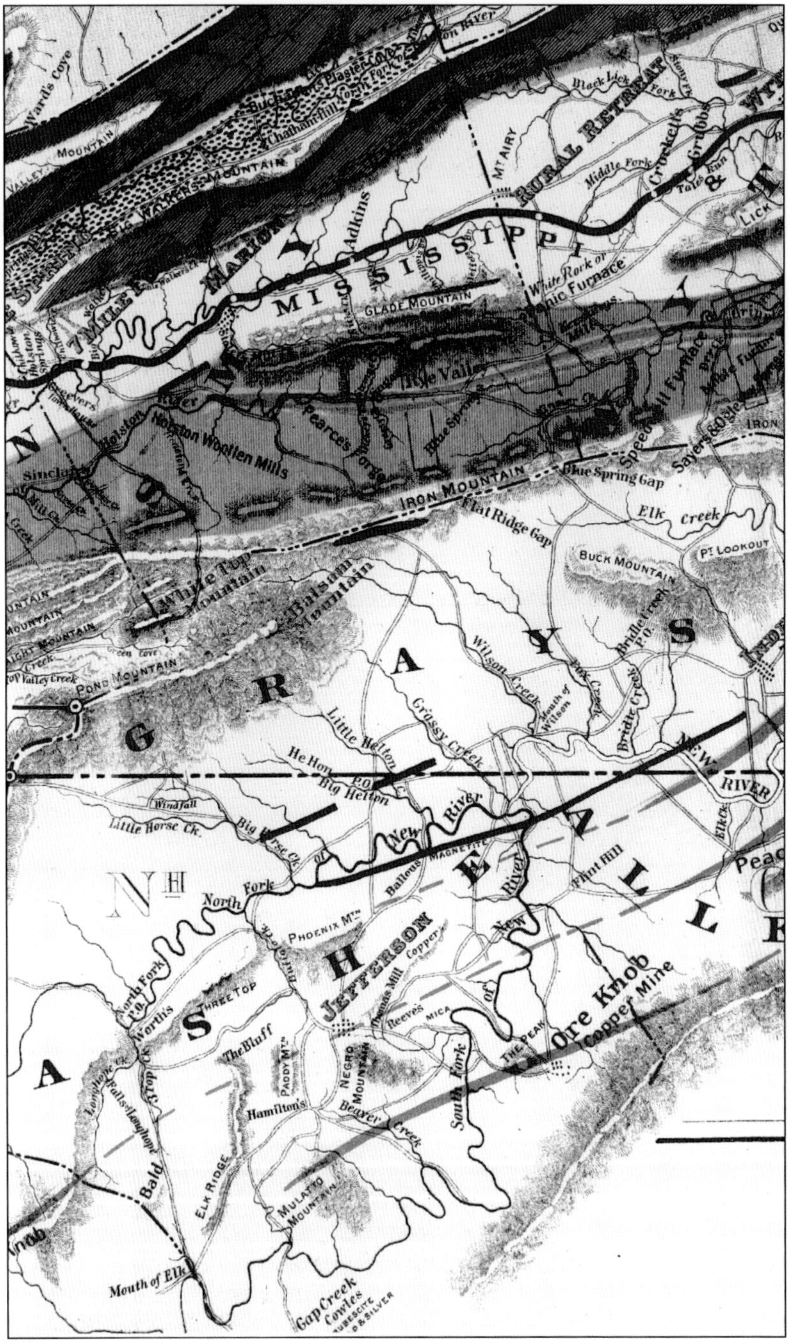

ASHE COUNTY, 1880. This early map of Southwestern Virginia and Ashe County, North Carolina, identifies significant mountain ranges and peaks, rivers, streams, and mines.

COVER PHOTOGRAPH. It was a spring ritual in the Big Piney Creek area for young people to walk the one-half mile distance to Raven Rock (pictured here) or Peter Rock to have their pictures taken. The rocks are part of Roberts Knob on the old William Roberts farm.

IMAGES
of America

ASHE COUNTY
Revisited

Ashe County Historical Society

ARCADIA
PUBLISHING

ISBN 978-0-7385-1450-5

Published by Arcadia Publishing
Charleston, South Carolina

Printed in the United States of America

Library of Congress Catalog Card Number: 2002106359

For all general information contact Arcadia Publishing at:
Telephone 843-853-2070
Fax 843-853-0044
E-Mail sales@arcadiapublishing.com
For customer service and orders:
Toll-Free 1-888-313-2665

Visit us on the Internet at www.arcadiapublishing.com

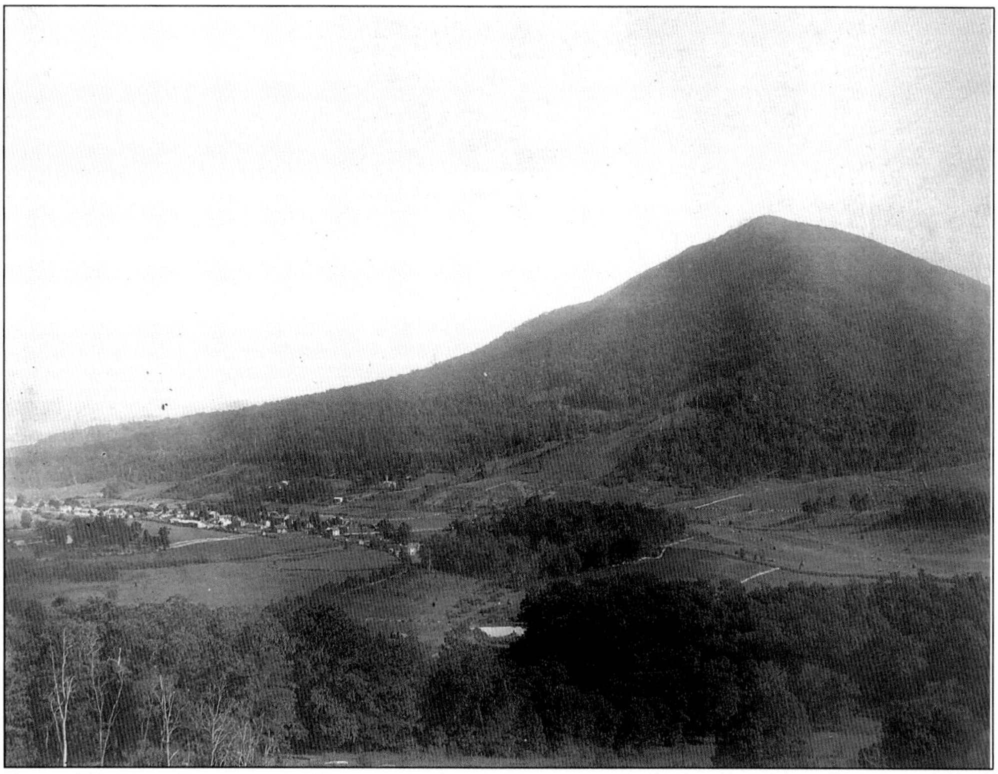

EARLY VIEW OF JEFFERSON. This picture, c.1885, was made from Neal Mountain behind the old Sara Lee plant, which is now Leviton. Mt. Jefferson towers over the landscape.

CONTENTS

ACKNOWLEDGMENTS

The High Country of Ashe County has long been known as "The Lost Province," referring to its inaccessibility. The nickname is a reminder of the physical difficulties that faced the early pioneers who settled in this region. Their descendants are justly proud of those who came before them, and as it turned out, one book was not enough to present their story visually.

To answer the call for more of the pictorial record of Ashe County, the Ashe County Historical Society has compiled a second volume, which contains different pictures reflecting life as it was in the distant and more recent past of Ashe County.

We are very grateful that so many wanted to submit their precious family photographs. Some contributors came through for us a second time, but photographs of many families represented in this volume were not available to us for the first volume. Contributors are as follows: Janet Auten, Sandra Church, Frank Colvard, Kenneth DeBoard, Charles Dolinger, Blanche Earvase, Pete Eller, Ruth Gambill, Dale Hamm, Annabel Harrill, Betsy Barber Hawkins, Mary Wilcox Herrin, Jenny Clyde Hightower, Sherry and John Houck, Ken Hurley, JoAnn Kemp, Shirley Killen, Iris Morphew, Frieda Blevins Patterson, Bruce Miller, Kathleen Perkins, Mary Gail Price, Ruth Rash, Virginia and Tom Roberts, Sam Shumate, Rufus Taylor, Leet Vannoy, Clarice and Jack Weaver, and Tom Worth. This volume offers a wide-angle perspective of the "Lost Province."

As he did for the first volume, Ed Reed gave us access to the fruits of his endless search for the pictures that tell the story of Ashe County. The library archives continue to be a rich resource and its staff is always helpful in our efforts to collect pictures and information.

Pictures alone cannot tell the whole story. Though this book is not in any way a history of Ashe County, the "wordsmiths" who wrote captions and introductions added important information to the visual feast. The "wordsmiths" are as follows: Frank Colvard, Lonnie Jones, Dolores Pitts, Sam Shumate, Ann Winebarger, and Sherry Winebarger-Houck.

The editors of Arcadia Publishing have once again been our trusty guides through the process. We appreciate the guidance of Laura New and Katie White.

The proceeds from the first book have made it possible for us to dream of an historical museum in the preserved and renovated 1904 Courthouse. Proceeds from this second book will also be used to further that dream, and to continue to aid the preservation and restoration of historical properties in Ashe County.

INTRODUCTION

The Celtic people who came to the mountains of Ashe County were drawn by the promise of land and an opportunity not found in the Piedmont and valleys of Virginia and North Carolina. From 1607 to 1725, there was little westward movement into this area. The values of the English and Dutch and other Europeans kept the settlers' gaze turned toward Europe for their inspiration. But during the next 50 years, from 1725 to 1775, the former indentured servants and the dispossessed, primarily the Scotch-Irish, Germans, and Welsh, looked to the south and west for a new life, one not shaped by European and English values.

Though access to the region was relatively easy from the north, it was almost impossible from the east and south. It would be years before wagons could come up the face of the Blue Ridge. Therefore, settlers spread southward from Pennsylvania and Maryland, following the Great Wagon Road through the Shenandoah Valley and the Old Warriors' Trail into a mountainous terrain, which, in many ways, was reminiscent of their homelands of Northern Ireland or Western England. Mountain peaks thrust 4,000 and 5,000 feet above a 3000-foot plateau, craggy rock masses, and rushing streams punctuated the sides of magnificent peaks—a land in which nature dominates the landscape.

Research by Dr. Charlotte Ross of Appalachian State University suggests that, contrary to a view of Appalachia as a land populated by an illiterate underclass, the Scotch-Irish, German, English, and Welsh settlers, though not of the landed class, were educated and had a history of a lifestyle uniquely suited to the mountains. The people and the geography were so compatible that, when other migrating settlers moved through the area heading further westward, most of these Celtic immigrants chose to stay and make the mountains their home. Living today in the valleys carved deeply into the plateau are descendants bearing the surnames of their ancestors who settled the valleys 300 years ago.

Throughout history, Celtic people have been primarily herding cultures, though quick to utilize elements of hunting-gathering, horticultural, and agricultural traditions to meet their needs. In the mountains of Ashe County, they were beyond the regulation of colonial governments and could build herds with a minimum of land. The herds were free to graze on open mountainsides and balds. The settlers supplemented their food needs with fish from abundant streams and fruit and crops grown in soil enriched by periodic flooding.

These hardy settlers built their homes and herded their cattle among some amazing geographical features, which in many ways influenced their development. The forks of the shallow river follow circuitous courses throughout Ashe County before joining just south of the

Virginia line to form the New River, one of those rare rivers to flow due north. In antiquity, these lovely streams were part of the mighty Teays (teez) River, which formed thousands of years ago. In this ancient period, both the Ohio and Mississippi Rivers were tributaries of the Teays, a truly huge river. In fact, there are those who believe the New to be even older than the Nile, commonly accepted as the oldest river in the world.

In some ways, the New River was a problem for early pioneers in the area. But the Native Americans and buffalo and other game they tracked had found the river and creek beds helpful, their paths along them ultimately becoming early trails, then roads and highways still in use today. The river and many creeks, all of which flow eventually into one of the New River forks, provided fertile soil to benefit the herders and farmers.

The mountain peaks became like friends. Early settlers, the Ellers, named one of the largest mountains Phoenix Mountain in memory of the ship that had brought them to the New World. The Peak towers over one of the more remote areas of the county, an attraction for local people since settlers first came into the county. Though the view from the top is spectacular, no roads go to the top; it is only accessible on foot. Traditionally, church and school groups have made annual pilgrimages up its slopes. Climbing the Bluff (Bluff Mountain) is part of the growing-up experience in the Buffalo Creek valley, and local residents have moved log cabins to its sides to allow closer communion with its unusual features.

This collection of pictures is assembled according to their proximity to the geographical marvels that exist in the Ashe County corner of the High Country. Within each chapter, pictures are arranged chronologically to give a sense of how, even though the lives of Ashe Countians have changed in many ways, the rhythms and rituals of their lives would be largely recognizable to the ancestors who first settled this area.

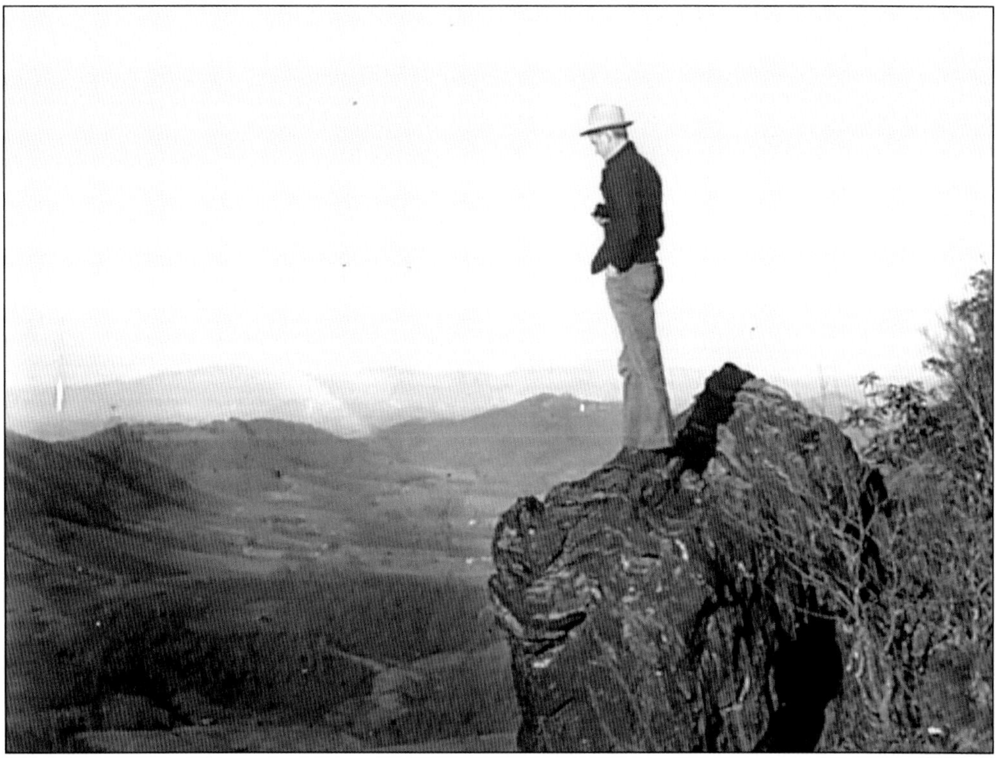

VIEW FROM MT. JEFFERSON, C. 1920S. A visitor enjoys the view of Jefferson in the valley below.

One

Rugged and Secluded

Northwest Ashe County

This area, which lies on and around Pond Mountain, is perhaps the most rugged and secluded section of the county. Though sparsely populated, it encompasses a large land area. It is blessed with scenic mountain roads, Big Laurel Creek, and several streams in an area that is rich in mountain heritage. There is a breathtaking view of four counties in North Carolina, Virginia, and Tennessee from the top of Pond Mountain.

The first people probably settled in this area between 1750 and 1760. Most of the first land grants mention that the owner was going to establish a sugar camp. Apparently, all of the original settlers were living off the land by hunting, trapping, and selling maple sugar. As a community developed, Thomas Sutherland was one of those early settlers leading the way to self-sufficiency by establishing businesses that would utilize the raw products that they produced.

Here, farming and agriculture is still a way of life. Growing Christmas trees, pasturing cattle, and raising tobacco are how many people make a living. There are no retail businesses located in the area. At one time, there were several country stores, but they have been closed for many years and, for the most part, the buildings were torn or burned down. Major shopping is usually done in Mountain City, Tennessee, which is closer than either of the Jeffersons. The community is made up of mostly full-time residents with a few retirees and people for whom these are second homes. One of the most famous of inhabitants in this area was Wilburn Waters, who achieved a widespread reputation as a hunter and trapper of dangerous wolves, bears, and other animals that preyed on settlers and their livestock.

Peter Jefferson, Thomas Jefferson's father, is believed to have named Pond Mountain. He surveyed the Virginia and North Carolina line in 1749. It is possible that the mountain was named for the two ponds that rest on the range.

—Joe Morgan

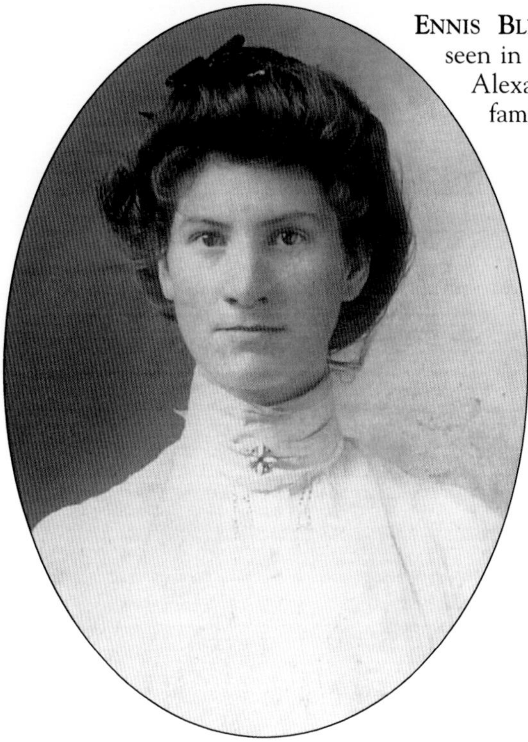

ENNIS BLEVINS OF LITTLE HORSE CREEK. Ennis, seen in this 1800s photograph, was the daughter of Alexander and Mary Miller Blevins, a pioneer family in Little Horse Creek.

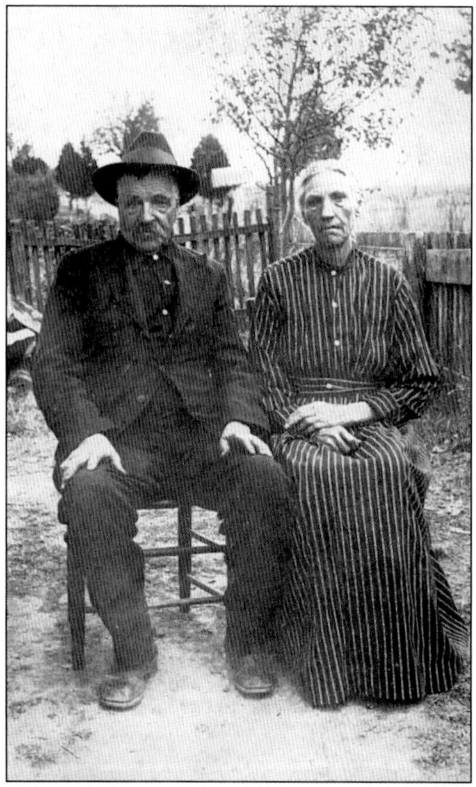

HORSE CREEK PIONEERS, C. LATE 1800S. Dave and Betsy Greer take time for a formal picture in their yard in Horse Creek.

THE SUTHERLAND SEMINARY HANDBOOK, 1887. Mrs. Mary Sutherland started North Fork School in 1866 at which time students paid tuition to attend. The school was college preparatory and offered a traditional classical education. Between 1866 and 1869, the North Carolina legislature enacted laws to support public education through tax monies.

SUTHERLAND SEMINARY 11

BOARD.

Good board, including room, lights, wood, etc., may be had at from $4.00 to $6.00 per month. Rooms may be rented for students to board themselves, making the expenses much less.

DISCIPLINE.

To accomplish the highest results good order and constant application are necessary. Hence the discipline will be mild and firm. Pupils will be expected to comply with the regulations more from a sense of honor, propriety and duty than from fear of punishment.

TEXT BOOKS AND METHODS.

In addition to those recommended by the State Board of Education the following will be used: Tarbell's Language Lessons, Robinson's and Well's Algebras, Well's Geometry, Collar and Daniel's Latin for beginners, Harkness' Latin Grammar and Exercise Book, Steele's Popular Physics, Shaler's Geology, Hill's Rhetoric and Literature.

That mode of instruction is adopted which will impart clear ideas and encourage a spirit of enquiry after knowledge. Thoroughness is insisted upon. Pupils will not be allowed to take up a new study without having thoroughly mastered the subject in hand. To test the pupils and to enable them to keep well in hand the work just done monthly examinations (oral or written) are held. The blackboard is costant-

SUTHERLAND SEMINARY 13

for the best oration delivered at the close of the school year

THE CARSON MEDAL.

This medal is given by Mr. A. S. Carson, of Sparta, N. C., and is awarded to the young lady who excels in elocution. Other prizes will also be given.

BUILDING.

The Academy is a large two story building furnised with all necessary furniture, and in every respect is a most complete and comfortable house.

LOCATION.

Sutherland is a beautiful village situated on the North Fork of New River, 20 miles West of Jefferson and 20 miles North of Boone. It is remarkably free from temptations to vice and extravegance. No intoxicating liquors are sold near the village, while the moral and religious advantages are the best.

With our success in the past and our hope for the future, we respectfully solicit the patronage and co operation of the surrounding country and no pains will be spared to make the school in every respect worthy of the highest praise.

REGULATIONS.

1. Recitations, prayers in the morning and other regular exercises shall be punctually attended by each student.

2. During study hours students are not allowed to visit each other's rooms nor to visit

THE SUTHERLAND SEMINARY HANDBOOK, 1887. Even though taxes had begun to pay for public education in North Carolina, in 1887 the Sutherland Seminary enrolled 143 students for the year, and, according to the handbook charged fees for grades 1 through 6, the college preparatory program, the music program, and room and board. Courses of study included business, teaching, and music programs.

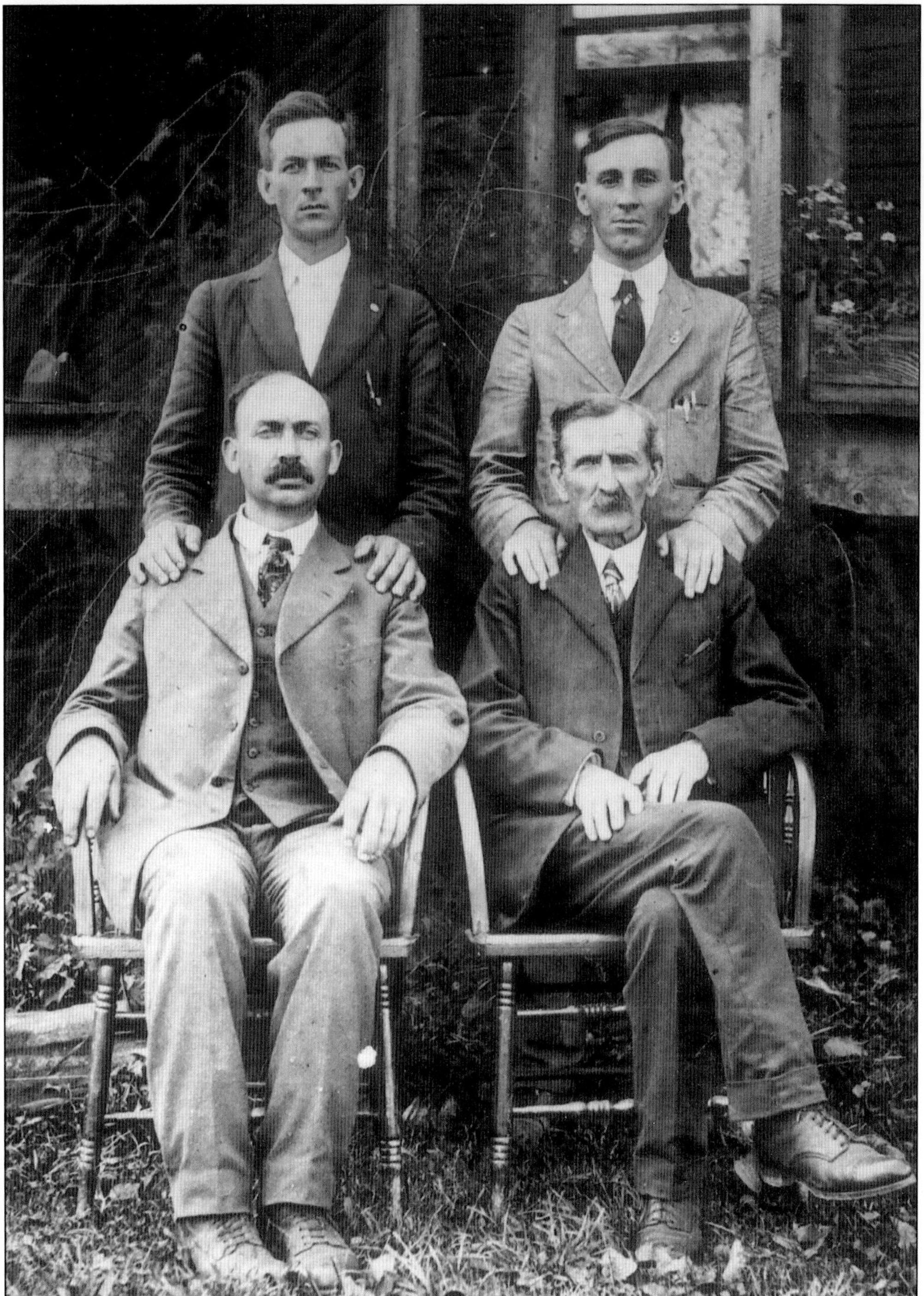

FOUR DISTINGUISHED BAPTIST MINISTERS. Pictured in this *c.* 1920 photograph from left to right are the following: (front row) Rev. Lee Dollinger and Rev. Franklin Barker; (back row) Rev. W.E. Denny and Rev. LeFord Stike. W.E. Denny, who served 18 different churches during his career, was an influential member of the Baptist Association from 1912 until 1962.

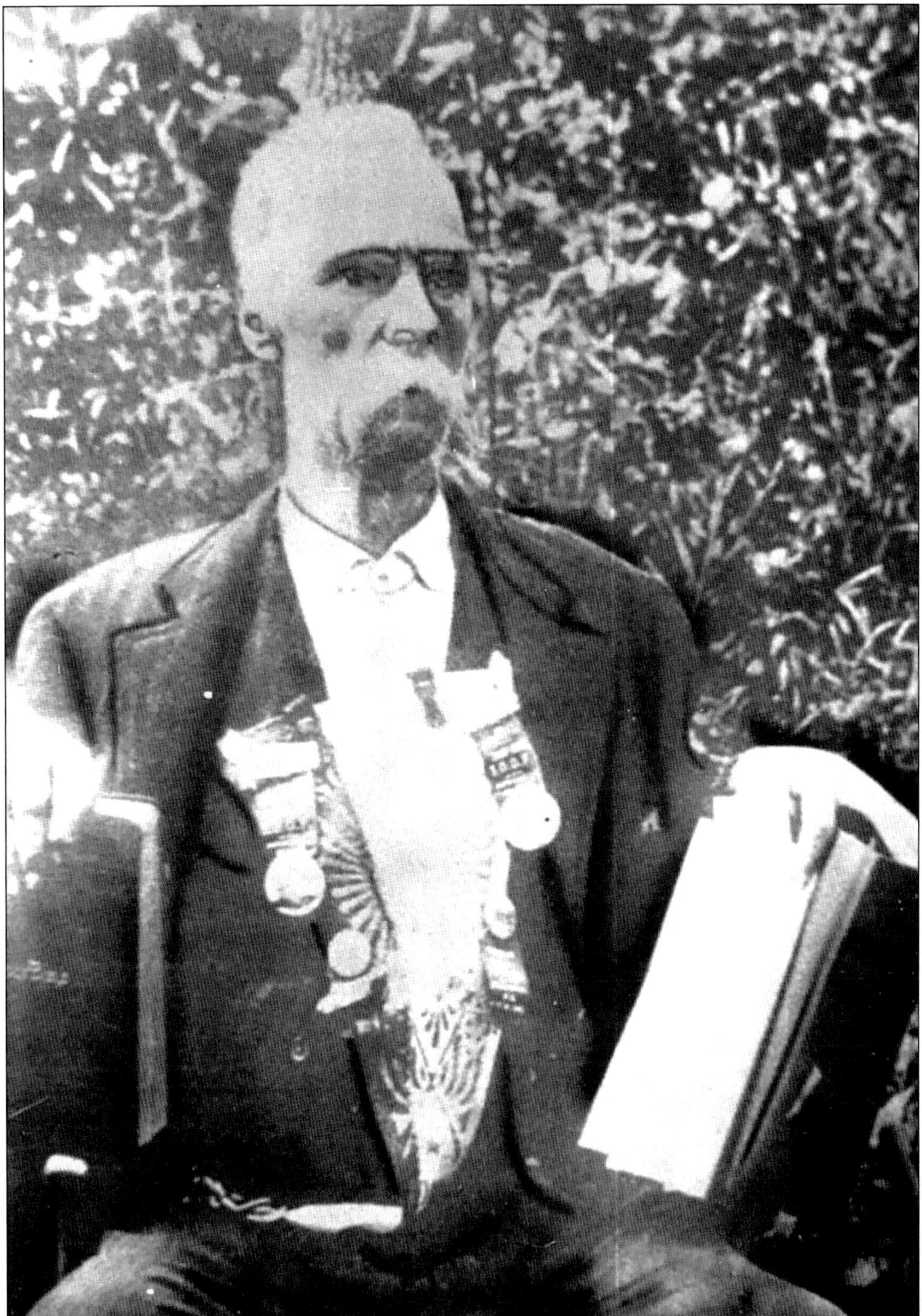

WILLIAM JOHNSTON ROBERTS, C. 1900. Roberts was a Civil War veteran and 32nd degree Mason. He operated the Roberts Post Office, which later became part of the Grassy Creek Post Office and the Lansing Post Office.

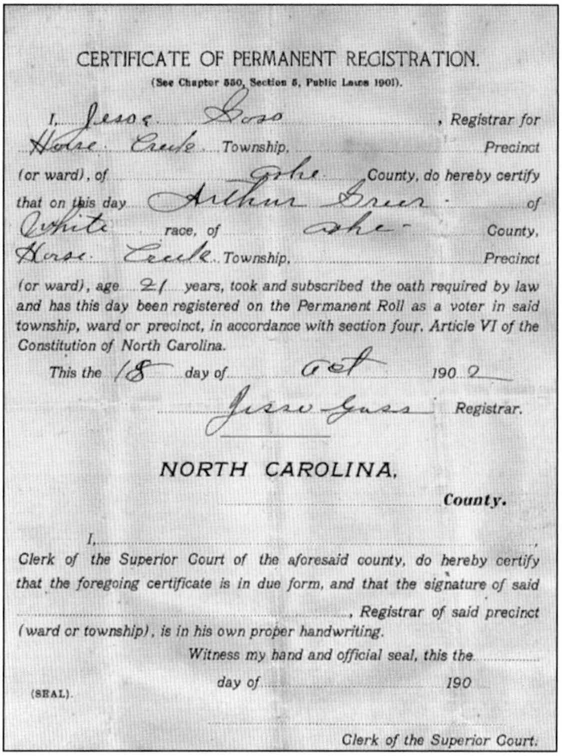

CERTIFICATE OF PERMANENT REGISTRATION.

(See Chapter 550, Section 5, Public Laws 1901).

I, Jesse Goss, Registrar for Horse Creek Township, Precinct (or ward), of Ashe County, do hereby certify that on this day Arthur Greer of White race, of Ashe County, Horse Creek Township, Precinct (or ward), age 21 years, took and subscribed the oath required by law and has this day been registered on the Permanent Roll as a voter in said township, ward or precinct, in accordance with section four, Article VI of the Constitution of North Carolina.

This the 18 day of Oct 1902

Jesse Goss Registrar.

NORTH CAROLINA,

County.

I, ..., Clerk of the Superior Court of the aforesaid county, do hereby certify that the foregoing certificate is in due form, and that the signature of said ......, Registrar of said precinct (ward or township), is in his own proper handwriting.

Witness my hand and official seal, this the ...... day of 190

(SEAL).

Clerk of the Superior Court.

CERTIFICATE OF REGISTRATION. In 1902, on his 21st birthday, Arthur Greer placed his name on the official voter roll of Horse Creek Township.

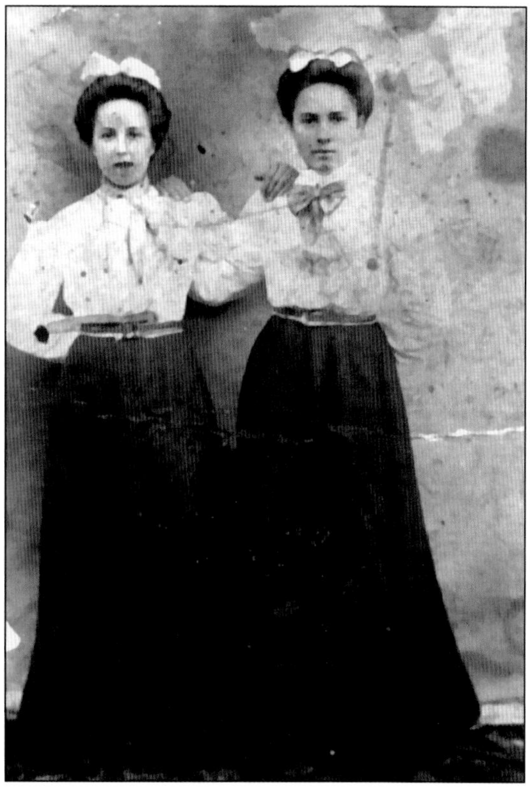

HATTIE AND MINNIE GREER. Hattie and Minnie, pictured here *c.* 1911, were the daughters of Alex and Lou Glenn Greer. These two young ladies were raised in the Fairview community.

CHARLES MILLER, EARLY RESIDENT OF LITTLE HORSE CREEK. Miller, pictured here *c*. 1900, was both a musician and carpenter. He built his home in 1905 with timber cut from the mountain. He also helped build the wooden barracks at Fort Bragg in the early 1940s. He made musical instruments and furniture and was the leader and guitarist of the band, the Carolina Night Hawks, which recorded "Governor Al Smith for President" on the Columbia label.

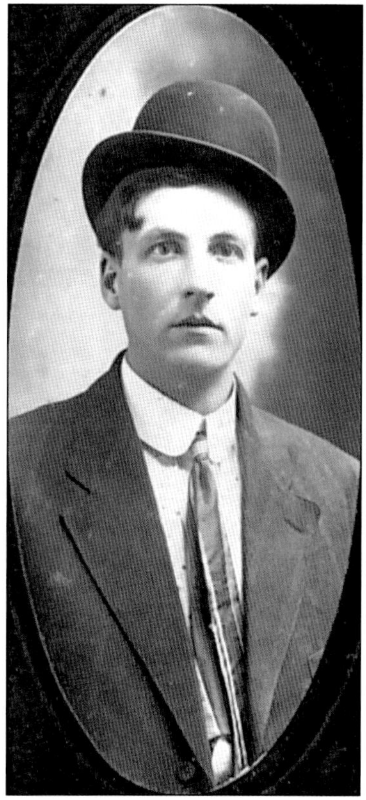

THE MILLERS OF STAGG CREEK, C. 1900. Pictured from left to right are (seated) Monroe Miller, Amanda, and Robert; (standing) Vaughn, Charles, Mary, and Mattie. The oldest son, James, is not pictured.

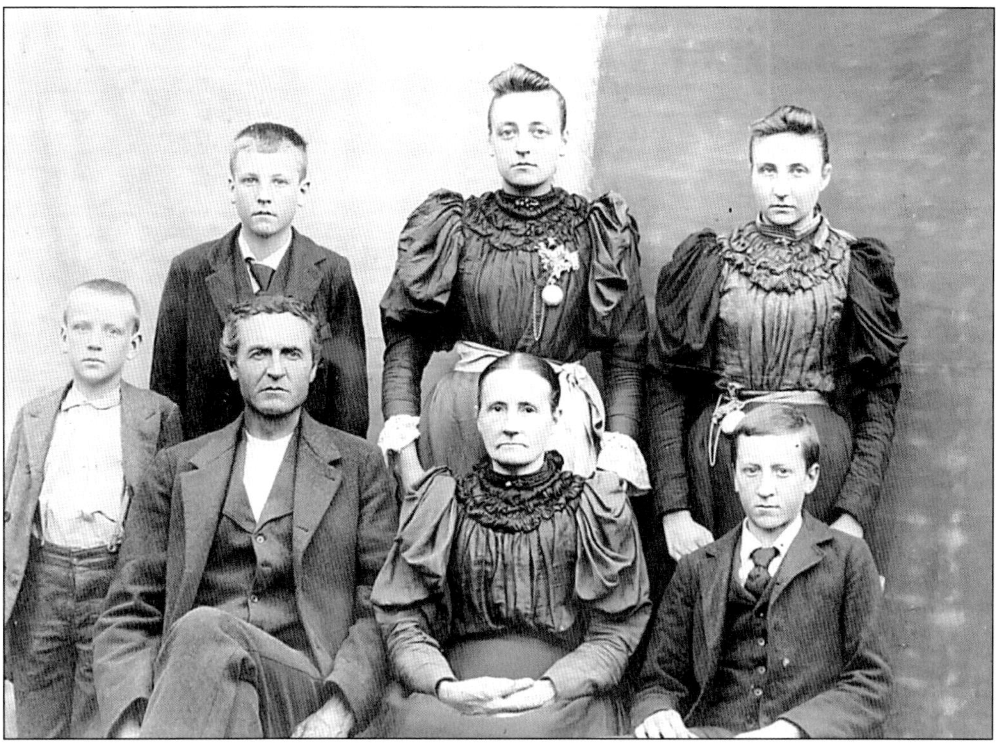

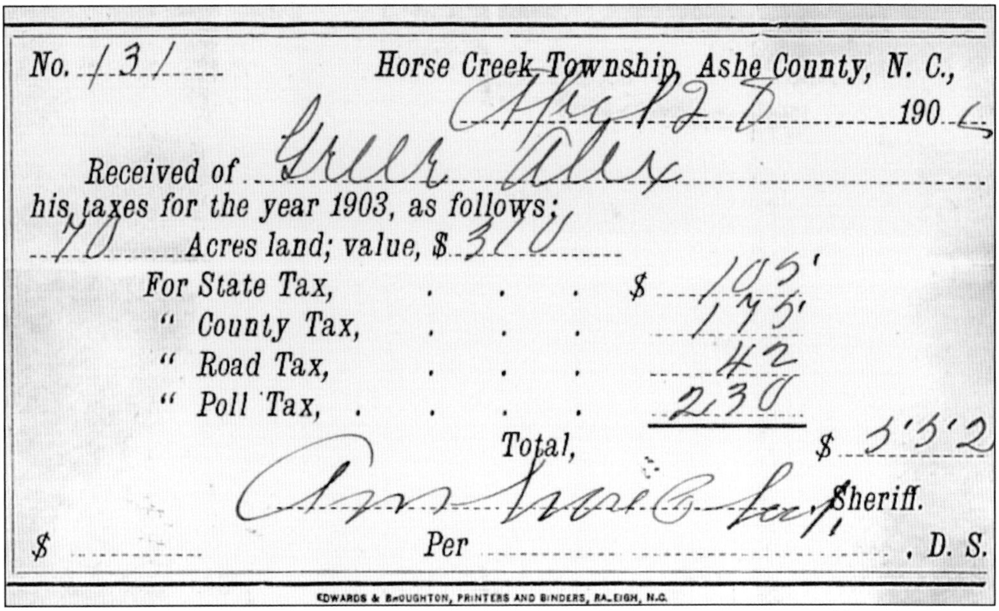

No. 131 Horse Creek Township, Ashe County, N. C., Apr 28 1906

Received of Greer Alex

his taxes for the year 1903, as follows;

70 Acres land; value, $ 310

For State Tax,	$	105
" County Tax,		175
" Road Tax,		42
" Poll Tax,		230
Total,	$	552

[illegible], Sheriff.

$ Per , D. S.

EDWARDS & BROUGHTON, PRINTERS AND BINDERS, RALEIGH, N.C.

MANY TAXES IN 1903. Alex Greer's receipt for taxes is based on the 70 acres of land he owned in Horse Creek Township. The importance of building new roads and improving existing ones is reflected in the road tax.

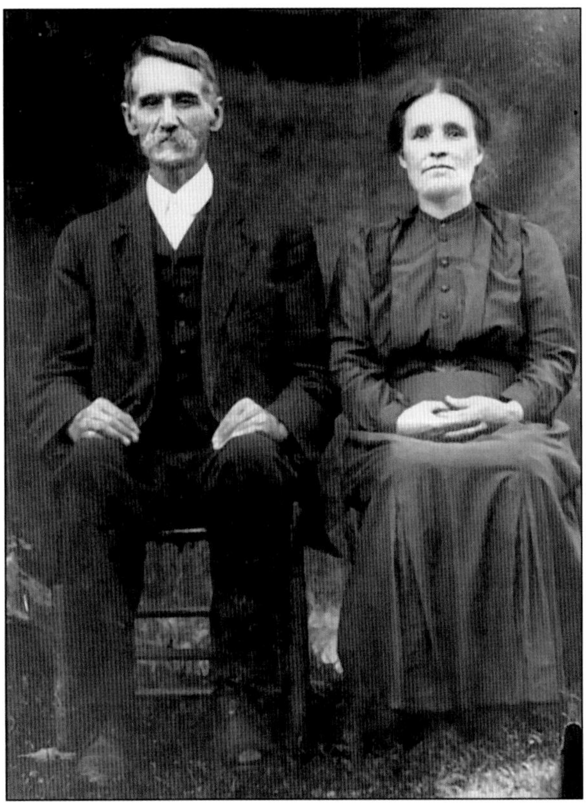

HUGH AND SARAH PORTER BARKER, C. 1900. The Barkers, who lived in the Hurricane Township, had five sons in the Civil War. Only two returned from the war to Ashe County.

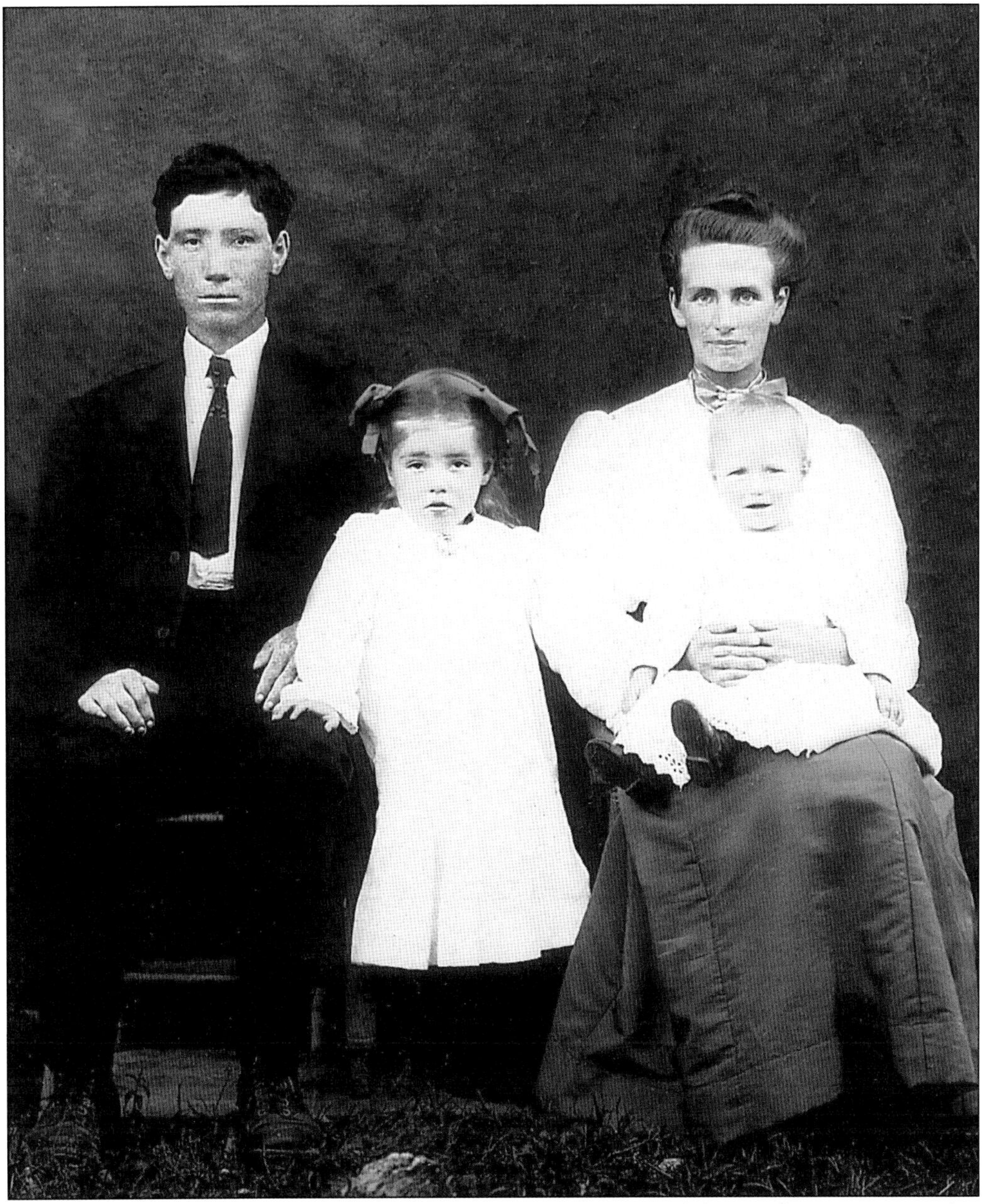

TAYLOR FAMILY OF POND MOUNTAIN, C. 1913. Pictured from left to right are H.H. Taylor, Lura, and Eliza Jane holding Rhea.

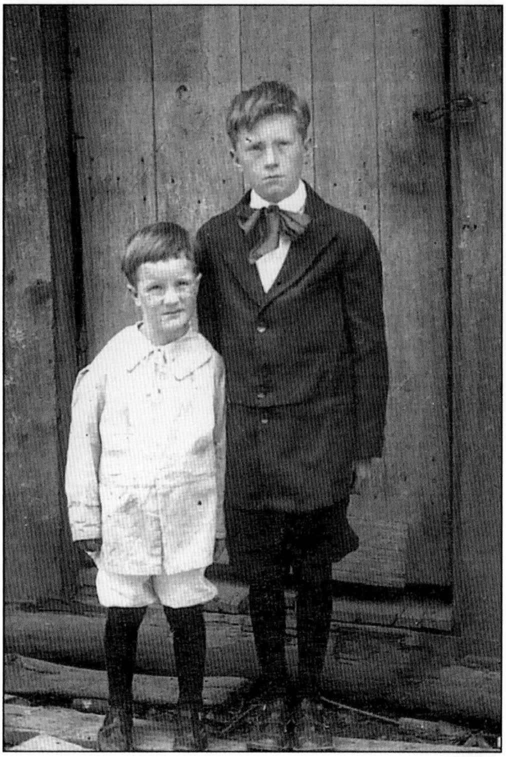

STANTON AND WORTH BLEVINS. Pictured above, *c.* 1910, from left to right are Stanton and Worth Lambert Blevins, sons of Ennis Blevins. They lived in the Little Horse Creek community.

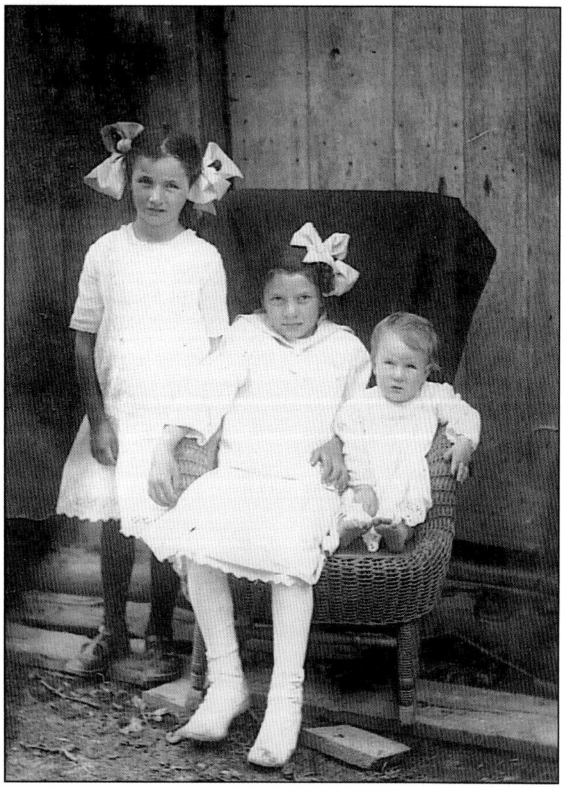

ENNIS BLEVINS'S DAUGHTERS, C. 1918. Pictured from left to right are Eileen Gladys Blevins, Vivian Arlene Blevins, and Violet Blevins.

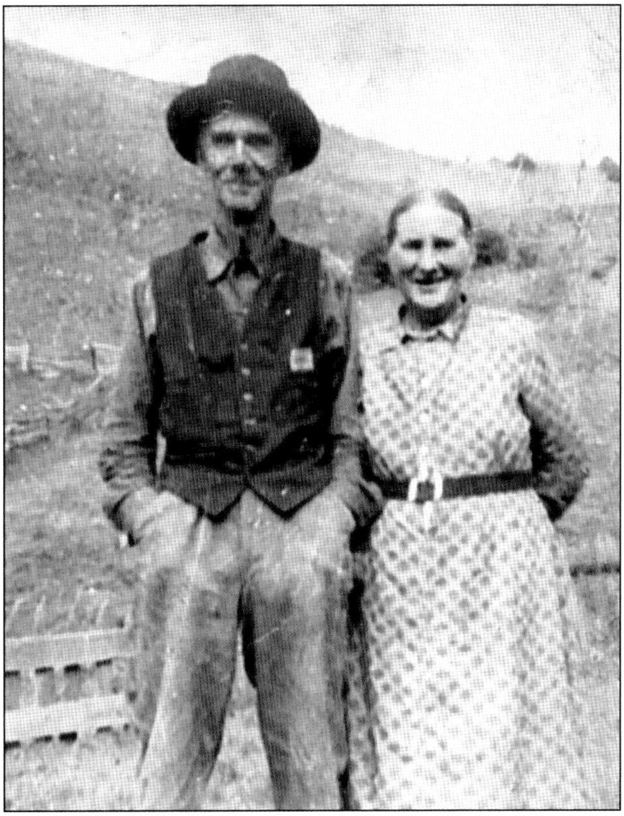

ALEXANDER AND LOUCRECIA GREER OF FAIRVIEW. Lou, pictured here c. 1918, was known as "Aunt Lou." She was a midwife who assisted with the births of more than a thousand babies. Her yard was a gathering place for her grandchildren and neighborhood children.

FOUR TUCKERDALE FRIENDS, C. 1915. Sam Gambill, pictured on the left holding his son Scott, died during the Bataan death march early in World War II. The picture includes Cleve Jones and Zeke Powers.

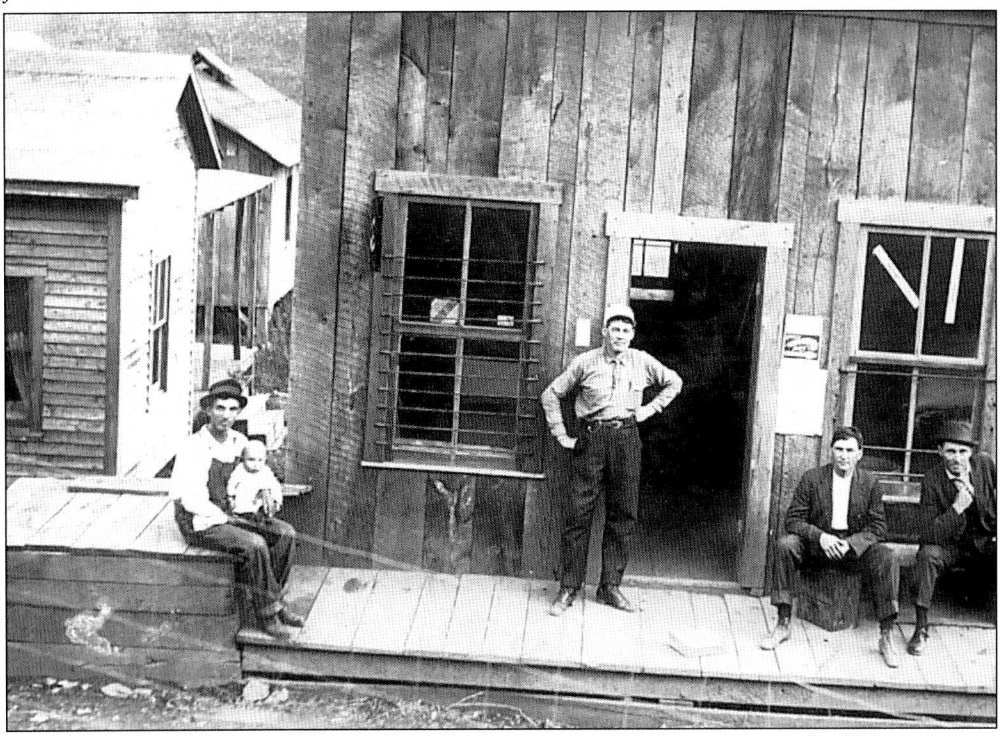

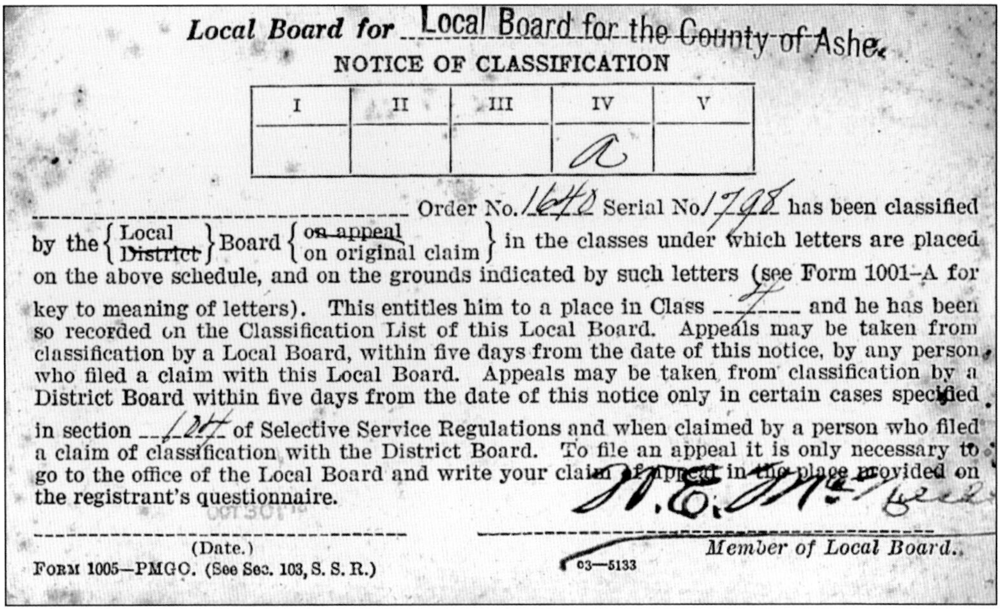

Local Board for Local Board for the County of Ashe

NOTICE OF CLASSIFICATION

I	II	III	IV	V
			a	

________________ Order No. 1640 Serial No 1798 has been classified by the { Local / ~~District~~ } Board { ~~on appeal~~ / on original claim } in the classes under which letters are placed on the above schedule, and on the grounds indicated by such letters (see Form 1001-A for key to meaning of letters). This entitles him to a place in Class 4 and he has been so recorded on the Classification List of this Local Board. Appeals may be taken from classification by a Local Board, within five days from the date of this notice, by any person who filed a claim with this Local Board. Appeals may be taken from classification by a District Board within five days from the date of this notice only in certain cases specified in section 124 of Selective Service Regulations and when claimed by a person who filed a claim of classification with the District Board. To file an appeal it is only necessary to go to the office of the Local Board and write your claim of appeal in the place provided on the registrant's questionnaire.

(Date.) *Member of Local Board.*

FORM 1005—PMGO. (See Sec. 103, S. S. R.) 03—5133

WORLD WAR I DRAFT NOTICE. Harrison Taylor of Horse Creek is notified he is IV A in 1918. Because of poor health, he was never drafted.

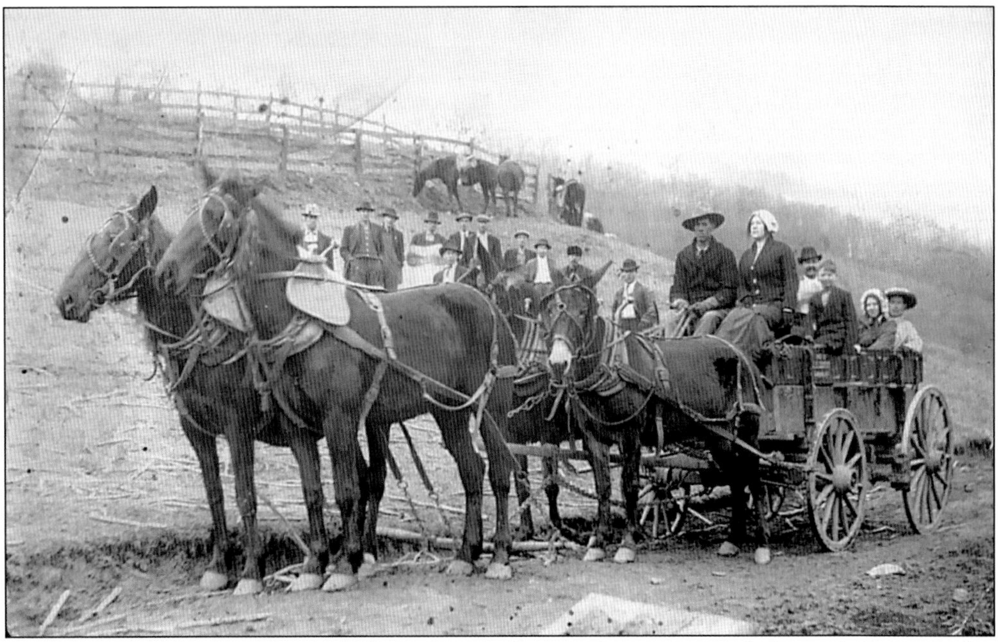

GOING TO CHURCH, 1916. Charles Davis is driving the wagon with his wife Betty Miller Davis seated beside him. They are going to Lansing to bid on lots.

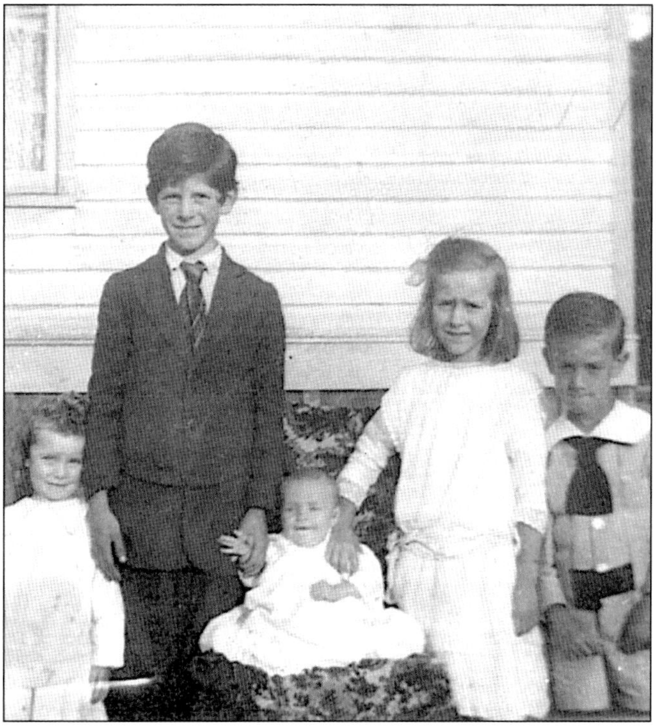

FIELDON AND SIRENA THOMAS SHEPHERD'S CHILDREN, C. 1928. Pictured from left to right are Ruby Elizabeth Shepherd, Roy Stacey Shepherd, Lenna Florence Shepherd Drain, Flossie Amanda Shepherd Wade, and Grady John Shepherd.

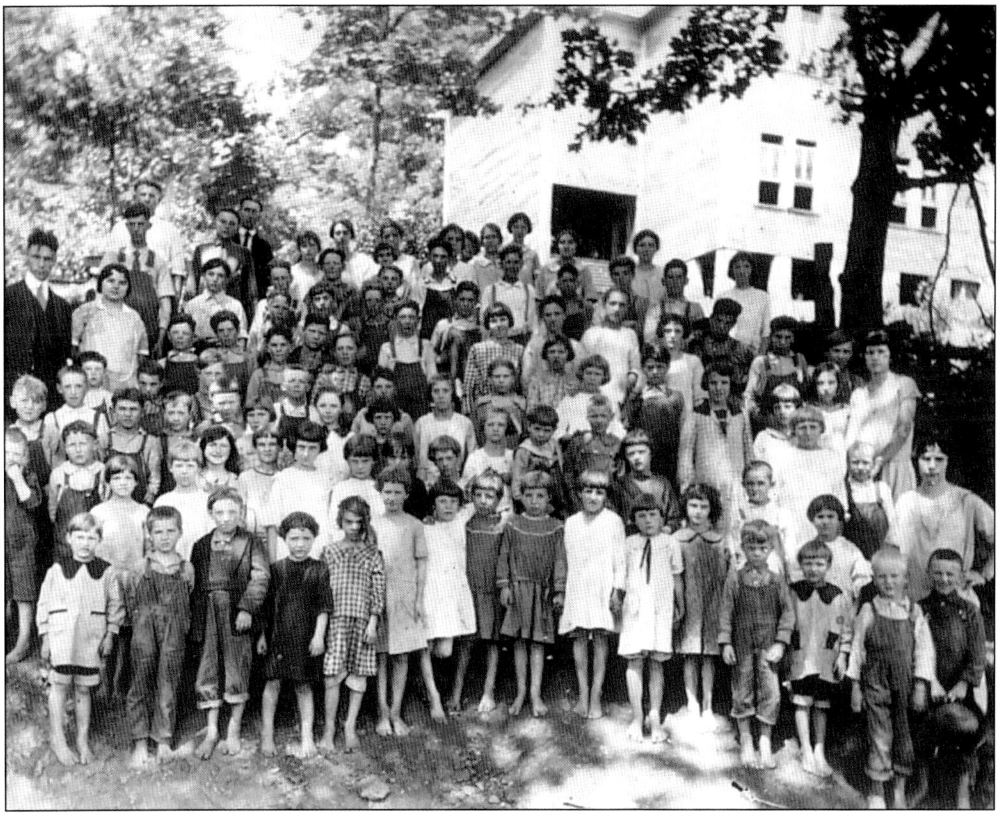

STAGG CREEK SCHOOL GROUP. The schoolhouse, pictured here in the mid-1920s, was located near the Comet Post Office on Stagg Creek Road.

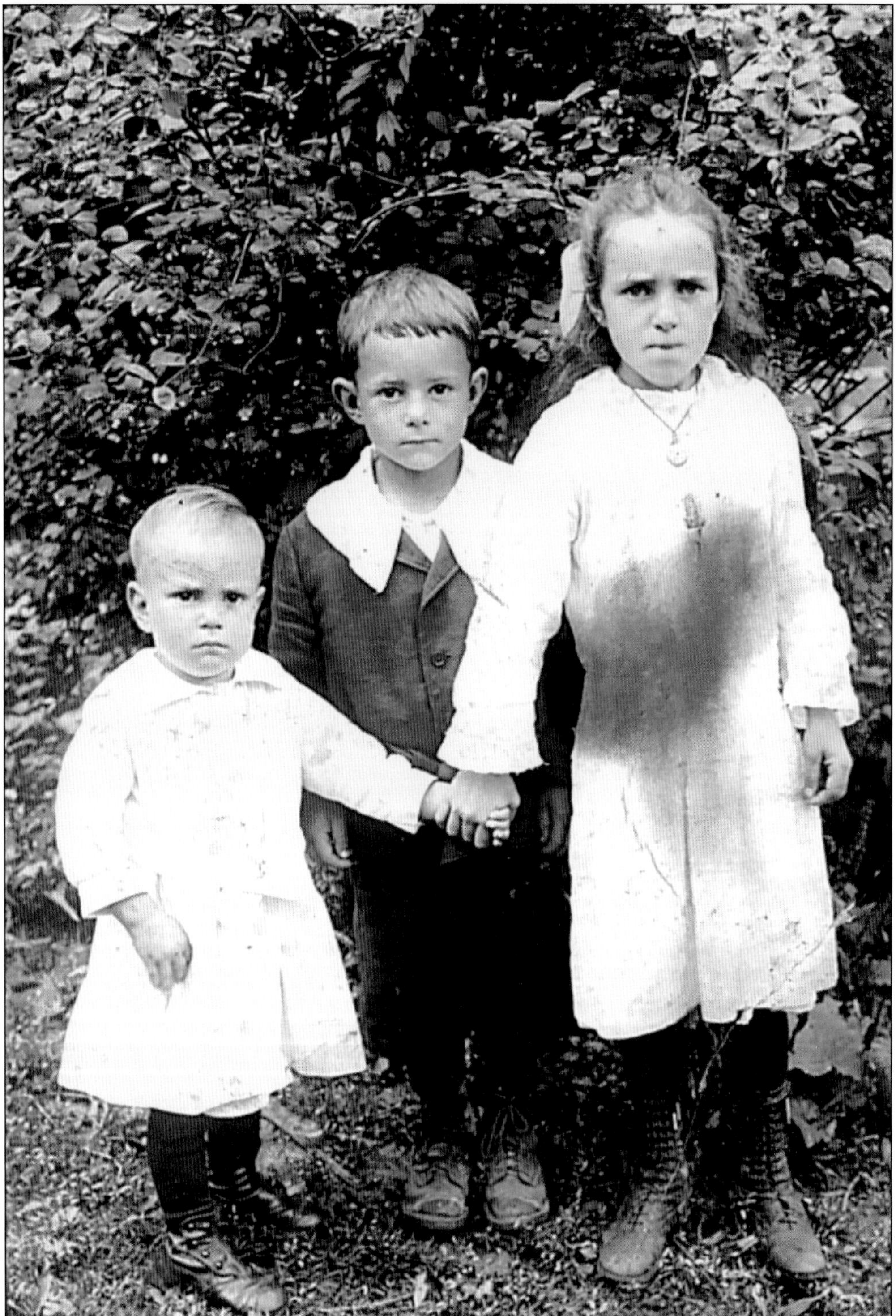

CHILDREN OF LITTLE HORSE CREEK, C. 1921. Pictured from left to right are Gaither Lee Barker, Blaine Barker, and Stella Barker Hamm, children of Lester and Minnie Greer Barker.

CHARLES MILLER'S HANDIWORK. Made of cherry wood, this chest is an example of the fine furniture created by mountain craftsmen. Miller also made musical instruments and other types of furniture. Though the chest was constructed in the 1920s, the picture dates from 1960s.

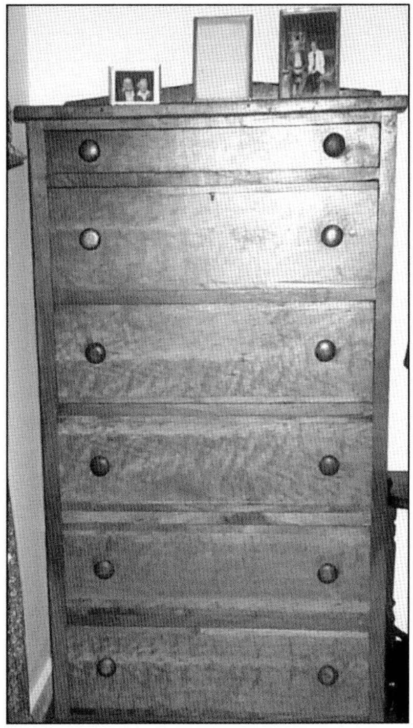

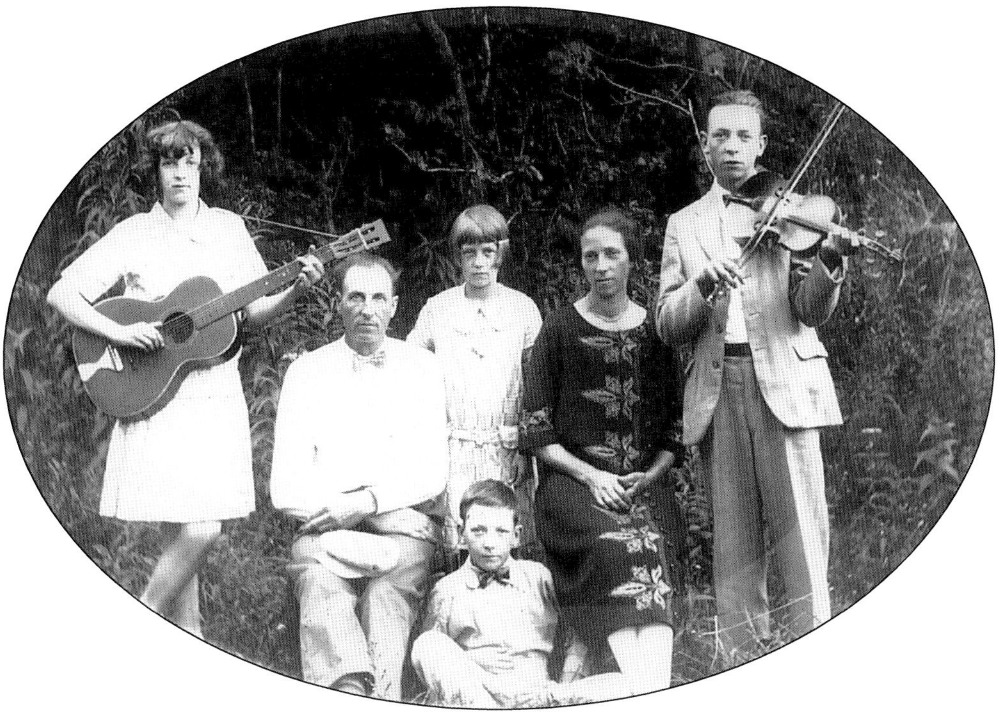

THE MUSICAL MILLER FAMILY, C. 1932. Pictured from left to right are Ella Mae Miller, Charles Miller (father), Lilly Miller, Clifford Miller (seated), Hattie Miller, and Howard Miller. Charles was the leader of the band The Carolina Night Hawks. Howard was the only other family member who also played in the band.

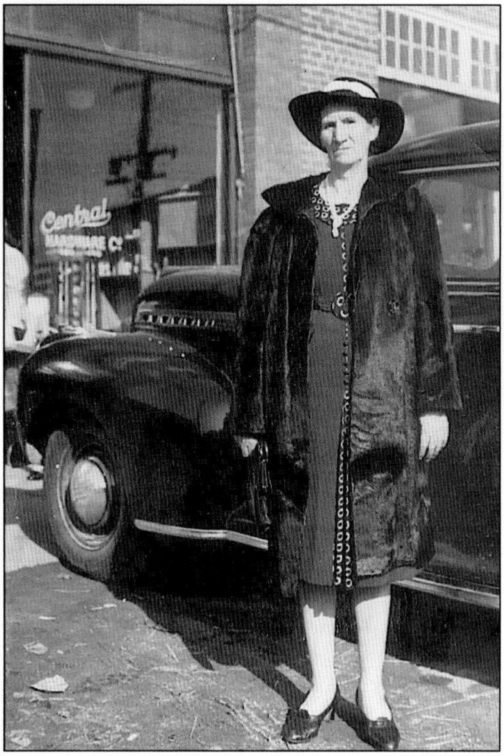

ENNIS BLEVINS OF LITTLE HORSE CREEK. Blevins, pictured here *c.* 1935, spent most of her life on Little Horse Creek, but she taught school for a number of years in West Virginia.

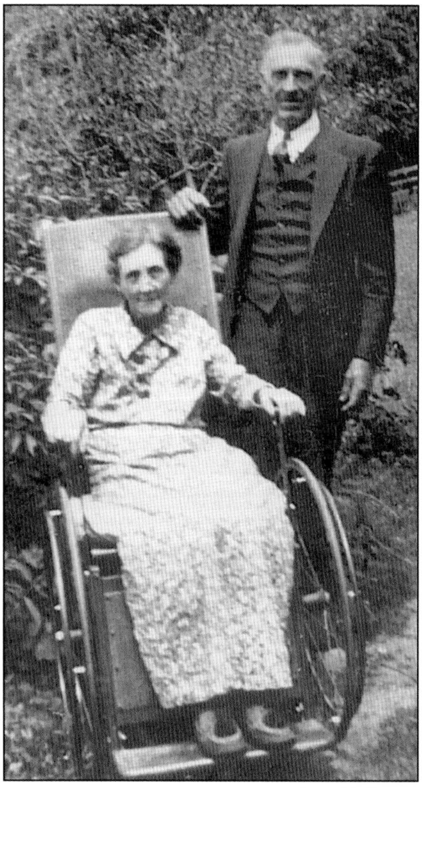

FIELDON AND SIRENA THOMAS SHEPHERD. Sirena, pictured here *c.* 1932, began her teaching career at the Flatwoods School in Little Horse Creek.

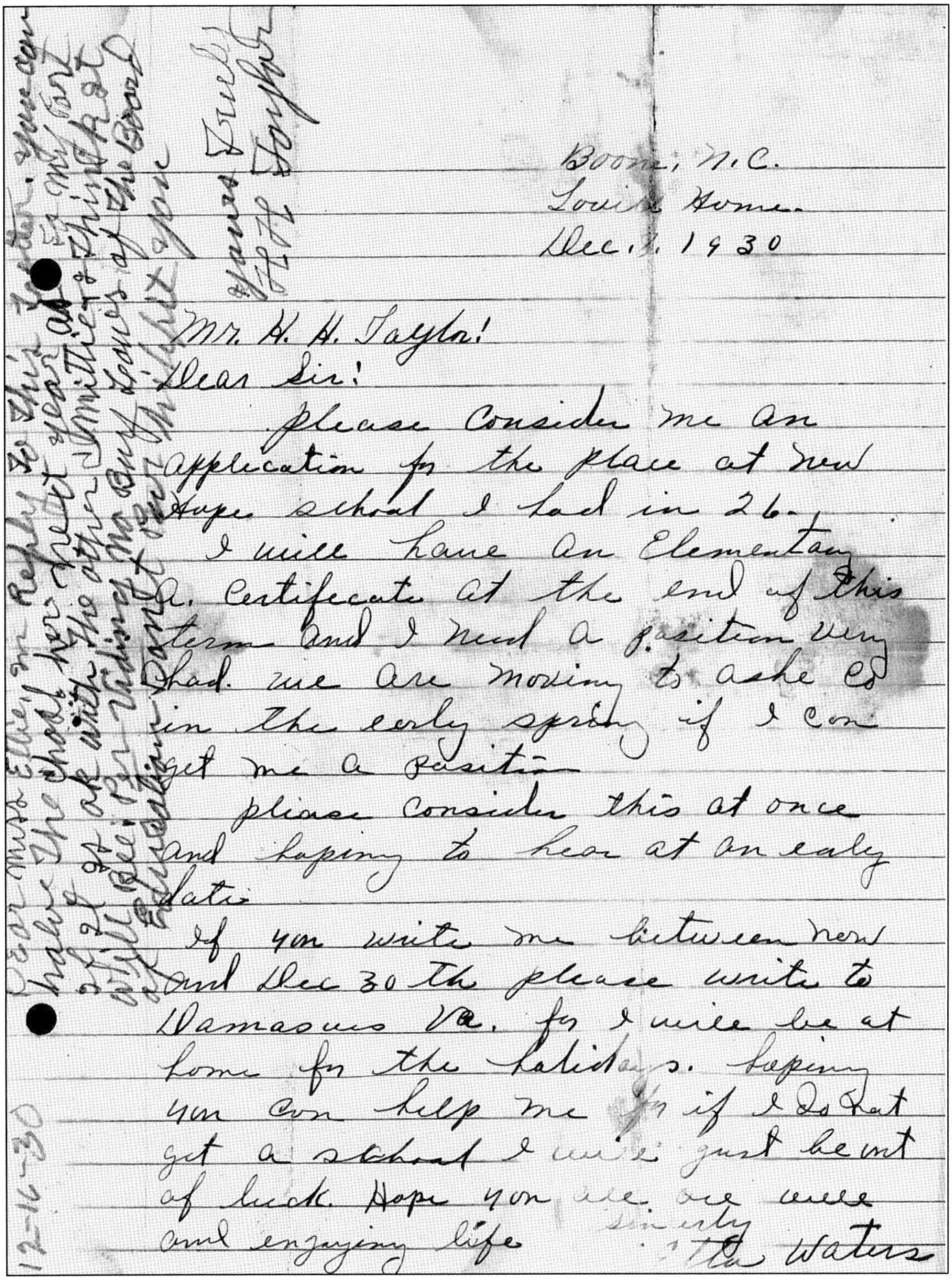

Boone, N.C.
Lovill Home
Dec. 1, 1930

Mr. H. H. Taylor:
Dear Sir:
please consider me an application for the place at New Hope school I had in 26.
I will have an Elementary A. Certificate at the end of this term and I need a position very bad. we are moving to ashe Co in the early spring if I can get me a position
please consider this at once and hoping to hear at an early date
If you write me between now and Dec 30th please write to Damascus Va. for I will be at home for the holidays. hoping you can help me for if I do not get a school I will just be out of luck. Hope you all are well and enjoying life
Sincerly
Etta Waters

SCHOOL EMPLOYMENT. A young applicant, wishing to work at New Hope School, writes to H.H. Taylor, who was school superintendent in 1930. Taylor's response is written on the other side of this letter.

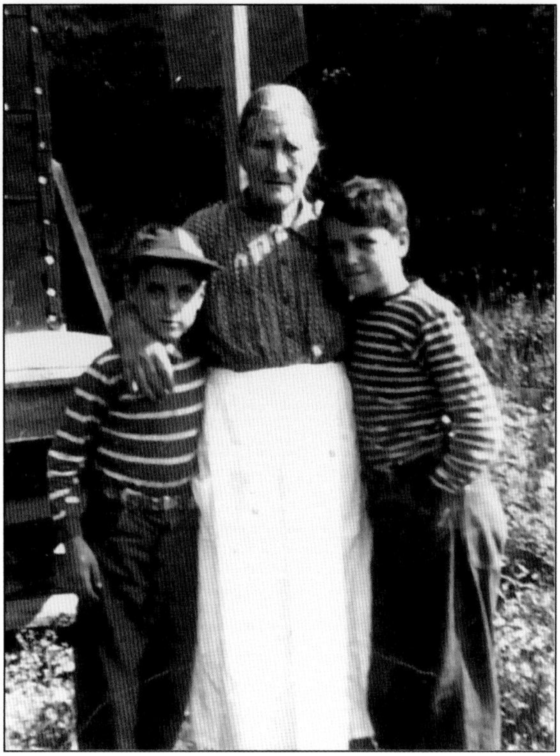

Lou Greer and Great-grandsons. Pictured from left to right in this c. 1945 photograph are John Hamm, Lou Greer, and Bill Hamm. The boys are sons of Stella Barker and Elmer Hamm. The photograph was taken in front of Lou Greer's home on Little Horse Creek.

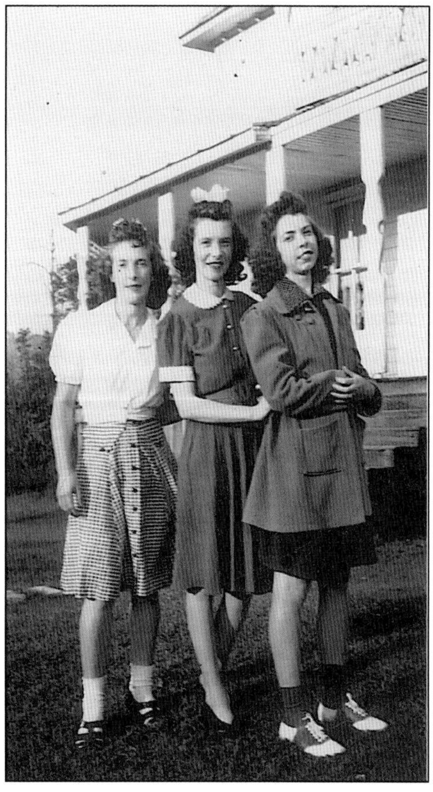

The Shepherd Girls. Pictured c. 1939 from left to right are Lenna Shepherd Drain, Ruby Shepherd Blevins, and Jewel Shepherd Wilcox. They lived in the Little Horse Creek Community.

WORTH BLEVINS OF LITTLE HORSE CREEK. Worth trained at the Great Lakes Naval Depot in Illinois during World War II, c. 1944.

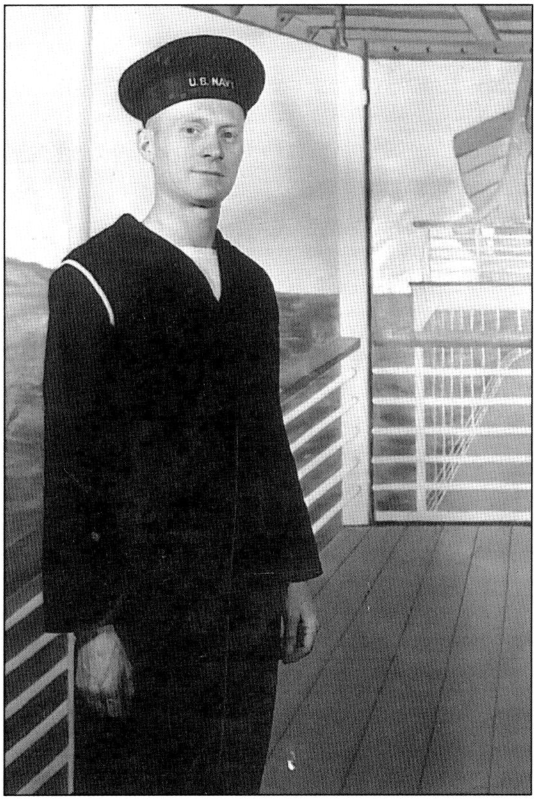

WORLD WAR II RATION BOOK. The U.S. Office of Price Administration controlled quantities and prices of rationed items. The policy was "no stamp, no purchase."

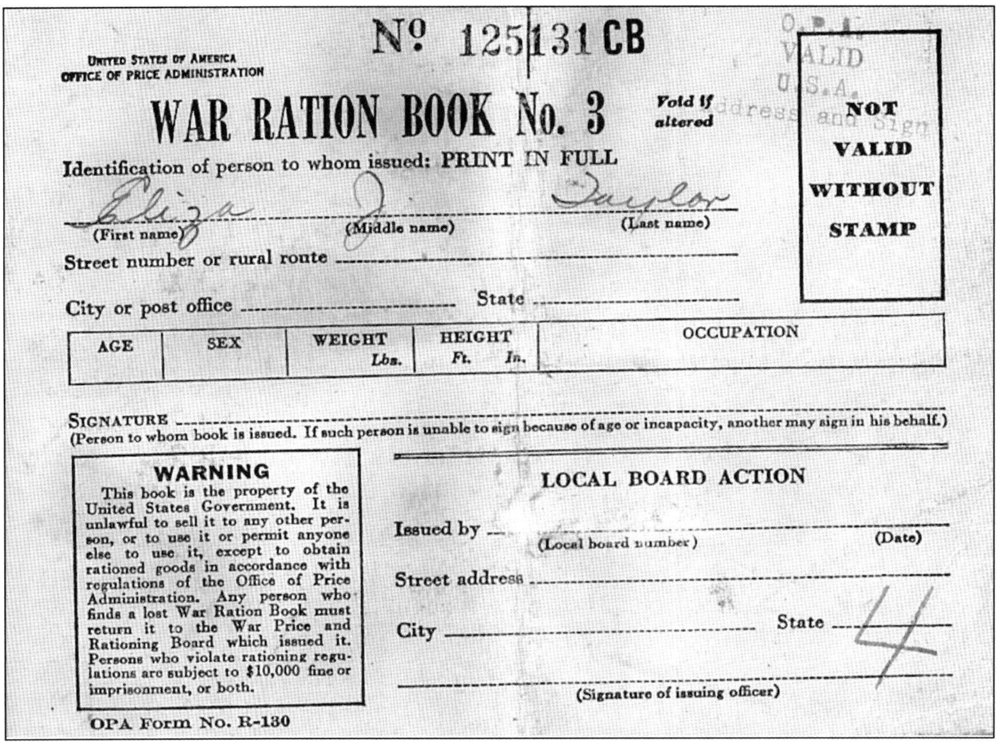

Nº 125131 CB

UNITED STATES OF AMERICA
OFFICE OF PRICE ADMINISTRATION

WAR RATION BOOK No. 3

Void if altered

NOT VALID WITHOUT STAMP

Identification of person to whom issued: PRINT IN FULL

(First name) (Middle name) (Last name)

Street number or rural route

City or post office State

AGE	SEX	WEIGHT Lbs.	HEIGHT Ft. In.	OCCUPATION

SIGNATURE
(Person to whom book is issued. If such person is unable to sign because of age or incapacity, another may sign in his behalf.)

WARNING
This book is the property of the United States Government. It is unlawful to sell it to any other person, or to use it or permit anyone else to use it, except to obtain rationed goods in accordance with regulations of the Office of Price Administration. Any person who finds a lost War Ration Book must return it to the War Price and Rationing Board which issued it. Persons who violate rationing regulations are subject to $10,000 fine or imprisonment, or both.

OPA Form No. R-130

LOCAL BOARD ACTION

Issued by (Local board number) (Date)

Street address

City State

(Signature of issuing officer)

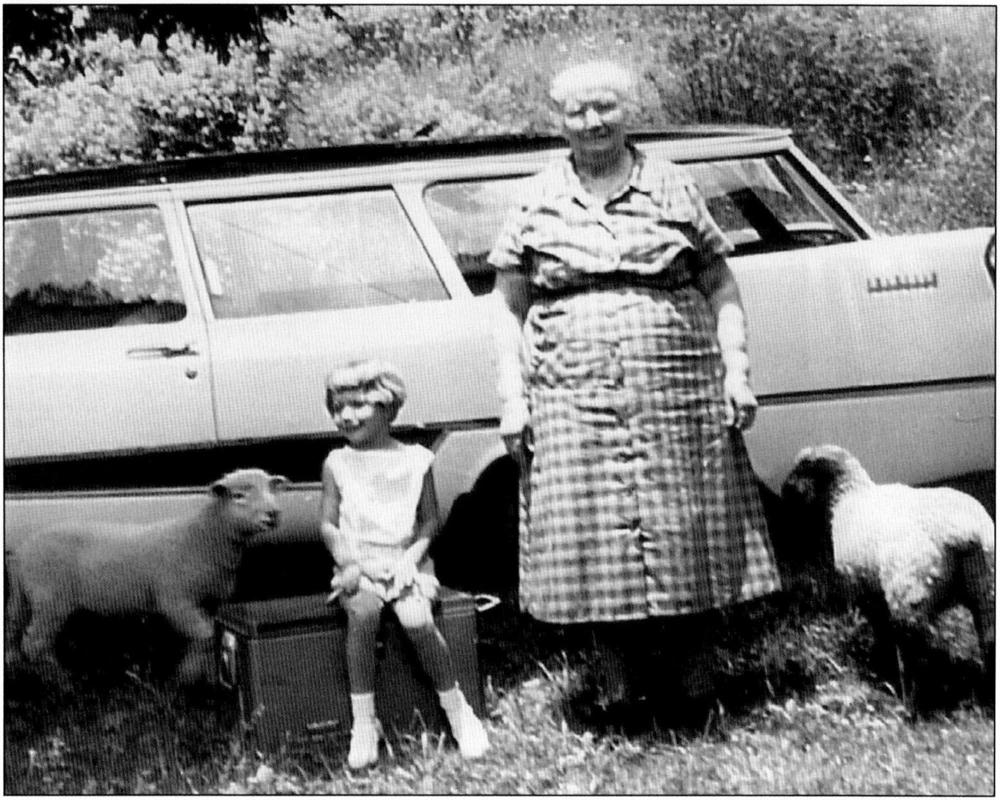

PICNIC WITH LAMBS, C. 1961. Pictured are Eliza Jane Blevins Taylor and her granddaughter Elizabeth Sue Taylor.

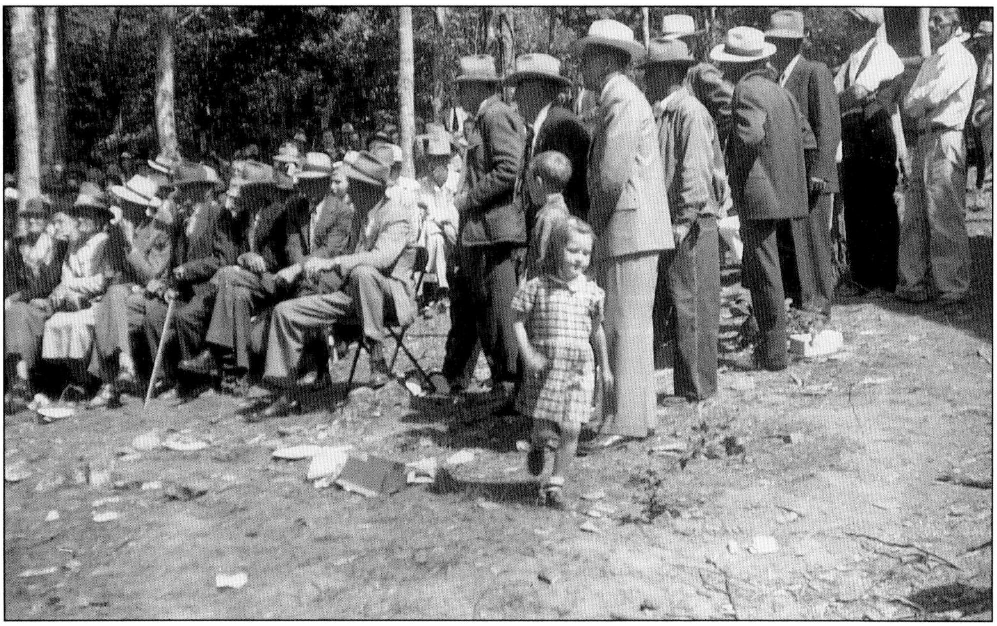

PRIMITIVE BAPTIST ASSOCIATION MEETING, SEPTEMBER 12, 1954. An overflow crowd attends the meeting on Pond Mountain.

Two

Friendly to Hunters and Settlers

The North Fork of The New River

As the first settlers walked to Ashe County from Virginia, "menacing" had to be the word to describe the mountains they faced. The rising mountains in the distance hid the rolling beauty of the fields, streams, and gentle hills on a plateau that eventually became the farms and homes along the banks of the North Fork of the New River.

The area was explored by Daniel Boone, who lived nearby for some time. Thomas Jefferson's father, Peter, surveyed the whole area and for a while owned adjacent land.

Hunters were the first to come. They pitched small hunting camps along the winding New River, which was originally called Woods River. They came to hunt the plentiful game. They fished from the river, trapped, and hunted until other people started to settle here.

These first settlers did enough farming to survive. Not much trading was possible unless you undertook an arduous journey either to Virginia or down the mountain to Rowan County. Mostly they grew what they needed, sold, or traded the rest to neighbors. They were a very hardy lot. They settled where the Indians and Long Hunters would not live. Isolated from the rest of the world they became a strong independent-thinking people. The tendency to be "independent" is still alive in their descendants today.

The people who came, stayed. From the days of the first census in 1790 until just recently, little change is noted; names and families were much the same. Many are related by marriage to other families in the area. For this reason and, due to isolation, the small rural communities along the North Fork became very close-knit.

Enjoy the pictures. Notice the people and the buildings. Most of them will show faces of a strong, wonderful people. The people who lived on the North Fork would want us to remember them as they are honestly portrayed here, just as they were. The buildings were for the most part simple, strong, and useful like their owners. Most of these old buildings are gone now, but a few remain, just around the next curve in the river.

—Lonnie Jones

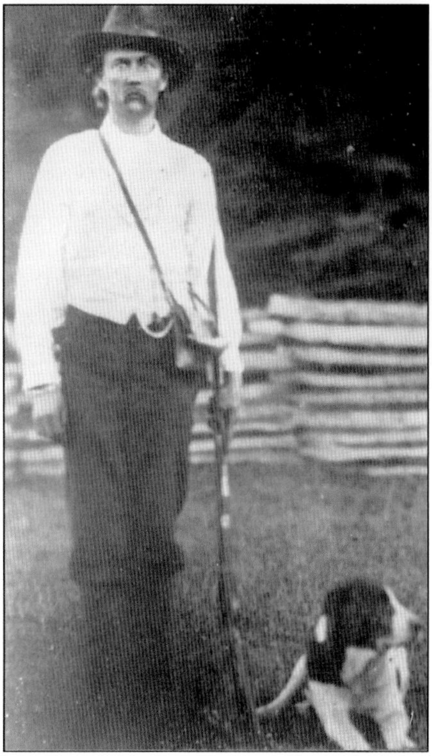

HUNTING IN THE MOUNTAINS. In the mid-1800s, Thomas Clarkson Worth was a pioneer of the Creston area.

LONG RANGE VIEW OF CRESTON, C. 1884. The Worth Chapel can be seen in the photograph, as well as the homes of various members of the Worth family.

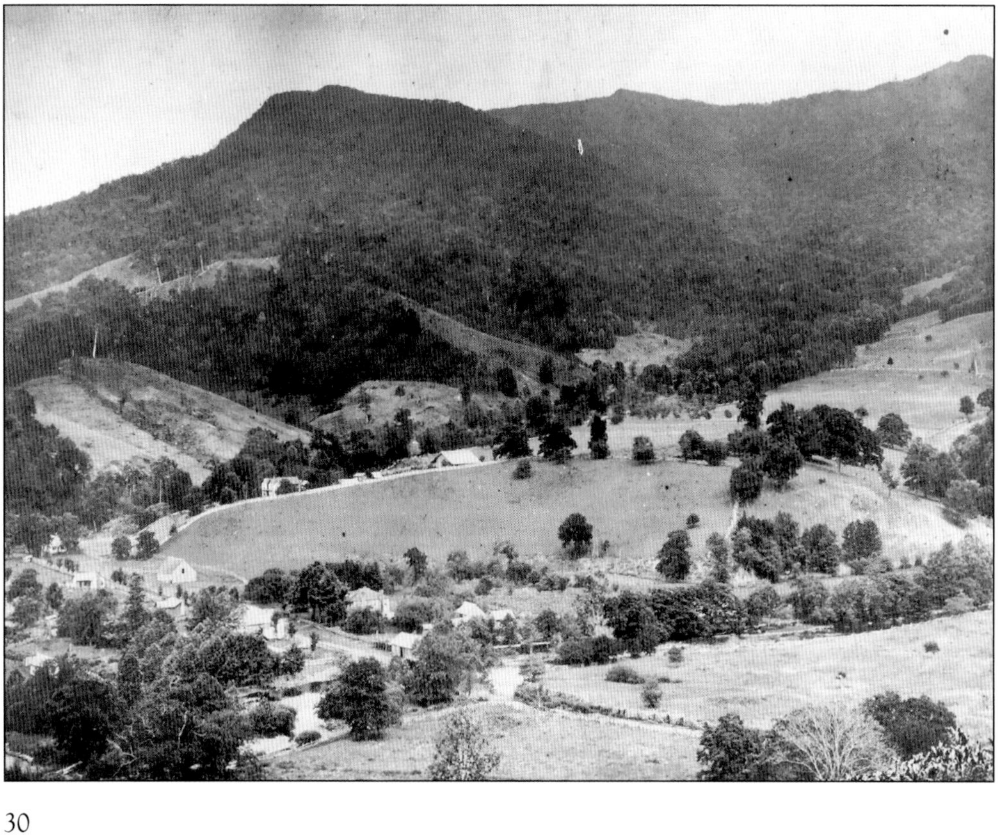

STEPHEN THOMAS, C. 1850. Thomas, who had various partnerships with David Worth, owned a tavern and inn in the early 1800s. Together they made Creston (then North Fork) into the largest business center in Ashe County with a larger population than Jefferson at the time.

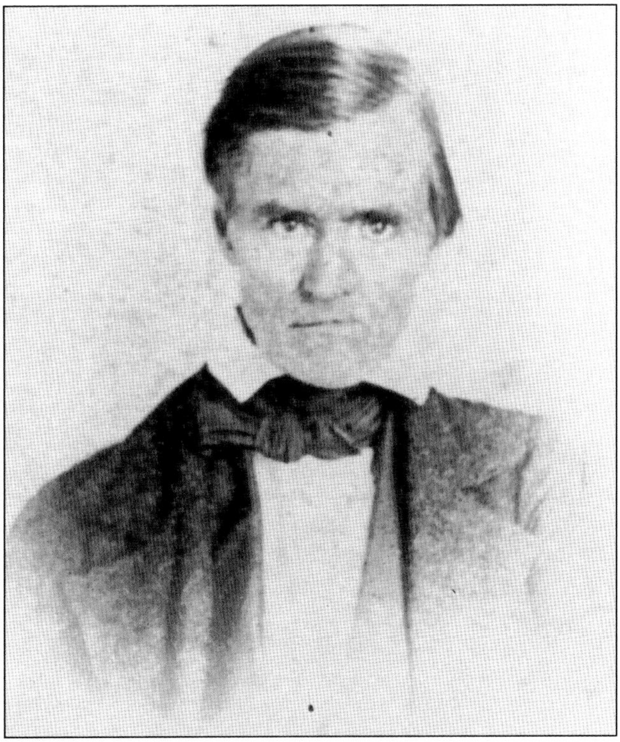

THE DAVID WORTH FAMILY, C. 1875. Pictured from left to right are Ada Worth (Penn-Coffey), David Worth, Elizabeth Worth, and Marianna Wilcox.

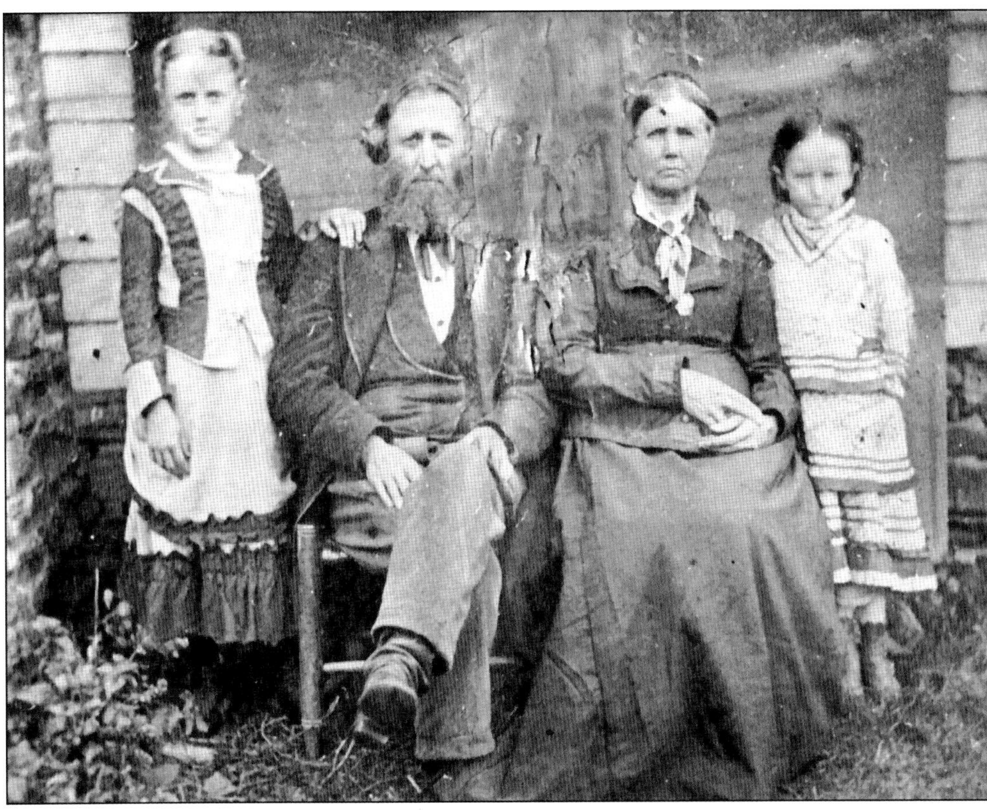

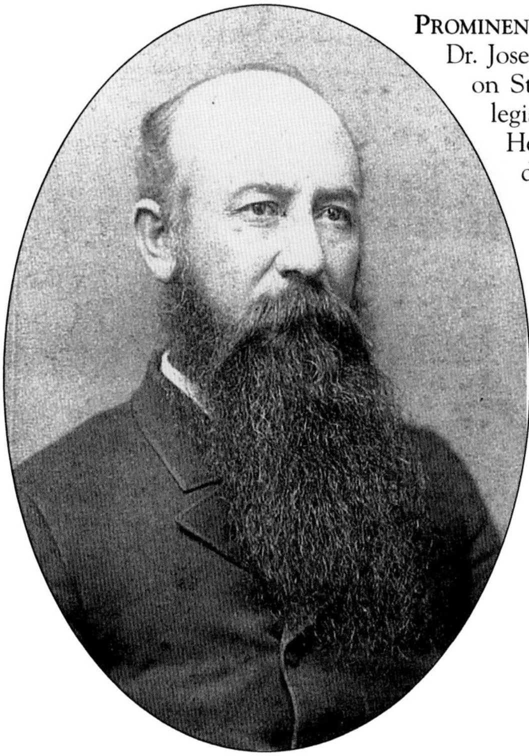

PROMINENT SETTLER OF THE DRESDEN COMMUNITY. Dr. Joseph Orrin Wilcox, *c.* 1890, lived at Dresden on Staggs Creek. He was a doctor, farmer, state legislator, and leader of the Republican Party. He was nominated for the U.S. Congress but died during the campaign in 1898.

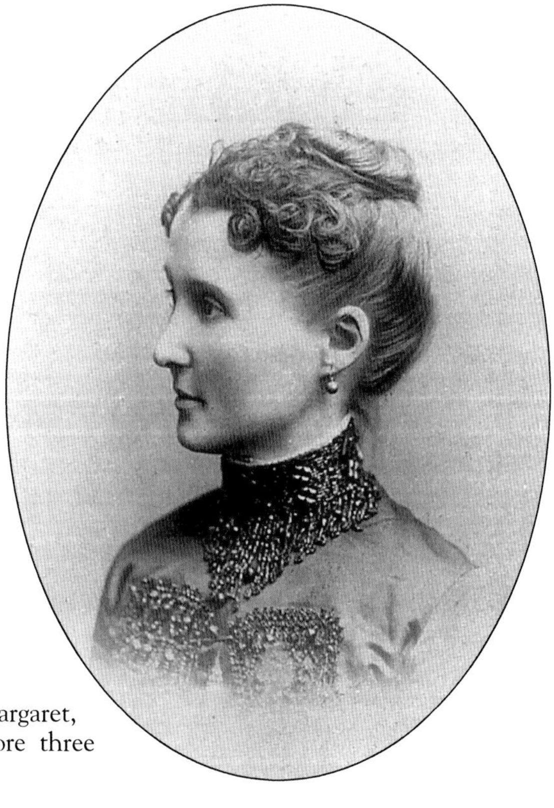

MARGARET HENRY WILCOX, C. 1900. Margaret, the second wife of Dr. J.O. Wilcox, bore three daughters and three sons.

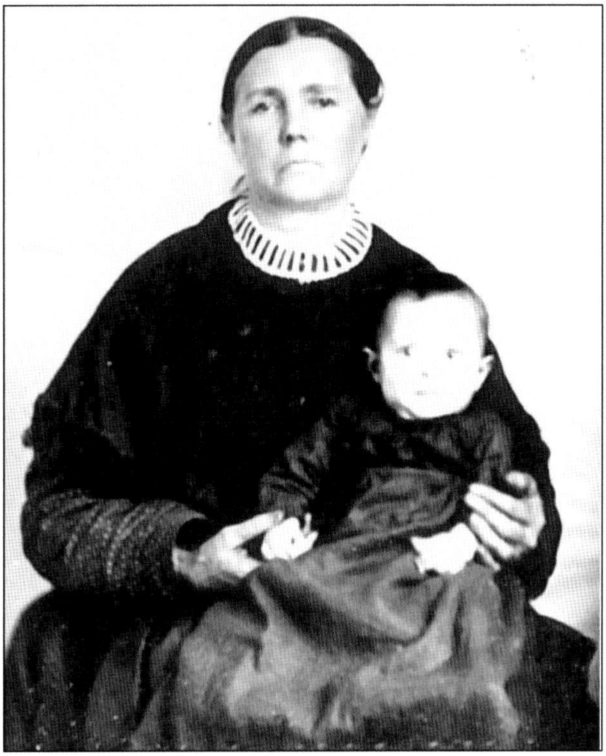

ELIZABETH THOMAS WORTH OF CRESTON. Mrs. Worth, pictured here around 1870, raised many orphan children. She reared the child on her lap, Mariana Wilcox Barber, after the death of her daughter, Martitia, in 1870. Mariana weighed only four pounds when Elizabeth took her home to Creston.

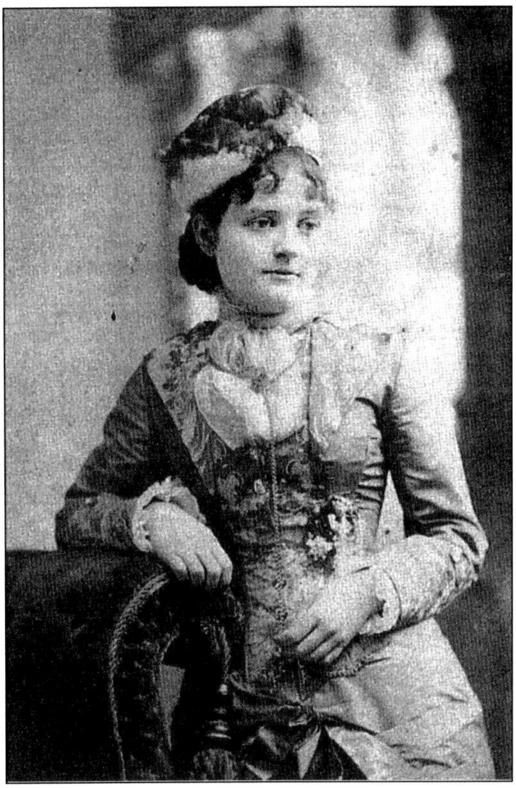

MARIANA MARTITIA WILCOX, 1889. Mariana was the daughter of J.O. Wilcox and Martitia Clemetine Worth. She was only six weeks old when her mother died and her Grandmother Worth took her to Creston to care for her. She returned to Dresden at age six when her father remarried.

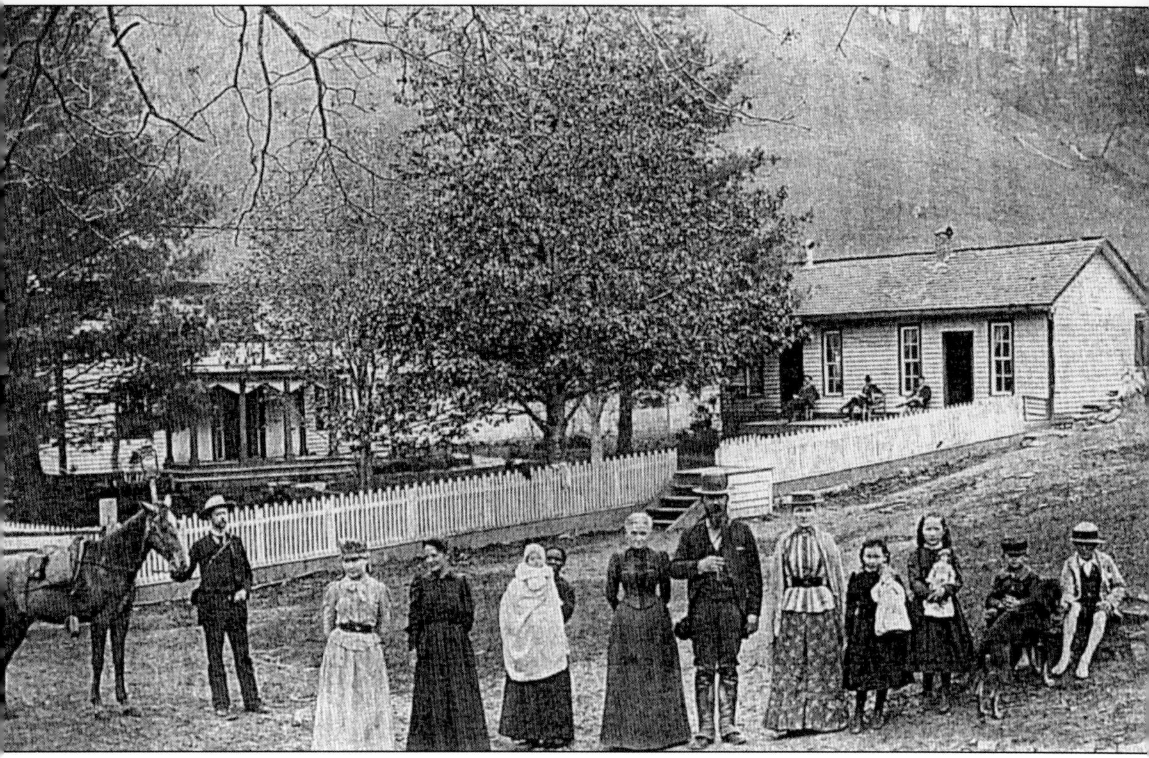

THE WILCOX ESTATE IN DRESDEN. Pictured from left to right in this *c.* 1892 picture are Orrin Wilcox, Maude Wilcox, Mariana Wilcox, Baby Margaret, Mrs. Henry (Margaret's mother), Dr. J.O. Wilcox, Margaret (J.O. Wilcox's second wife), Mayme, Dolly, Henry, and Edward.

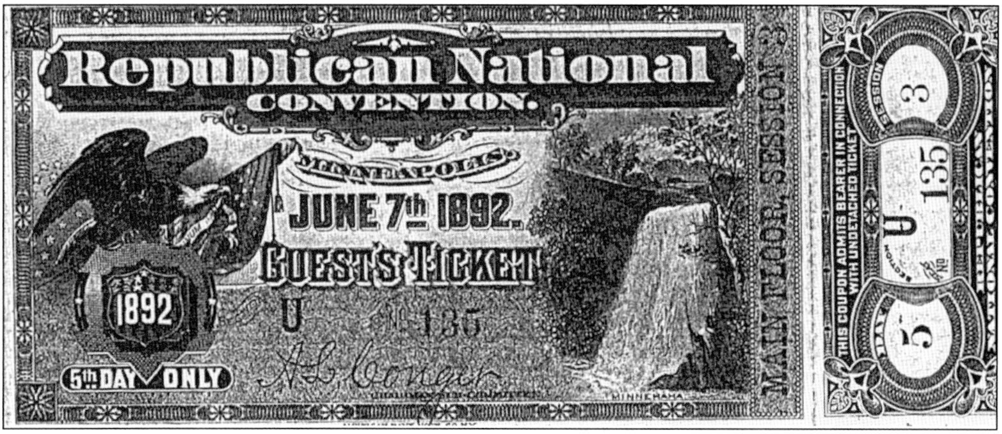

GUEST TICKET TO THE REPUBLICAN NATIONAL CONVENTION, 1892. In the possession of Dr. J.O. Wilcox, this ticket allowed one guest to the fifth day of the convention in Minneapolis.

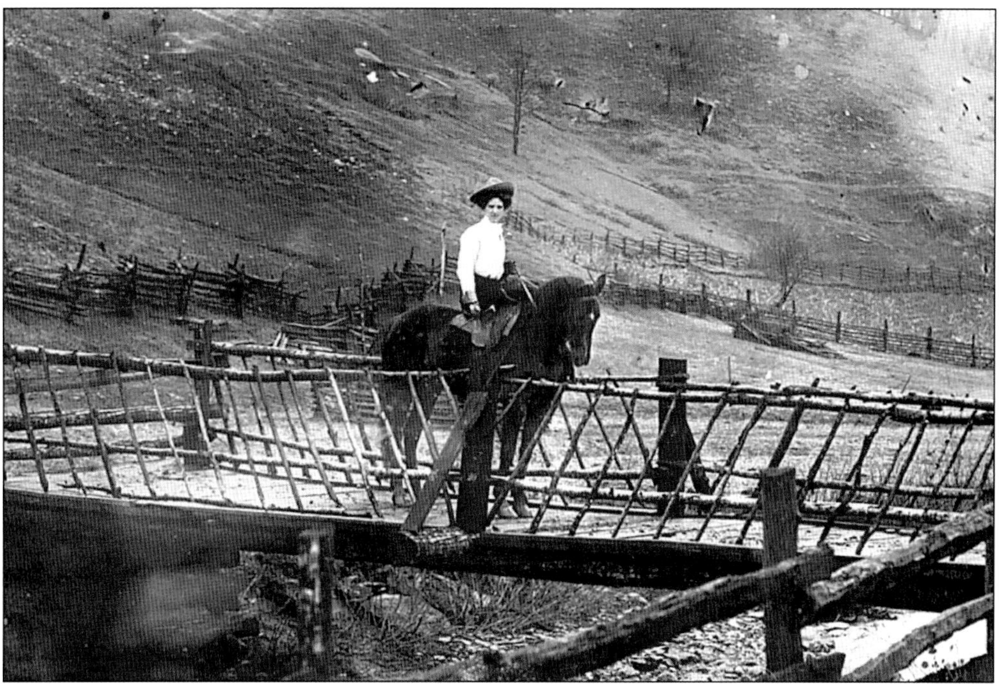
STAGGS CREEK BRIDGE. May Hamilton is out for a ride, c. 1892.

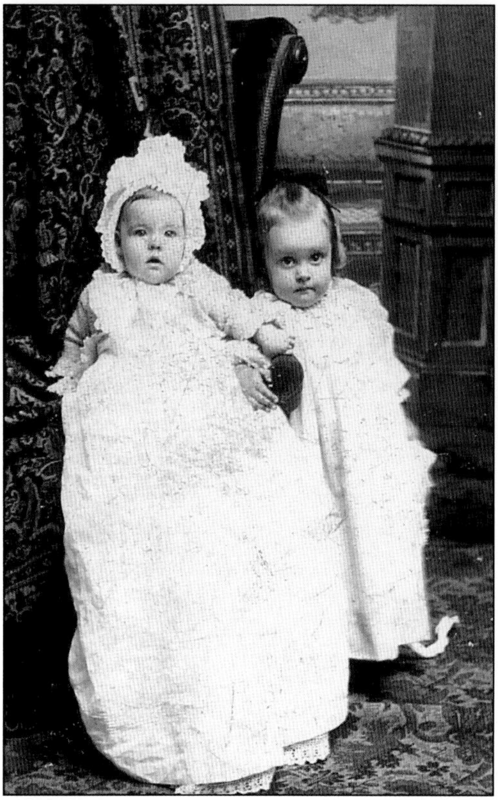

RUTH AND VIRGINIA LILLIARD, C. 1890. The girls were the granddaughters of David and Elizabeth Worth.

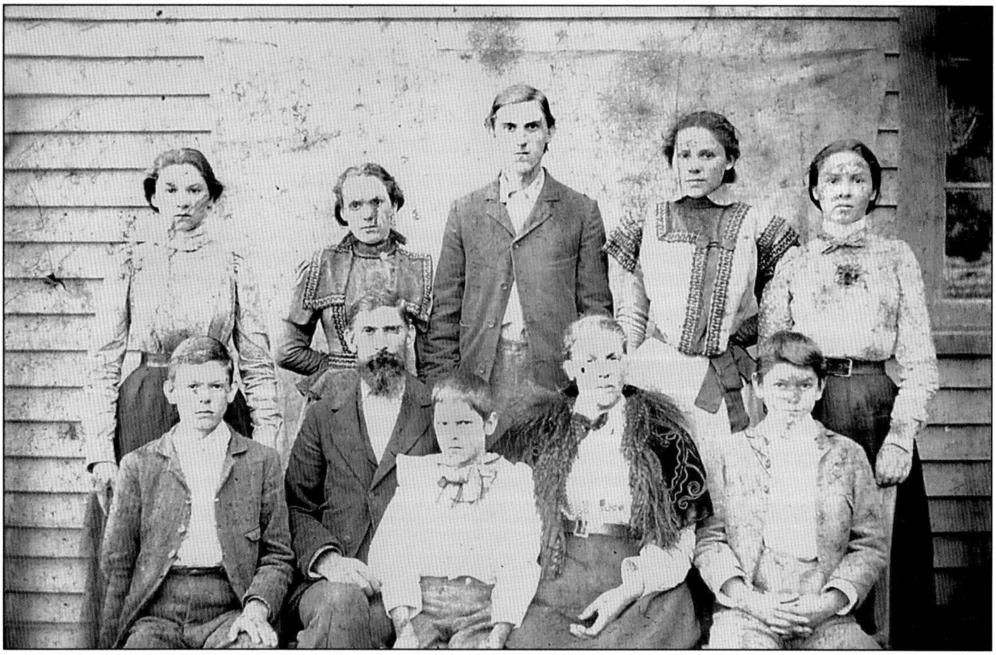

FAMILY OF THOMAS AND SALINA GAMBILL SUTHERLAND. Shown in this late 1890s picture are Robert (Bunk), Ola (Viola), Pearle, Elizabeth, Ella, Joe, John, and Will Sutherland. The Sutherland's fifth daughter, Della, died before the picture was made.

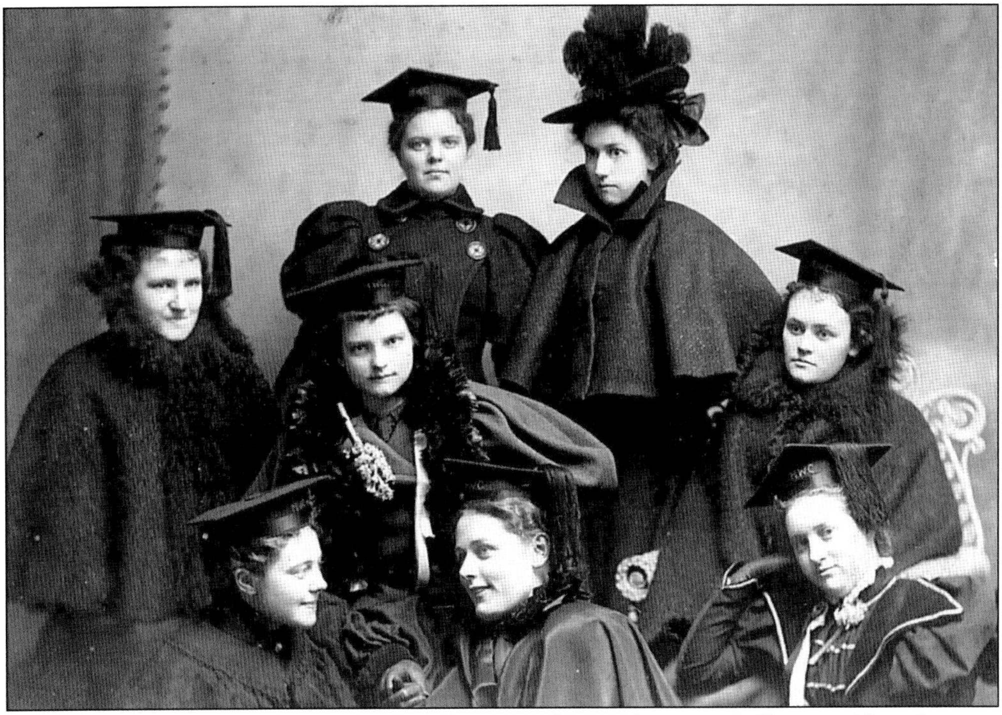

PROUD GRADUATES, 1897. Graduating from Martha Washington College in Abingdon are, from left to right, the following: (first row) DeEtte Benham, Carrie Flannery, and Laura Kilgore; (middle row) Jennie Maxwell, unidentified, and Jennie Worth; (back row) Lizzie Worth Benham and Clyde Worth.

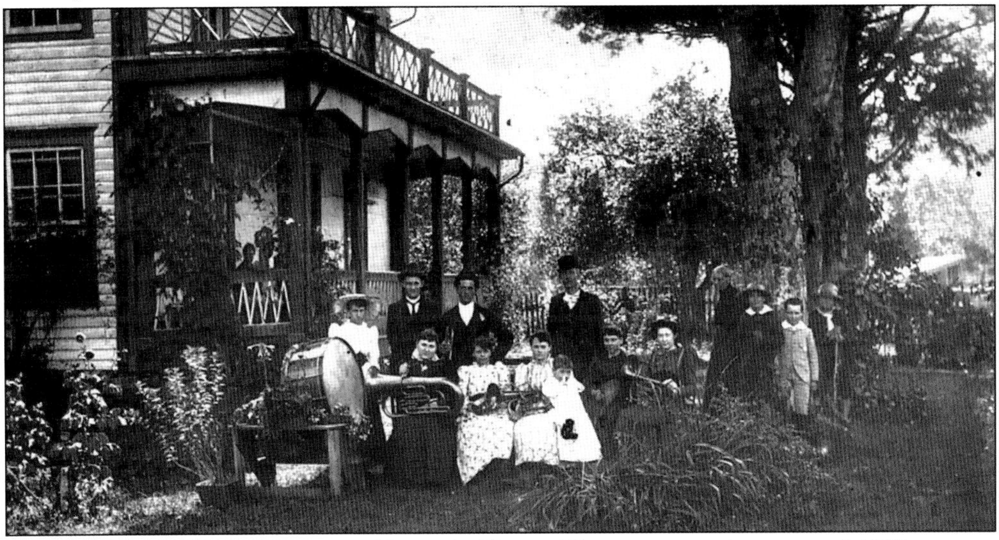

MUSICAL GATHERING AT DAVID WORTH'S HOME. This picture, taken around 1882, was on the cover of the author's first book in this series, *Images of America: Ashe County*. Pictured from left to right are the following: (by the tree) Mrs. Elizabeth Worth, Pete Lillard, John Lillard, and Edward Wilcox; (men standing) Jim Worth, Walter H. Worth, and Lillard Mason; (with instruments) Clyde Worth, DeEtte Benham, Lizzie Worth Benham, Jennie Worth, and Bess Lillard (leaning on Jennie), Hattie Wiley, and Maude Wilcox. Ruth Worth is on the porch.

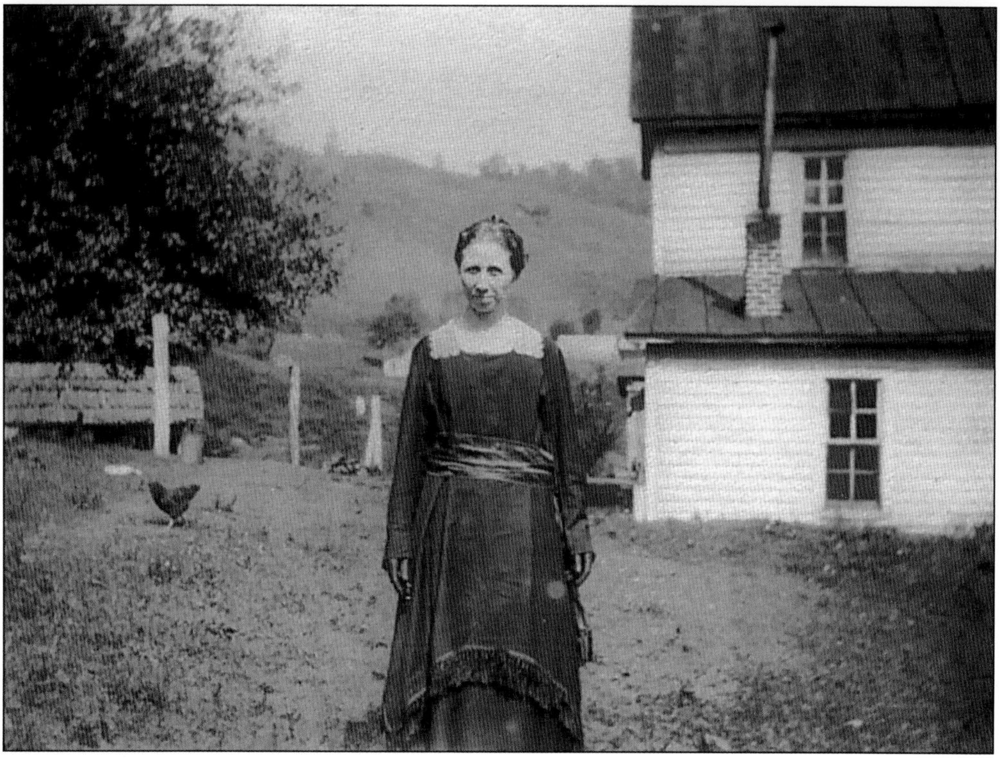

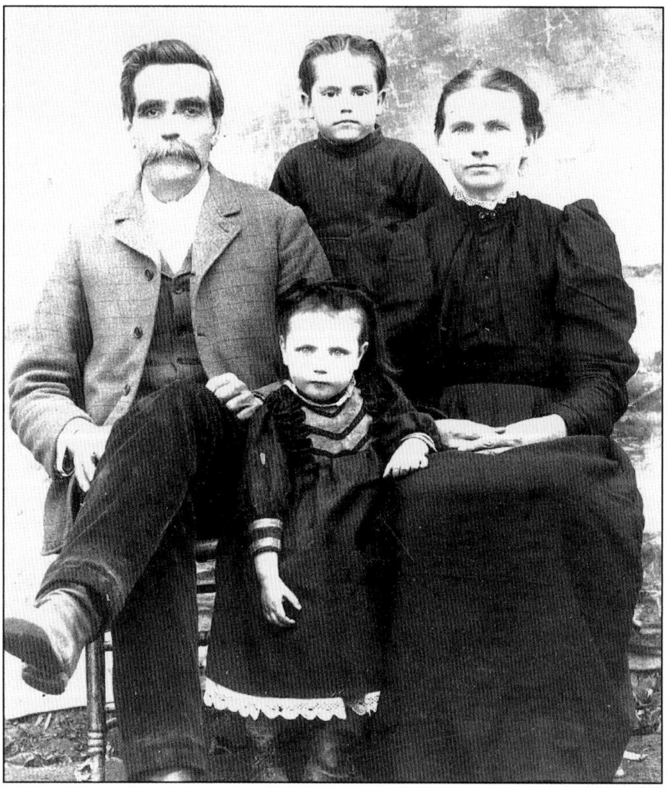

BINA GRAYBEAL SUTHERLAND. Bina Graybeal of the Riverview community is pictured above *c.* 1920. She was married to Emmet Sutherland.

THE LEWIN SEGRAVES FAMILY, 1902. Pictured from left to right are (front row) Jane; (back row) Lewin, Dewey, and Osena Segraves. Lewin was the first Segraves descendent in Ashe County, having come as a young man from Wilkes County during the Civil War.

THE ALFRED VANNOY FAMILY. Pictured from left to right, in this *c.* 1900 picture, are (front row) Alfred and Cynthia Ann Brown Vannoy; (back row) Nuba Vannoy Woodruff, Hartnese Vannoy Revis, Sally Vannoy Taylor, and June Vannoy.

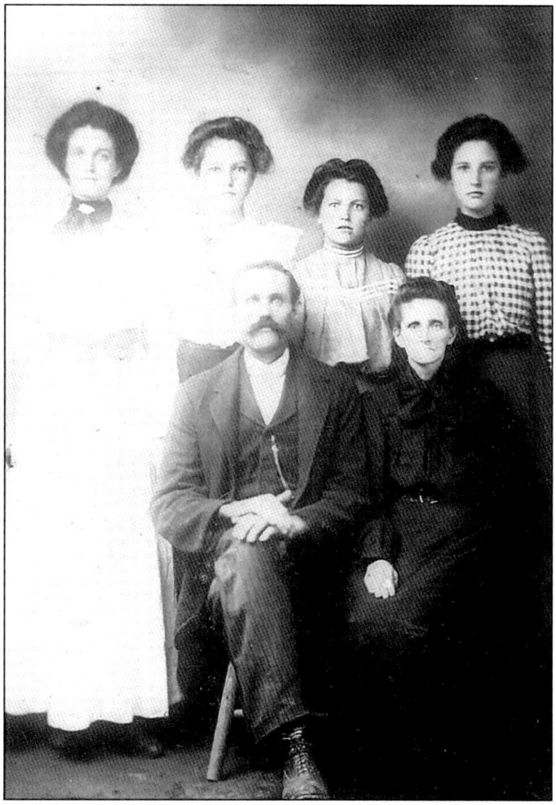

FAMILY REUNION AT A.P. HOWELL'S HOME. Alvin P. Howell and his wife Callie Blackburn Howell are standing in the center at the top of the steps of their Silas Creek home, *c.* 1903. Included in the picture are Welch Howell, Carola Howell Neaves, Robbie and Minnie Stike, and Judd and Gaither Howell.

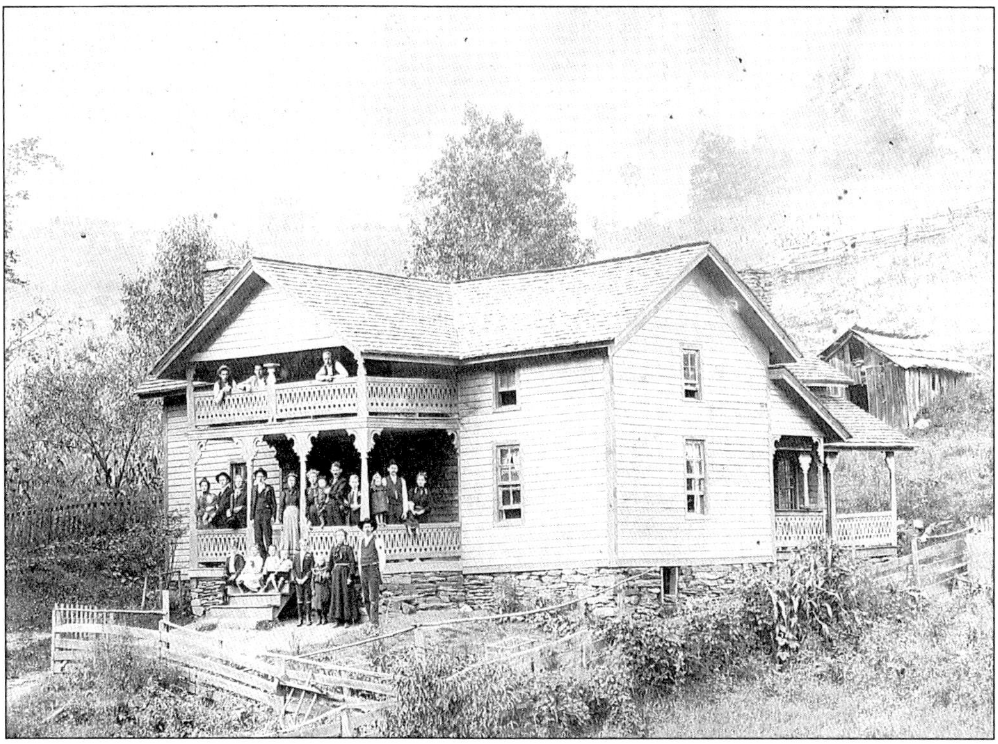

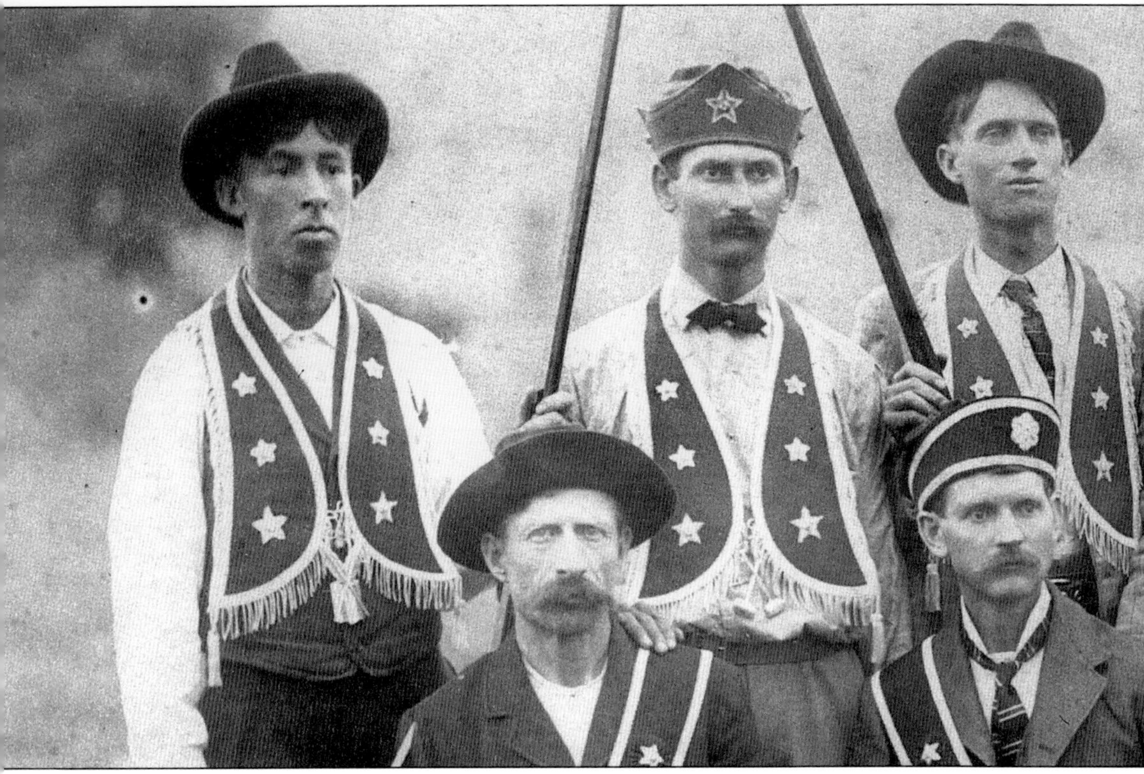

THE ODD FELLOWS OF HELTON, 1903. Like the Masonic Order, the Independent Order of Odd Fellows is a secret organization. The order came to America in 1819 and quickly became a nationwide organization. This group had a meeting house at Little Helton.

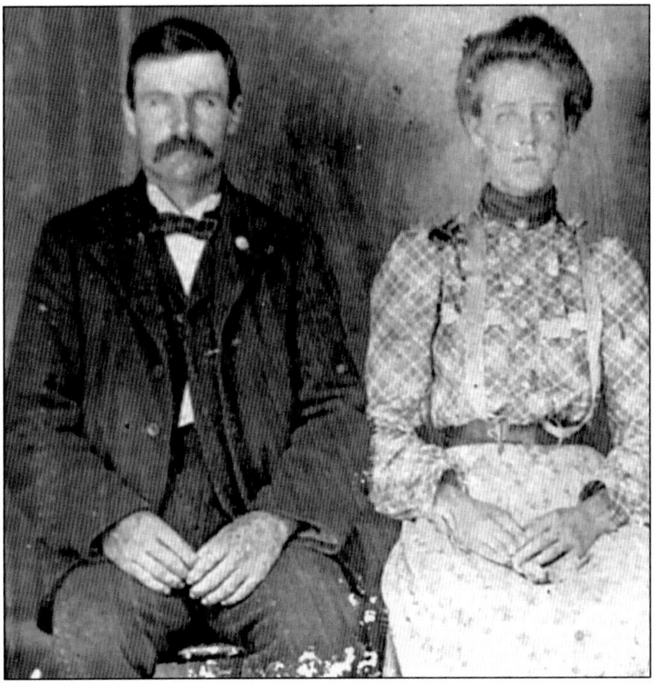

ARTHUR SAMUEL AND LILLIE OAKLY REESE WILCOX, 1904. Arthur was the son of Samuel A. Wilcox and his wife Lillie was the daughter of William and Sarah Church Reese.

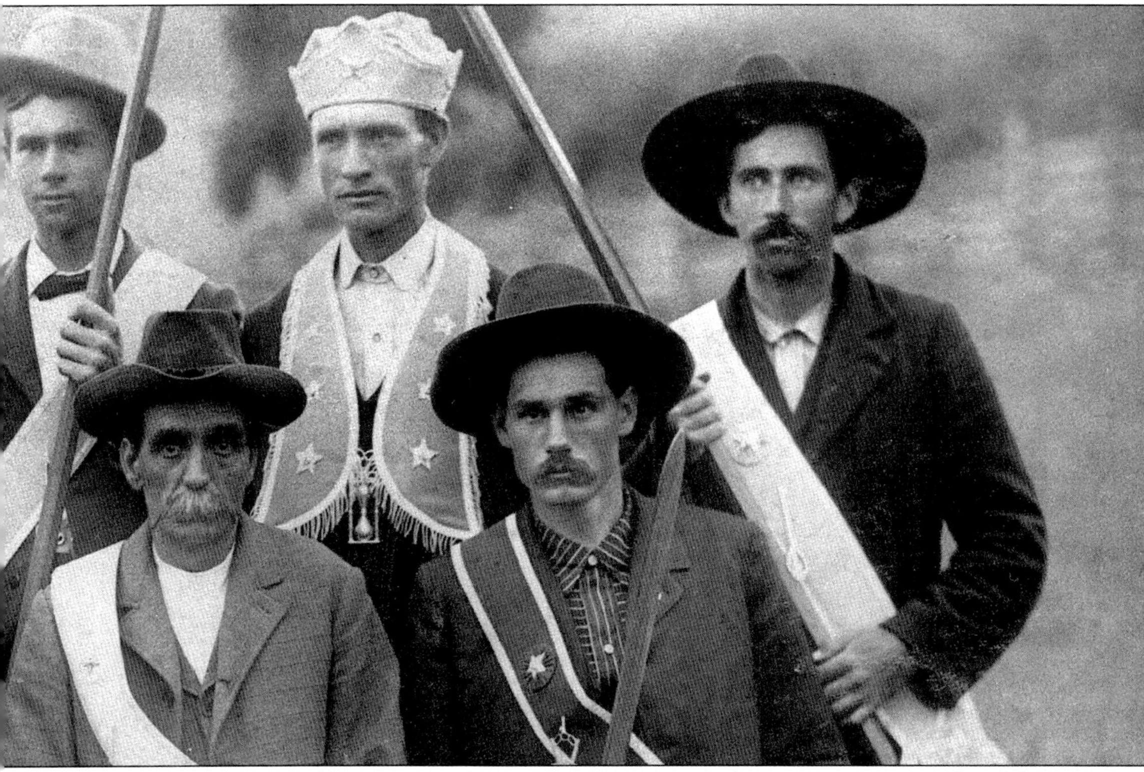

Pictured from left to right are (sitting) Gus Mock, unidentified, Lewin Segrave, and Dolphus Segraves; (standing) Claburn Baker, four unidentified, and Curtis DeBoard.

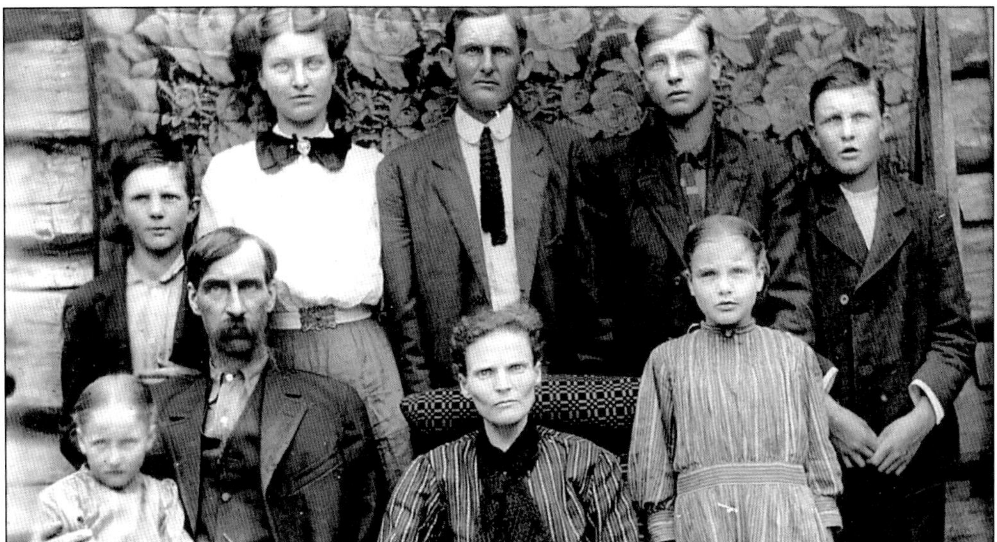

THE JAMES P. ROBERTS FAMILY, C. 1900. Pictured from left to right are the following: (front row) James P. Roberts holding Golda Roberts Blevins, Rozina Sheets Roberts, and Bonnie Roberts; (back row) George Conrad Roberts, Cordelia Roberts Testerman, Colar Testerman, Emory Roberts, and Austin Roberts. Rozina was the daughter of Henry Sheets, a Church of the Brethren minister who established the first Brethren Church in Ashe County.

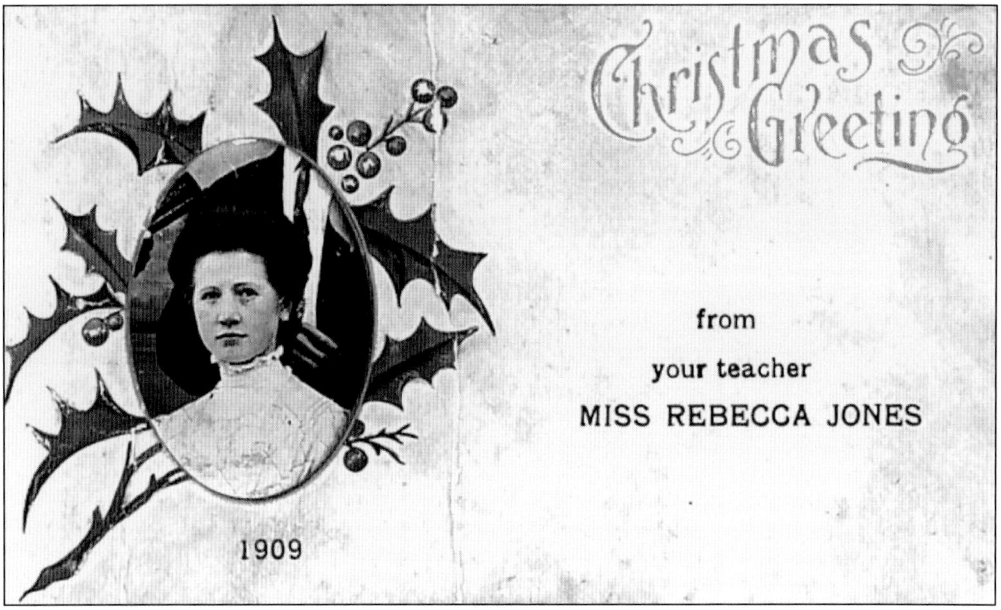

CHRISTMAS CARD, 1909. Rebecca Jones's Christmas card to one of her Piney Creek pupils is pictured above.

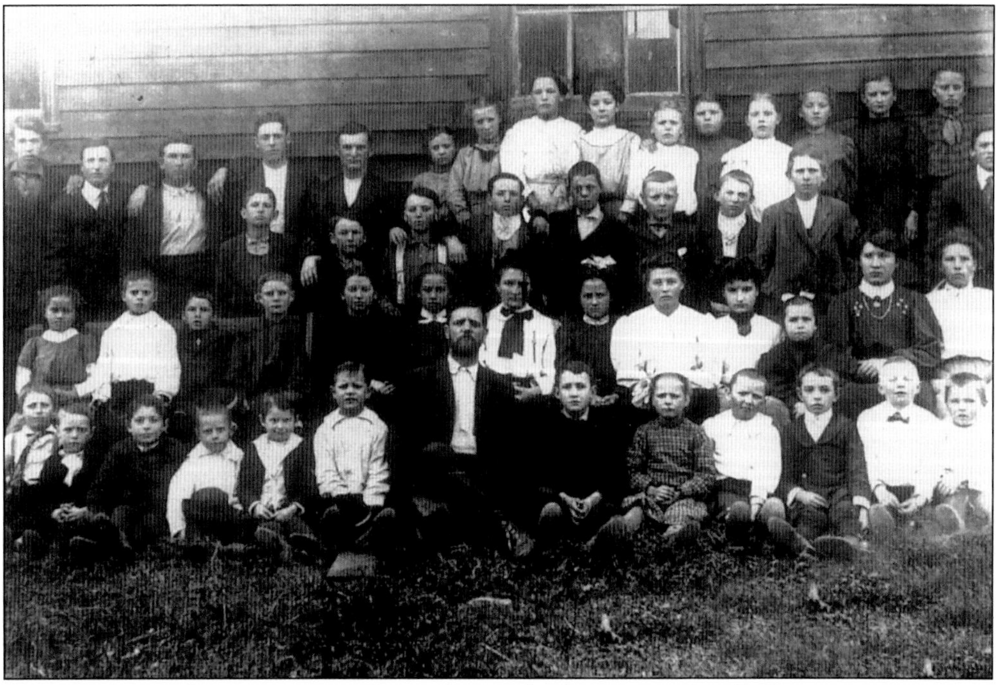

WILLOW GROVE SCHOOL, 1910. The teacher in the front row is Sam Robinson.

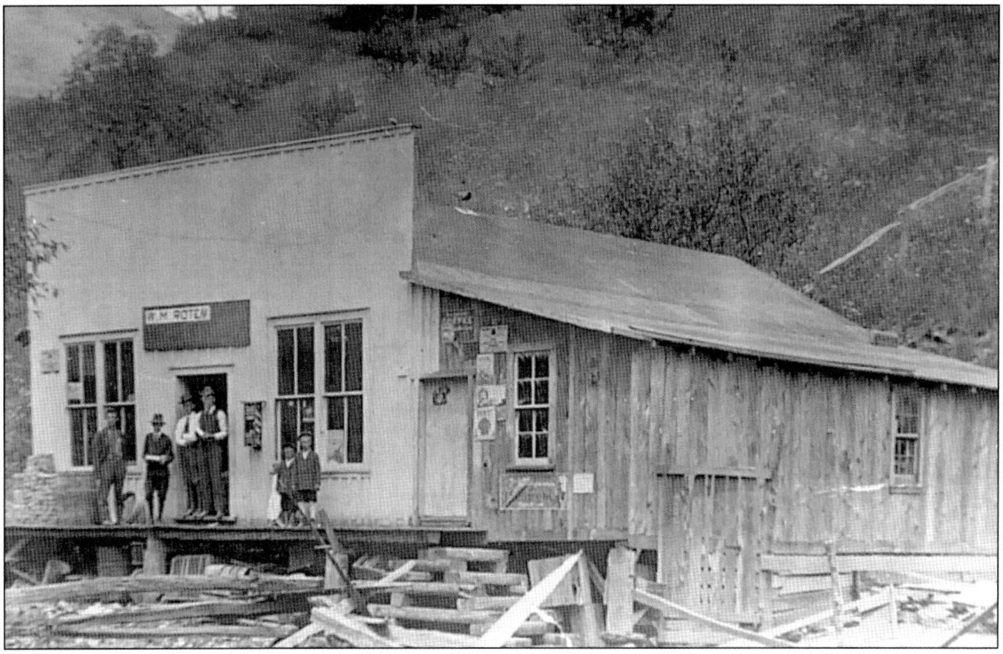

THE ROTEN GENERAL STORE. This store was located on Rich Hill Road in the Riverview community, c. 1915.

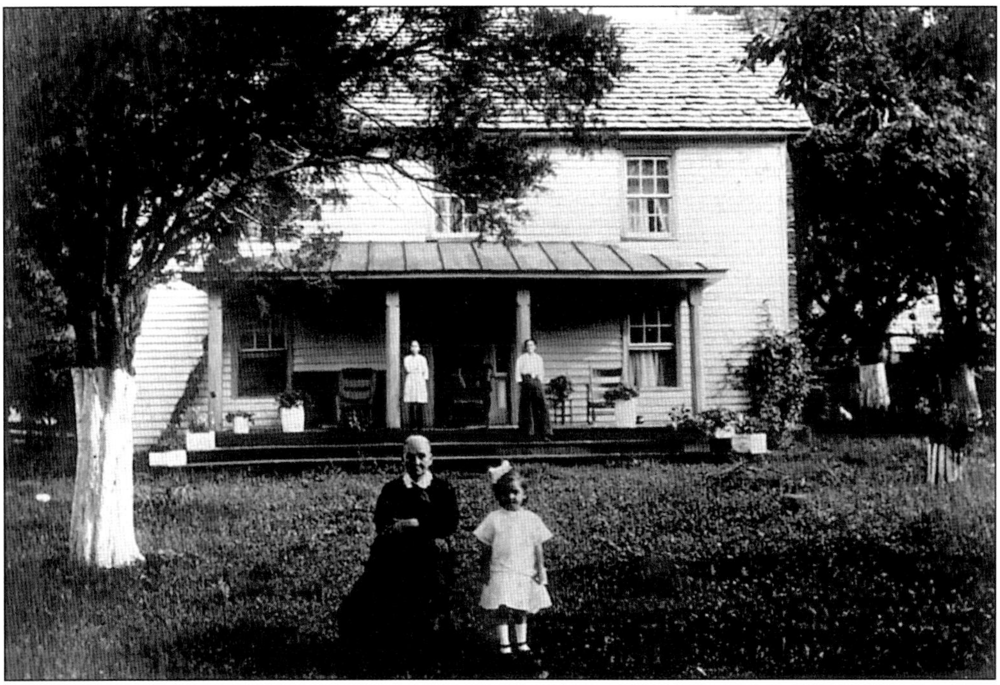

THE PRICE HOME IN RIVERVIEW, C. 1912. The Prices's built a central hallway to join two slave cabins to form one large home; they later added three bedrooms upstairs. The cedar tree is painted white so horses would not run into it at night. Pictured from left to right are (forefront) grandmother Elezy Jenkins Price and Ruth Tugman Draughon; (porch steps) Ruth Price Graybeal and Lizzie Price Jones.

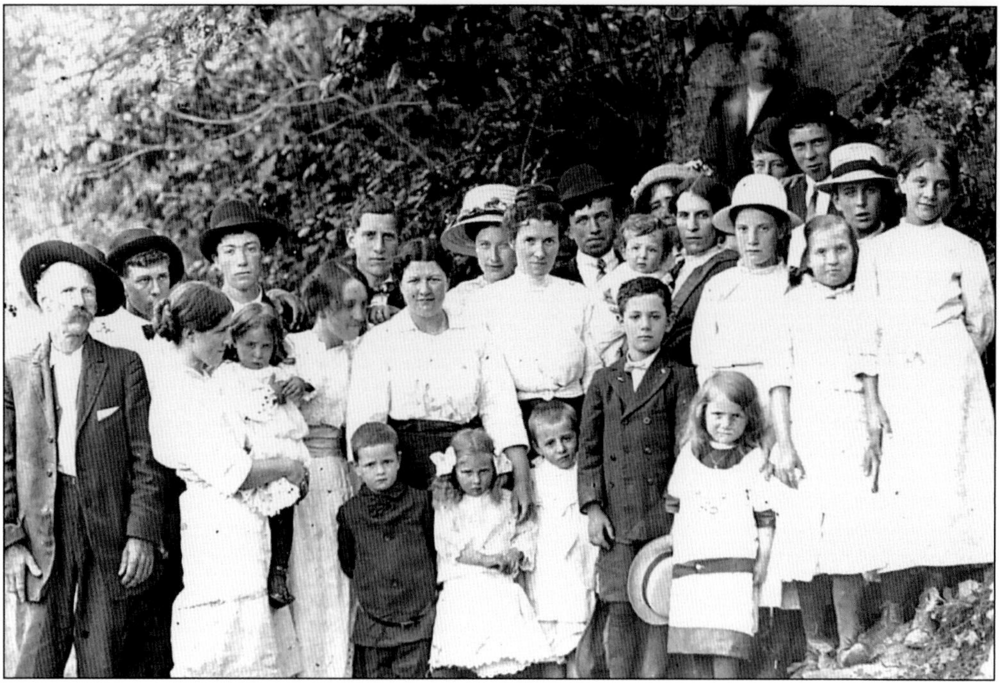

BAPTISM AT SILAS CREEK. Will A. Hurley is pictured in 1915 on the left as he poses with his two families. This baptism probably occurred at Landmark Baptist Church.

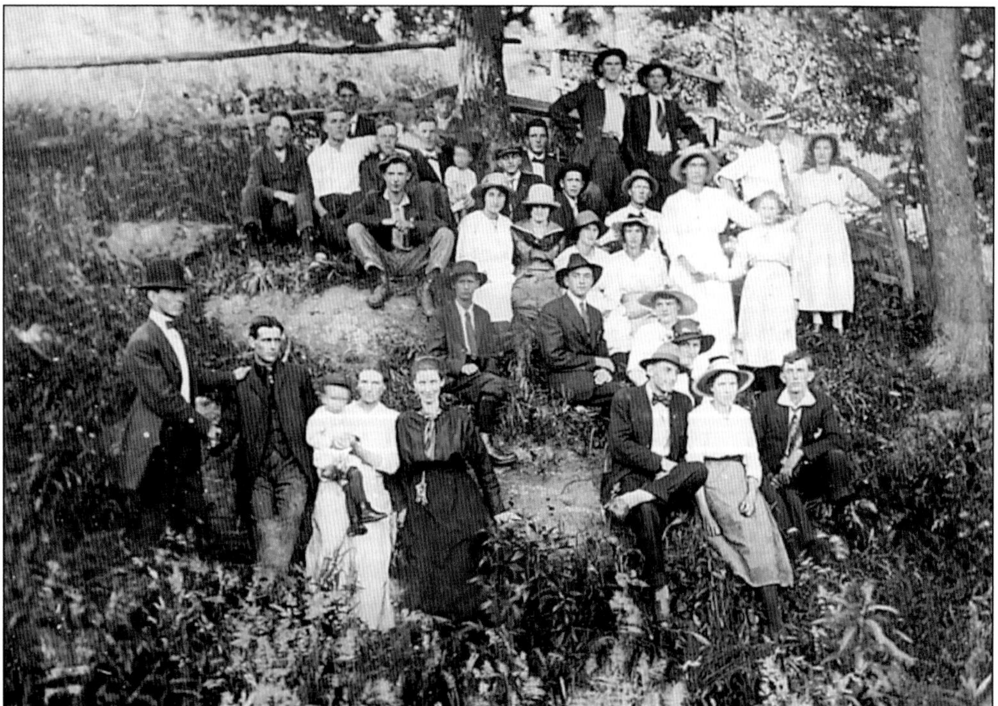

THE SILAS CREEK BAPTIST CHURCH SUNDAY SCHOOL, 1915. Teacher Sam Gambill is shown on the far left shaking hands.

THE DICKSONS OF HELTON TOWNSHIP, C. 1915. The adults pictured above, from left to right, are Mrs. Maude Dickson, Mrs. Clyde Franklin Dickson, and Mrs. Ruby Dickson. The children are unidentified.

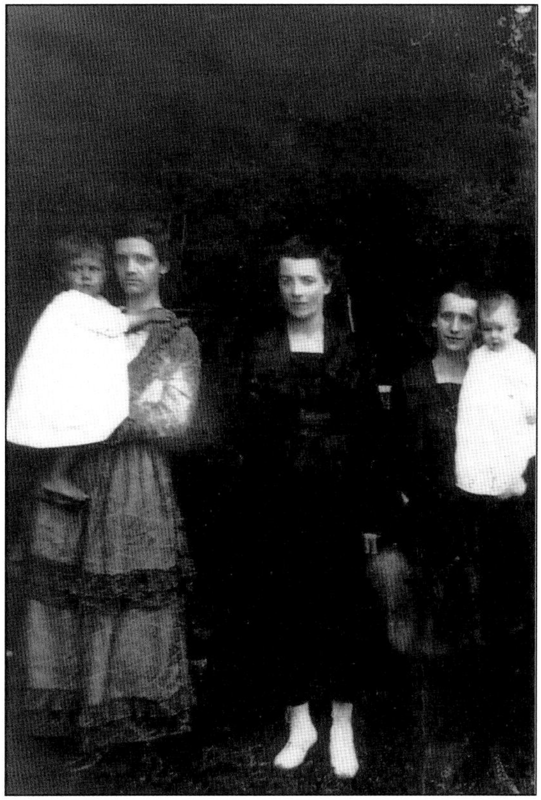

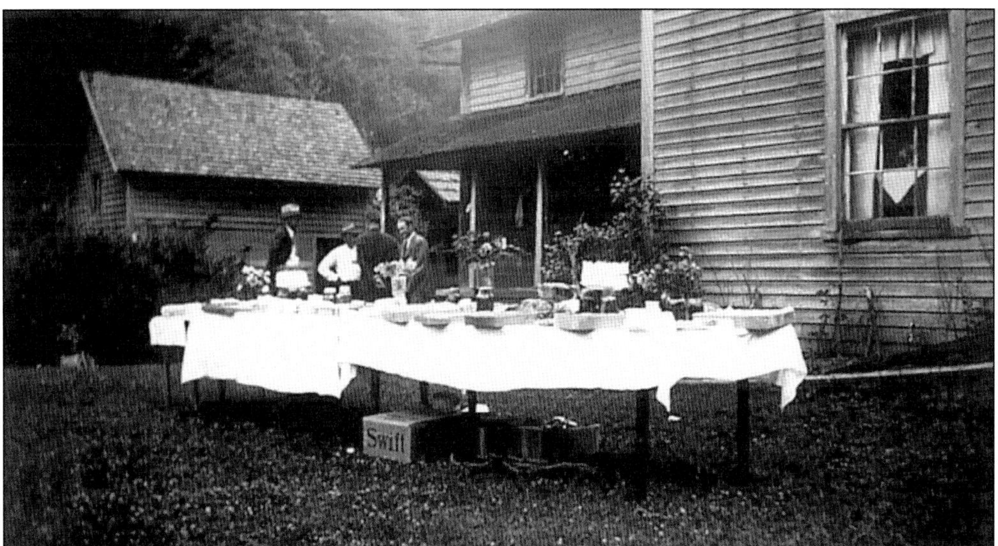

THOMAS SUTHERLAND'S BIRTHDAY. This 1924 birthday party was held at Blue Buck Cove at Sutherland on Thomas Sutherland's 78th birthday.

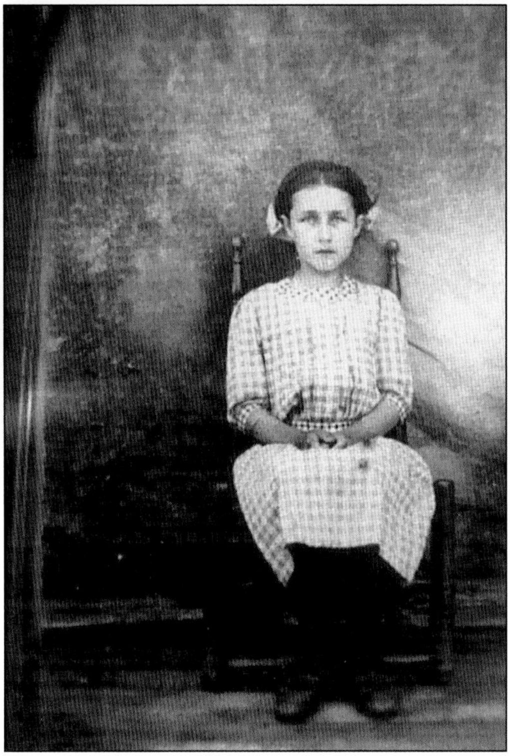

GERTIE GAMBILL ROBERTS OF PINEY CREEK. Gertie G. Roberts is pictured at left around 1919 wearing a dress made from hand-loomed cloth.

HELTON TEXTILE MILLS, C. 1920. During the 19th century, cloth was primarily carded and woven in the home. After the invention of carding machines, which could be operated by waterpower, many mills developed. The Helton mill is surrounded by chestnut rail fences.

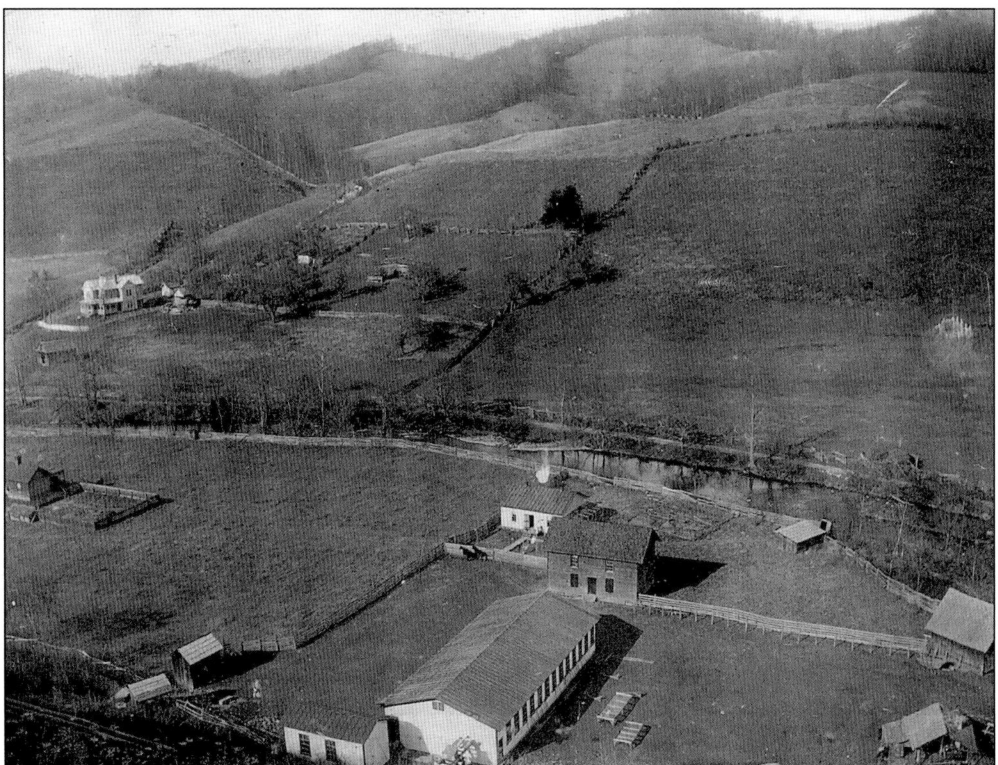

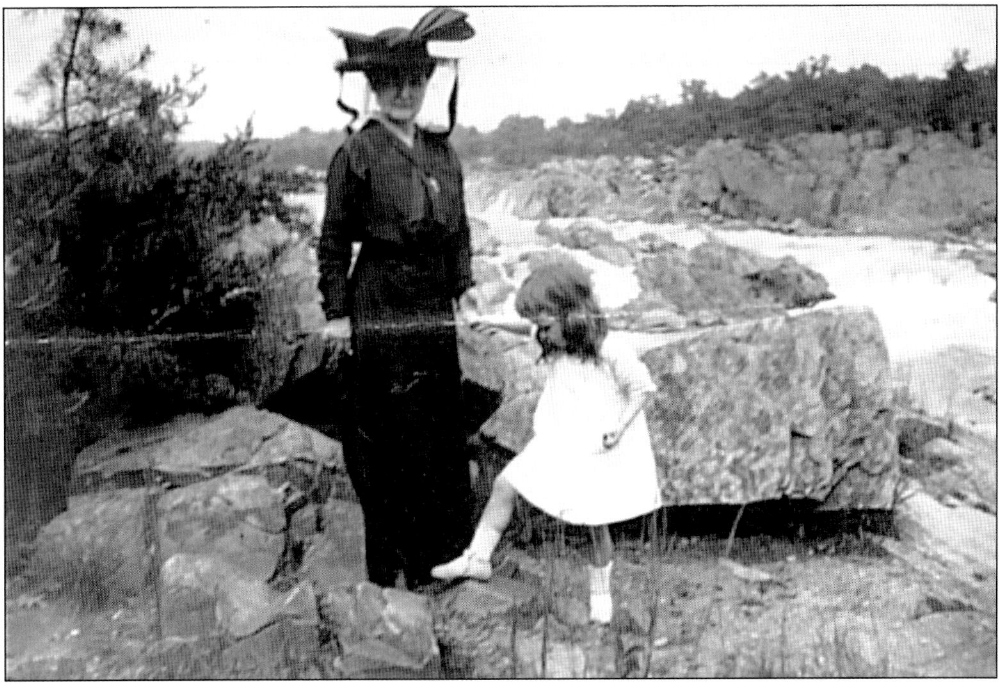

"Mama" Ashe and Margaret Newland, c. 1900. Margaret Newland died when she was only four years old because of diphtheria.

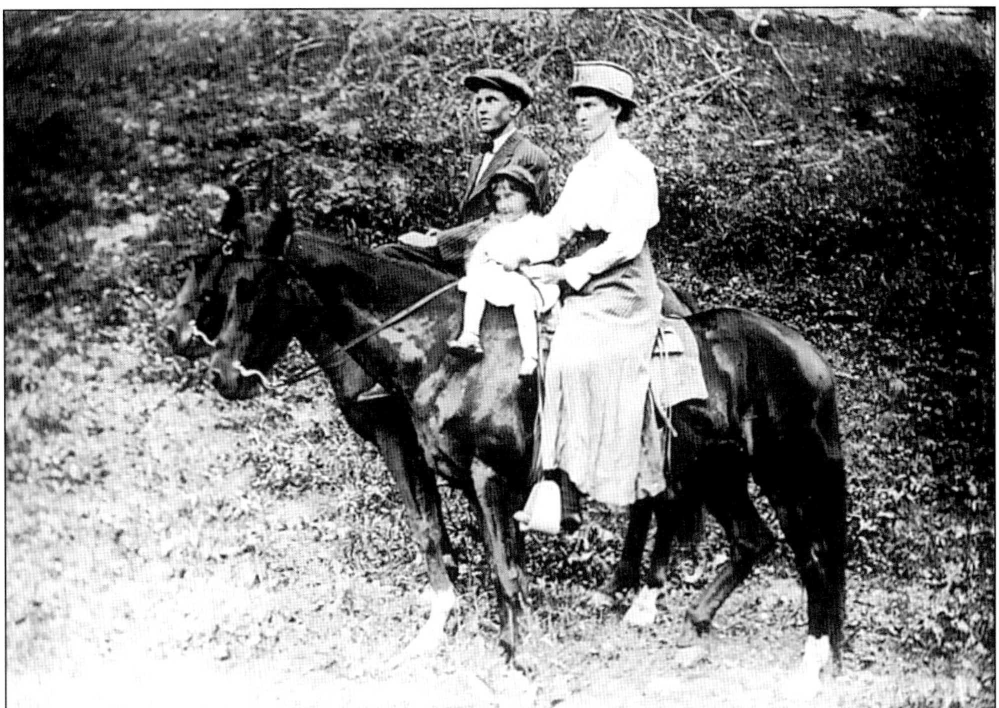

Sunday Ride, c. 1918. Austin Roberts and Cordelia Roberts Testerman are pictured above with their daughter Della Testerman.

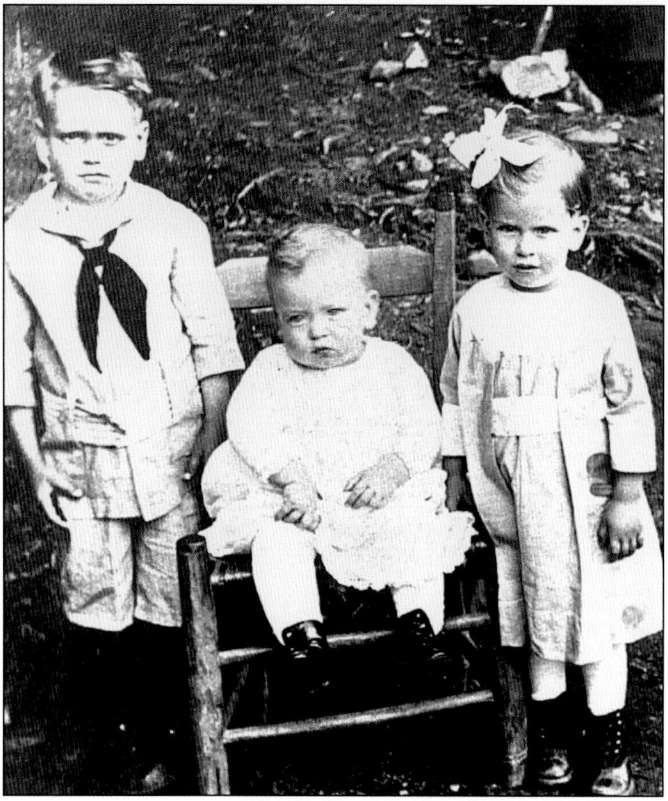

ROSCOE AND VIRGIE PEACOCK STURGILL'S CHILDREN. Pictured from left to right in this *c.* 1920 image are Henry, Earl, and Hazel Sturgill of the Lansing community.

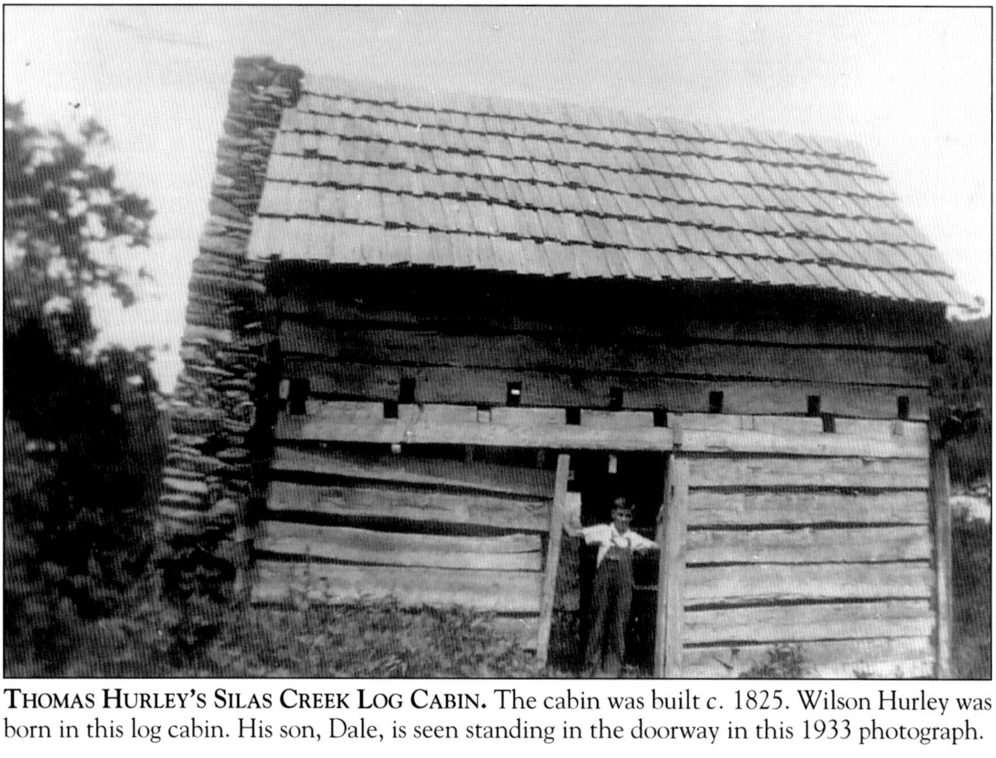

THOMAS HURLEY'S SILAS CREEK LOG CABIN. The cabin was built *c.* 1825. Wilson Hurley was born in this log cabin. His son, Dale, is seen standing in the doorway in this 1933 photograph.

PLAYING GAMES IN HELTON, C. 1925. Pictured from left to right are Blake and Walter Spencer in the front row; the children in the back are unidentified.

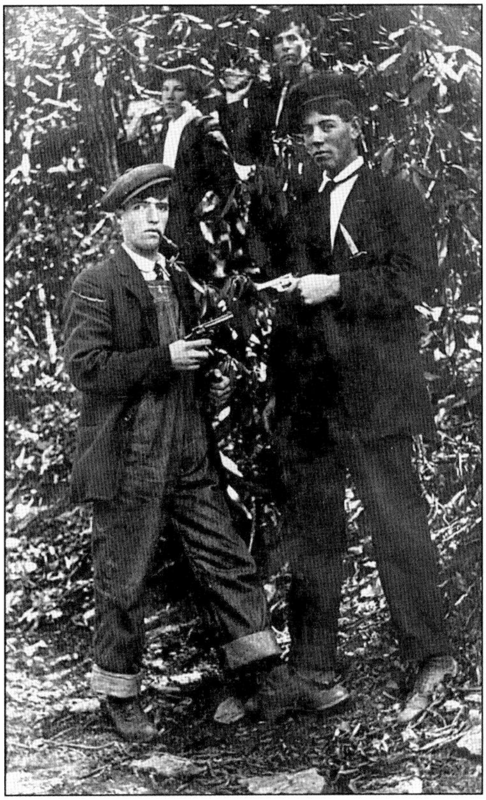

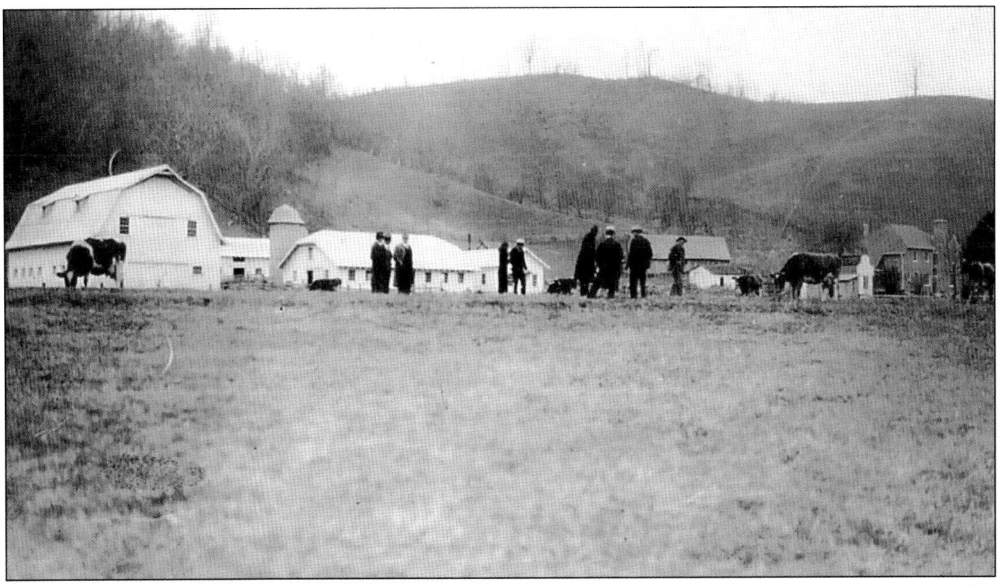

RICH HILL FARM FIELD DAY, 1937. Local gentlemen traditionally gathered to view the livestock, as seen in this photograph.

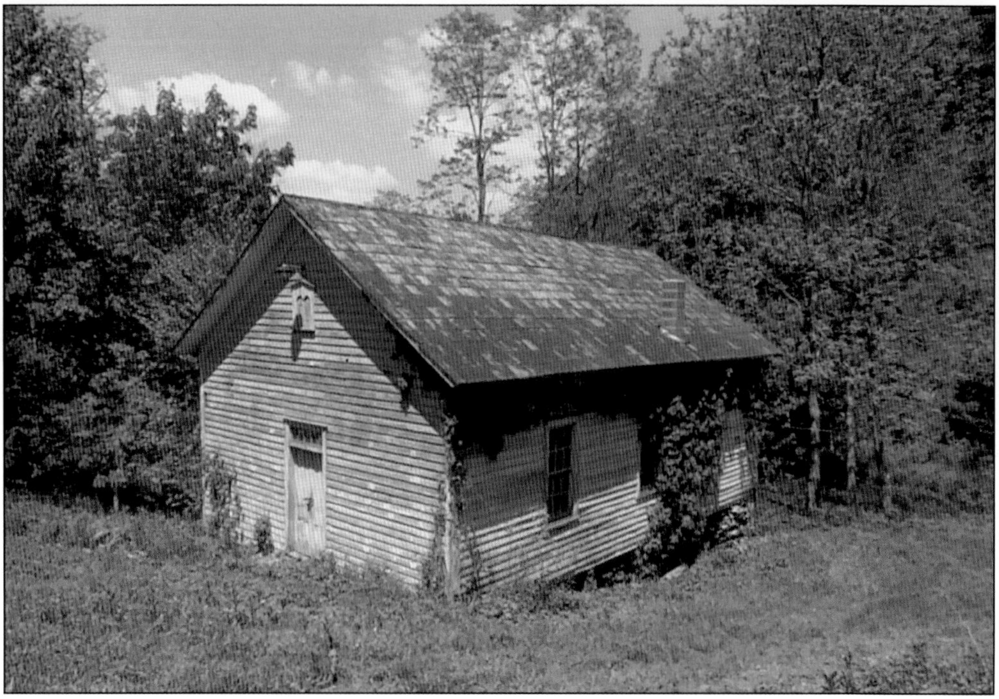

CHURCH OF THE BRETHREN NEAR WARRENSVILLE. During the 1920s, an ordinance was passed in Jefferson denying members of the sect a welcome to visit Warrensville.

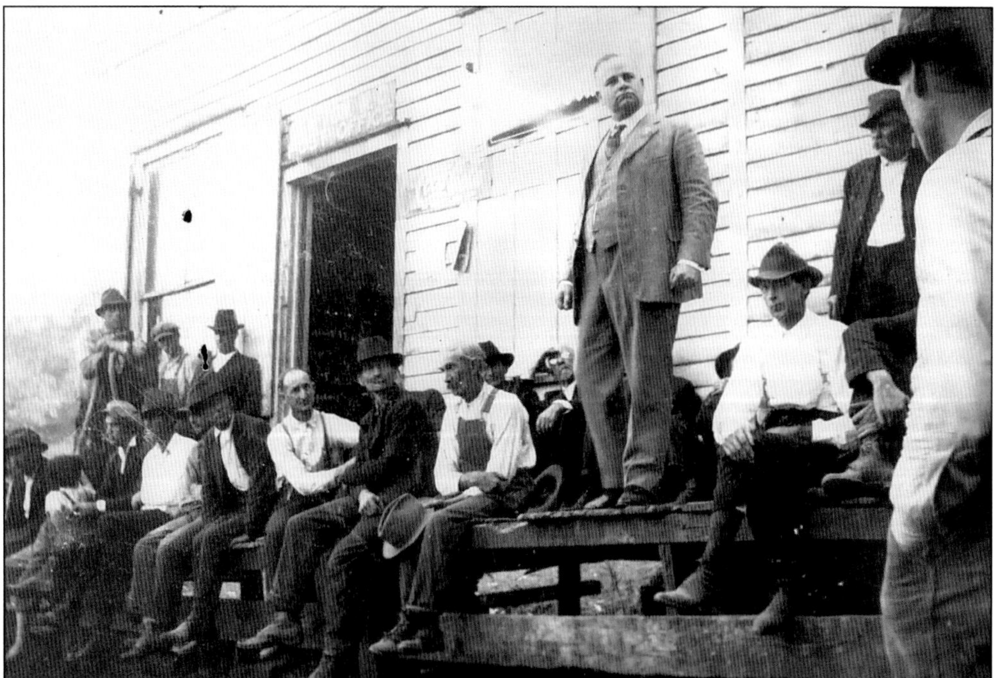

TOM "TAM" BOWIE. Bowie is speaking *c.* 1920 at the Clifton Post Office, and he is probably making a stump speech. A well-known attorney, Bowie's first elected post was to the House of Representatives in 1909.

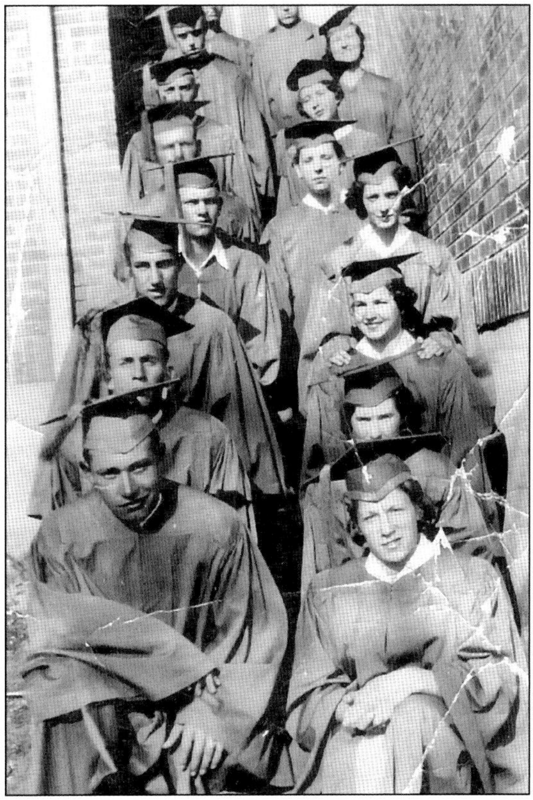

NATHAN'S CREEK HIGH SCHOOL GRADUATING CLASS OF 1936. Graduating students pictured from the bottom to top are as follows: (left side) Paul Shatley, Lonnie Bare, Grover Marsh, Osco Woodie, Bruce Shepherd, Mont Shately, Emerson Woodie, Everett Shepherd, Guy Shatley, and Russel Bard; (right side) Ala Sexton Lyalls, Myrtle Phipps, Edity Pierce Jones, Kathleen Woodruff Perkins, Pauline Blevins Leastry, Thelma McMillan, and Edit Yates Corbett.

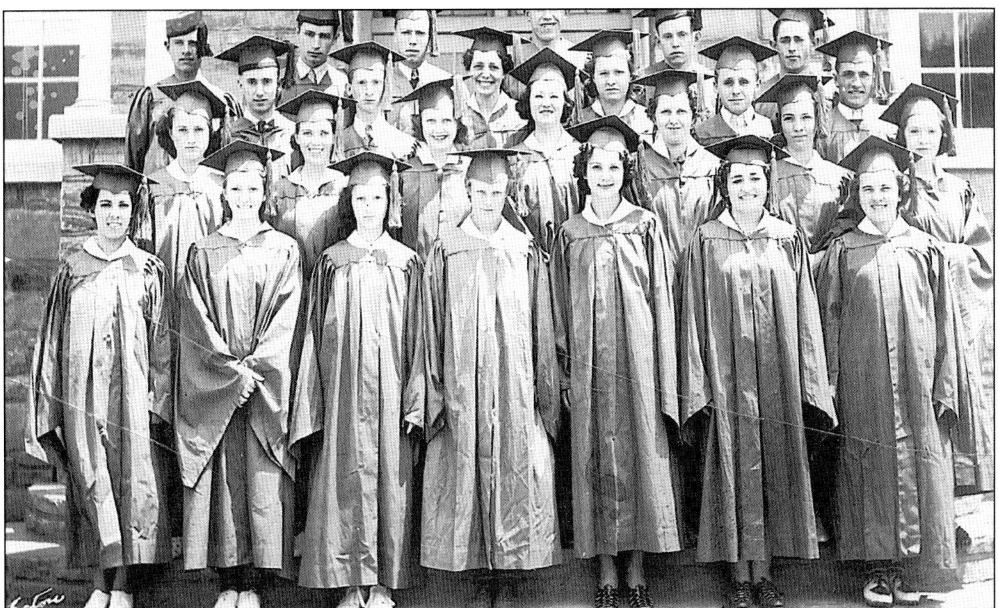

LANSING SCHOOL GRADUATING CLASS, 1939. This was the first graduating class in the new building constructed by the Works Projects Administration. Lansing became an accredited high school in 1927 when it was located in its original building.

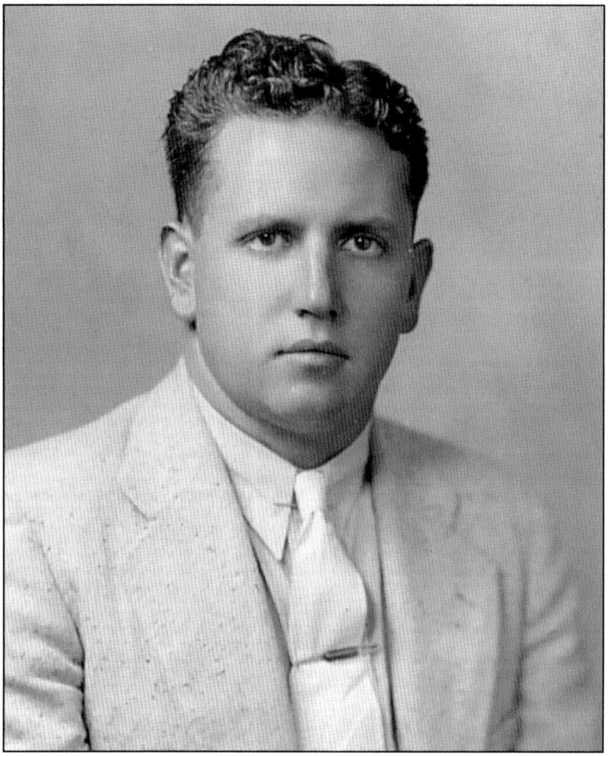

LANSING HIGH SCHOOL'S COACH MORPHIS. Morphis was a prominent football coach for Lansing High School. This photograph was taken *c.* 1944.

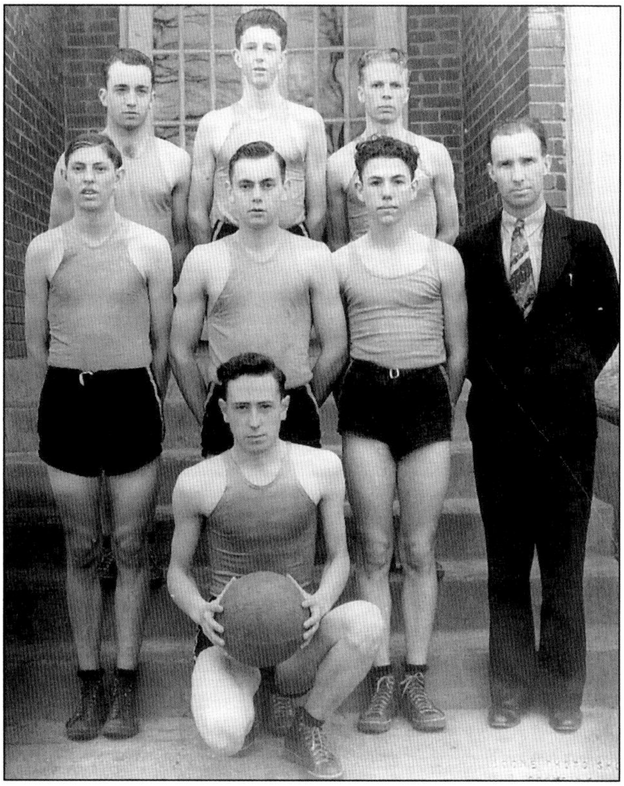

NATHAN'S CREEK BASKETBALL TEAM, 1939. Pictured from left to right are (front row, kneeling) Maynard Cox Gambill; (middle row) Blaine Ward, John Gentry, Dayne Saunders, and Coach Glen McGuire; (back row) Bill Pennington, John Woodruff, and Kyle Ward.

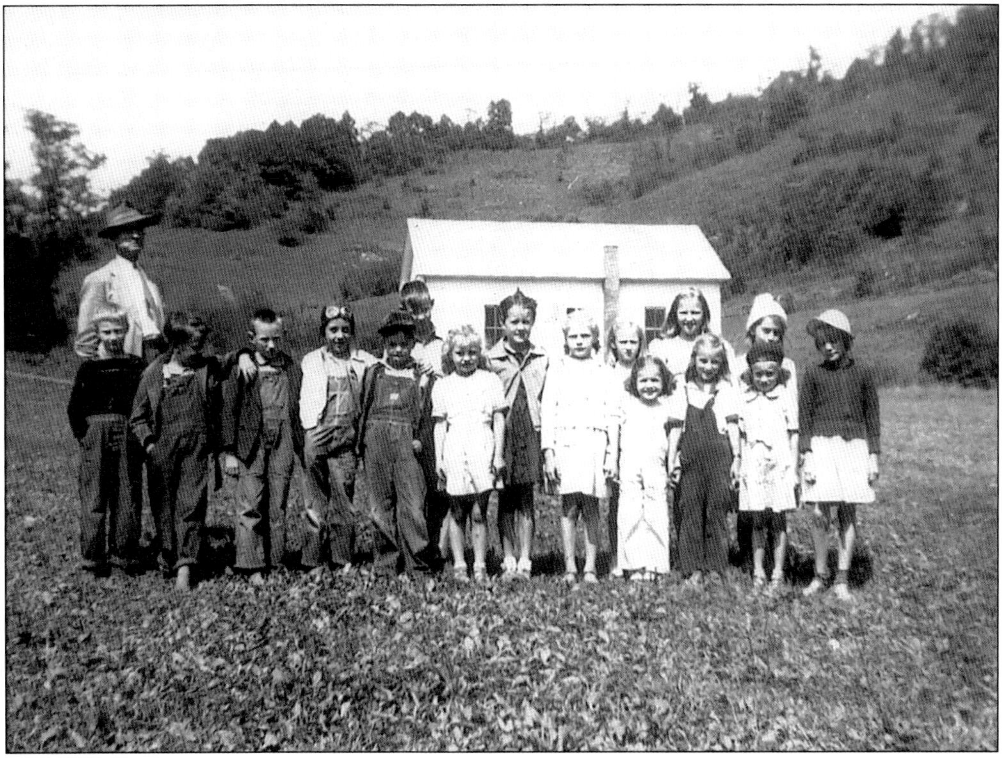

LANDMARK SCHOOL STUDENTS, c. 1946. Claude Franklin Dickson (pictured on the left) and his students, grades one through seven, pose for this photograph. He was the sole teacher in the one-room school. Landmark Baptist Church is in the background.

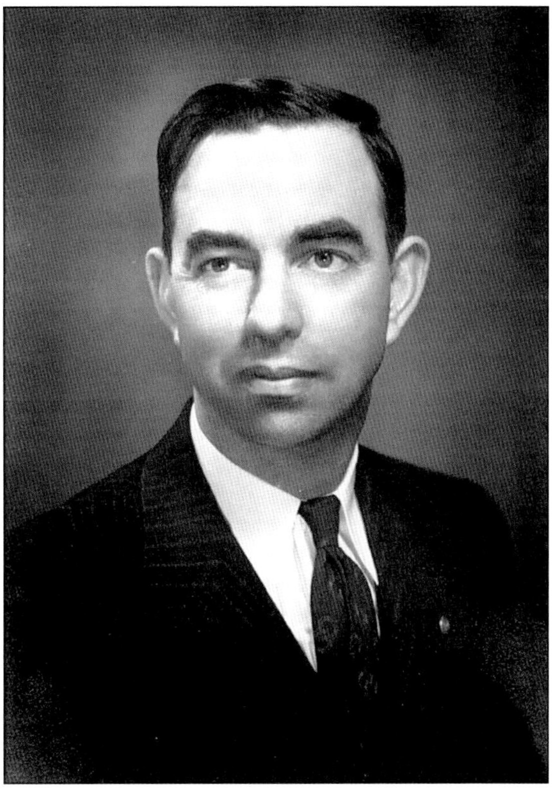

GWYN B. PRICE, c. 1930s. In addition to his career as dairy farmer, Price was a teacher and principal of the Jefferson Academy. Called the "father of North Carolina's cooperative movement," he guided development of electric and telephone co-ops throughout the state. He served on the North Carolina Rural Electrification Authority for 42 years.

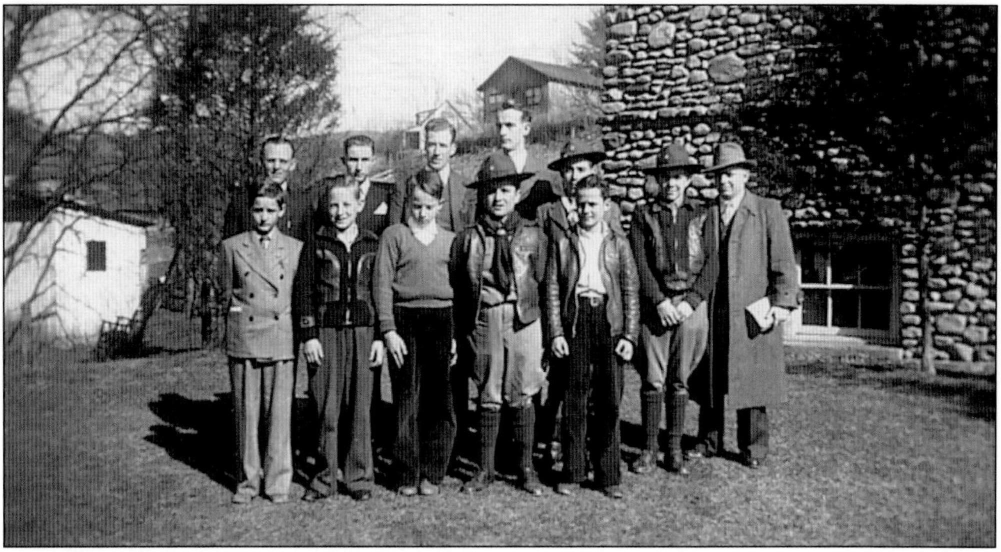

FIRST BOY SCOUT TROOP IN LANSING. The troop met at Lansing Presbyterian Church, which is pictured in the background. Pictured in this c. 1942 photograph are, from left to right, (front row) Ray Shepherd, Jack Baldwin, Pete Barr, Allen Weaver, Jack Poe, Harry Goss, and unidentified; (back row) unidentified, Tom Roberts, Walter Osborne, and Joseph Martin.

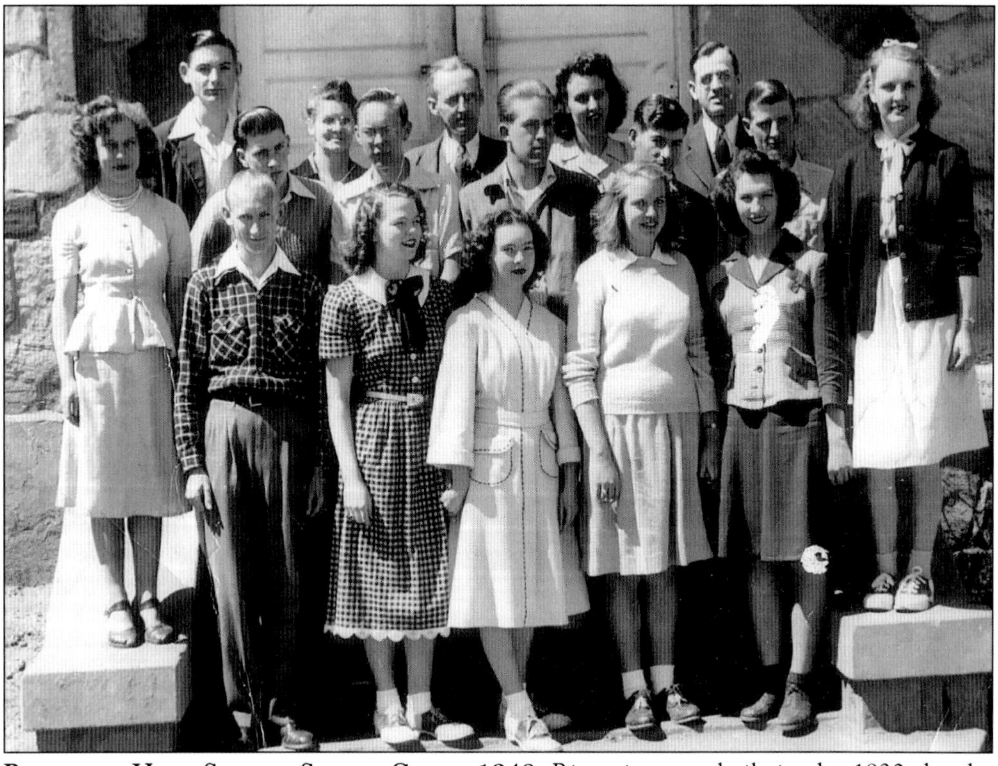

RIVERVIEW HIGH SCHOOL SENIOR CLASS, 1948. Riverview was built in the 1930s by the WPA and existed until the late 1950s when it consolidated with Lansing High School to form Northwest High School. Riverview and Lansing were the last two regional high schools to consolidate.

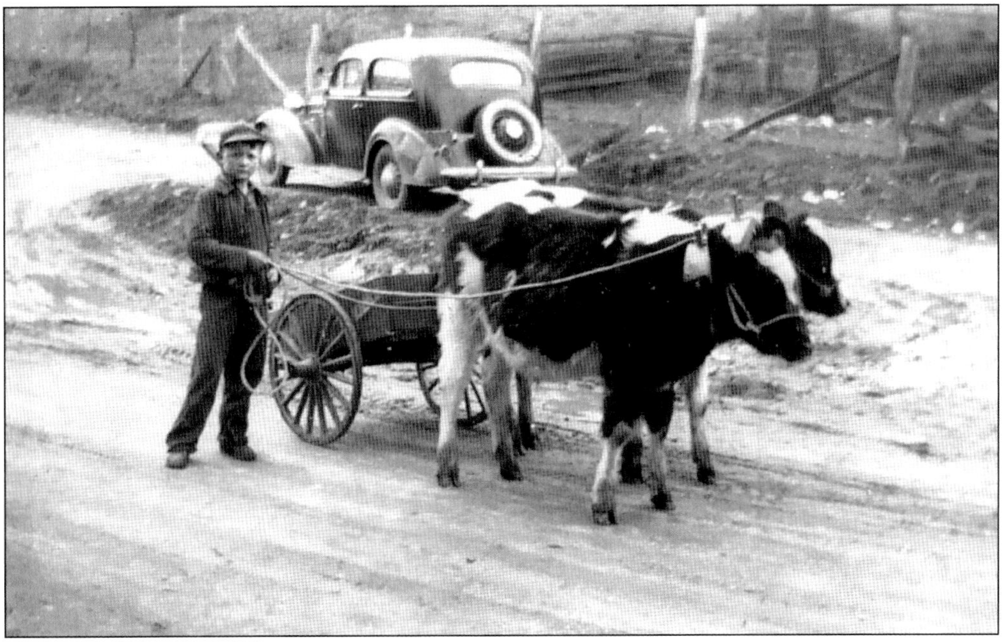

Young Entrepreneur Helps Neighbors. In Green Valley in the late 1940s, Tom Barlow cleaned people's barns and hauled and distributed the manure out to the fields for his neighbors.

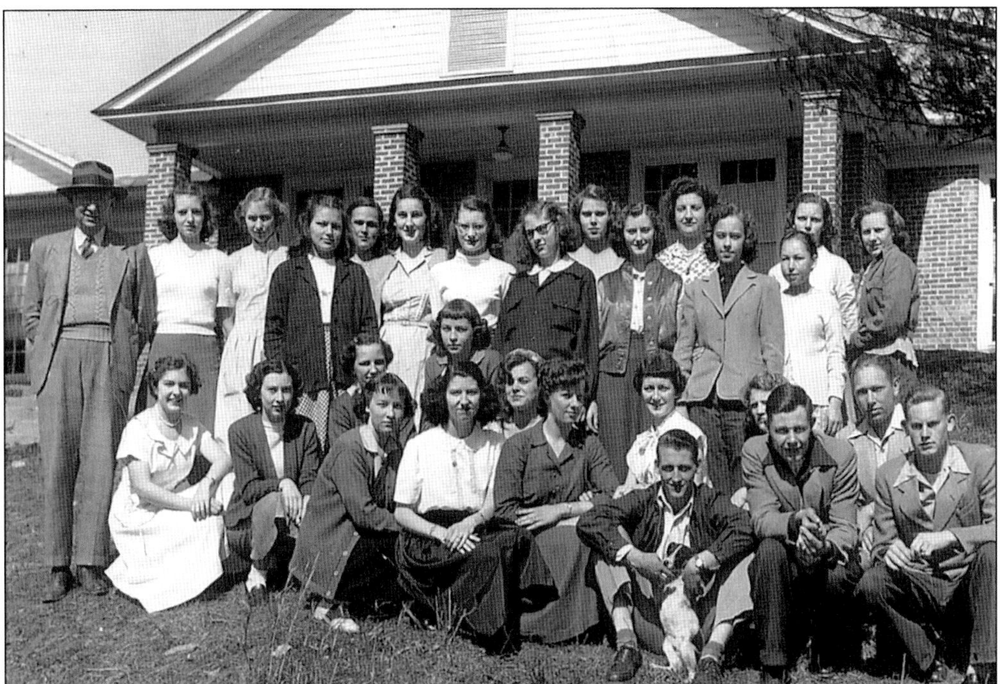

Healing Springs High School Drama Club, 1949. Club adviser William Lawton Woodie is pictured at the left.

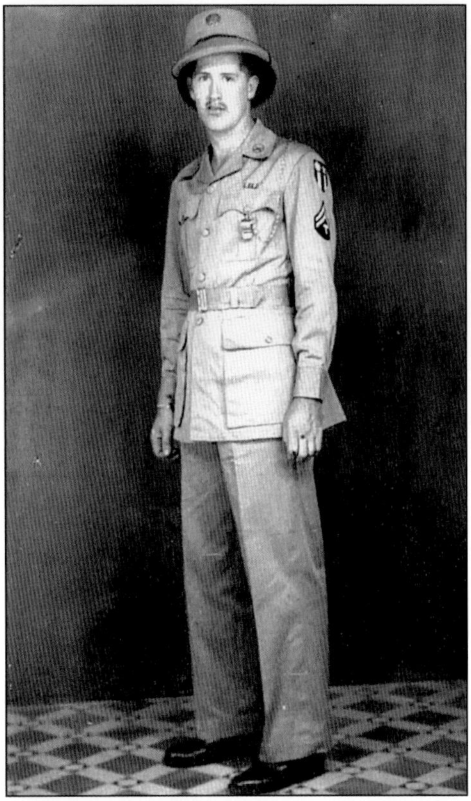

CPL. E. RICHARD JONES, C. 1942. Jones, who is pictured in his uniform as a member of the military police in India during World War II, is the son of Mr. and Mrs. W. Lee Jones.

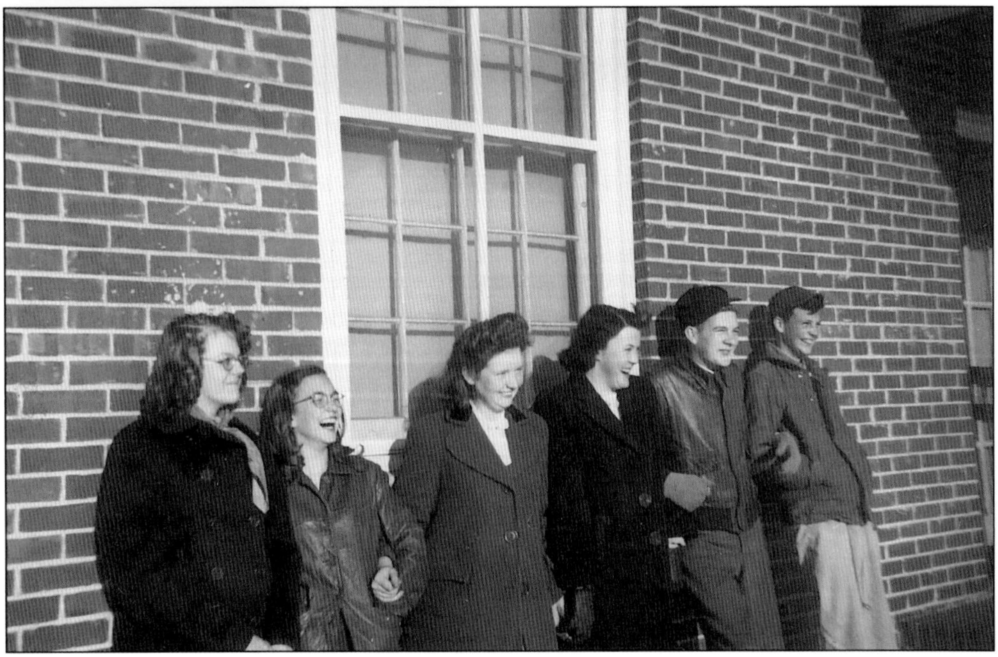

LANSING PRESBYTERIAN YOUTH GROUP. Pictured in this 1947 photograph from left to right are Allene Powers, Katherine Carter, Marlene Jones, Marilyn Farmer, Dawes Graybeal, and Charles Dolinger.

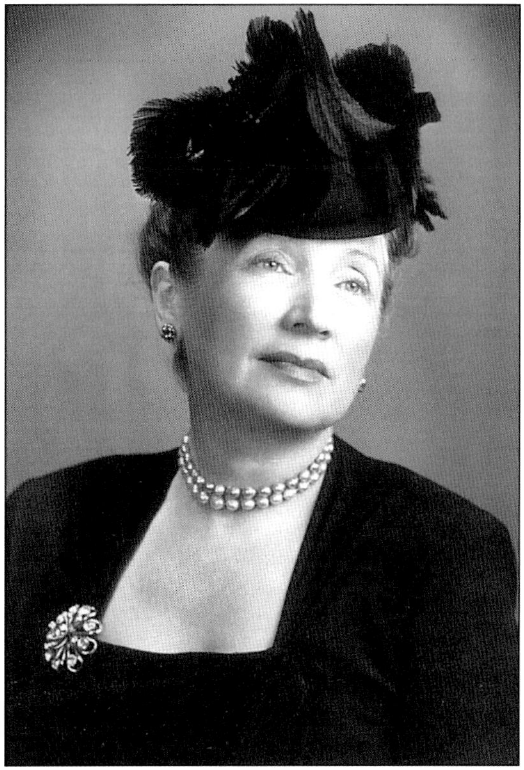

PAULETT LOUIS BERTRANDIAS SIMPSON DICKSON, C. 1940. Mrs. Paulett Dickson was the wife of Dr. Robert Lee Dickson. She was a native of Paris, France, and had lived in Philadelphia, Pennsylvania, before moving to her husband's native Ashe County.

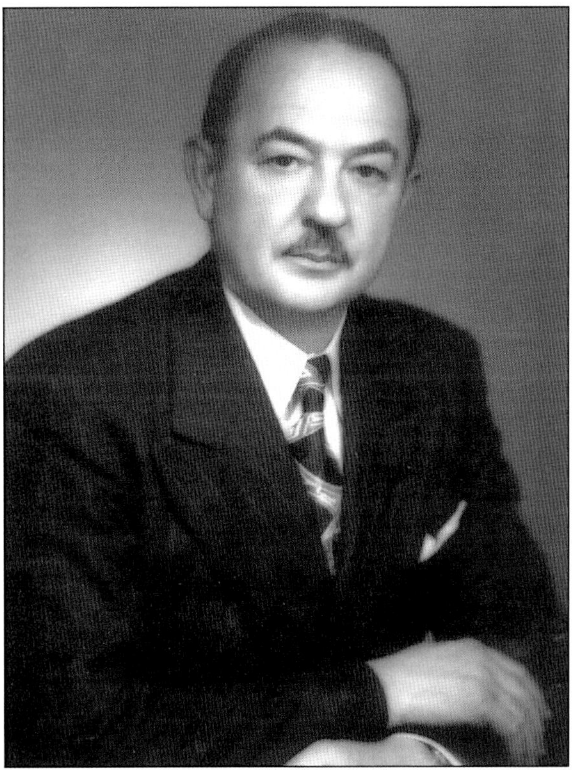

DR. ROBERT LEE DICKSON, C. 1940. Dickson purchased the Healing Springs Hotel when he retired to Ashe County. He became active with community affairs.

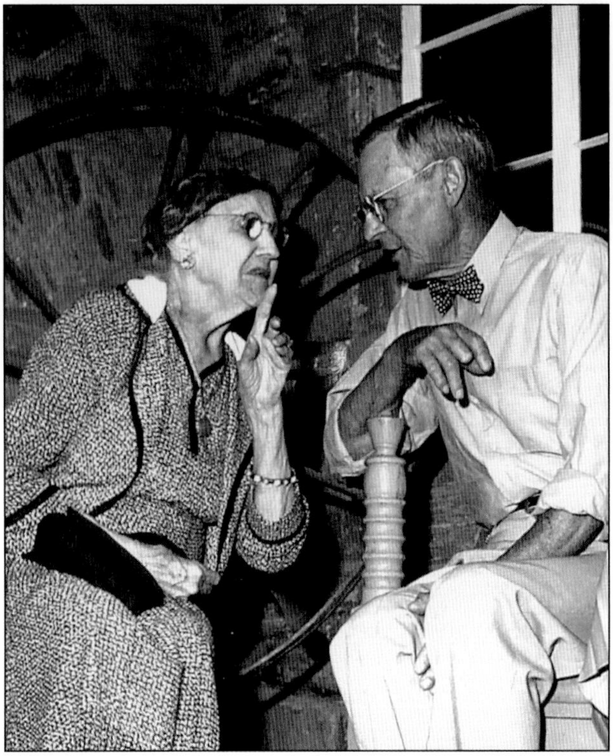

ADA WORTH PENN-COFFEY AND PETE HAMILTON. Ada and Pete are pictured conversing at a Worth family reunion around 1958. Ada is the youngest daughter of David and Elizabeth Worth of Creston. Hamilton bought the old David Worth home and farmed the surrounding land for many years.

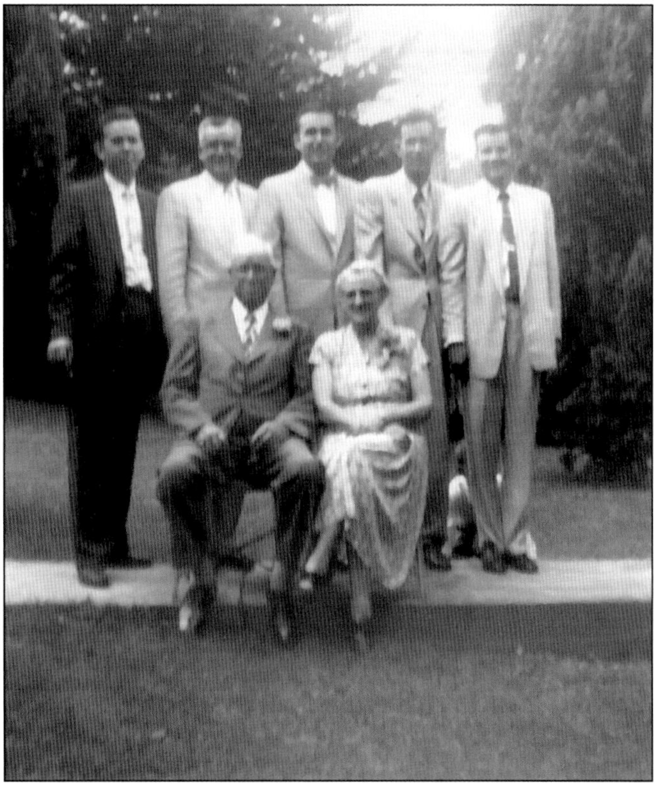

BEN AND EMMA DOLINGER CELEBRATE, 1958. Ben and Emma Dolinger are enjoying their 50th wedding anniversary celebration in this photograph. Pictured from left to right are (front row) Ben and Emma Dolinger; (back row) sons Kenneth, Lloyd, Ancel, Wade and Charles Dolinger.

Three

BETWEEN THE SUMMITS

JEFFERSON, WEST JEFFERSON, AND THEIR NEIGHBORS

The first settlers in what is now Ashe County came primarily from the North. Due to the terrain, the Helton and Creston areas were settled first. As more and more settlers arrived, migrations moved further into the region where good land was still available. The two commercial centers that developed over time nestled in a valley in the heart of Ashe County between the summits of Mt. Jefferson, Paddy Mountain, and Phoenix Mountain.

By 1799, the population had grown to a point that the area qualified for county status. Ashe County originally included all of Alleghany and a large portion of Watauga County. The General Assembly of 1799 appointed a special commission to select a site for the new county seat. Fifty acres were purchased from Adam Bowers for $100 and Jeffersontown was laid out with the courthouse in the center. The name was later shortened to Jeffersonton and again to Jefferson. In the early 1800s, Jefferson was the largest town in the North Carolina mountains.

The Virginia-Carolina Railroad (later Norfolk and Western), which entered Ashe early in the 20th century, brought with it modern transportation for people and their goods. It also brought with it a bitter pill for our county seat. The railroad company was not willing to spend an additional $5,000 to route the line through Jefferson on its way to Todd, its planned destination. As a result, the West Jefferson Land Company was formed by three prominent Ashe speculators and another town was laid out two miles southwest. West Jefferson soon grew to be the largest town in Ashe County.

The two towns on the valley floor are visible from the heights of the surrounding mountains, which like others in the county are remnants of a mountainous region that existed in the remote geological past. Weathering and erosion has worn away the softer rocks, leaving behind peaks rising above a plateau-like surface. A bonus of the past is abundant, unusual flora which make their peaks and slopes objects of much interest.

—Sam Shumate

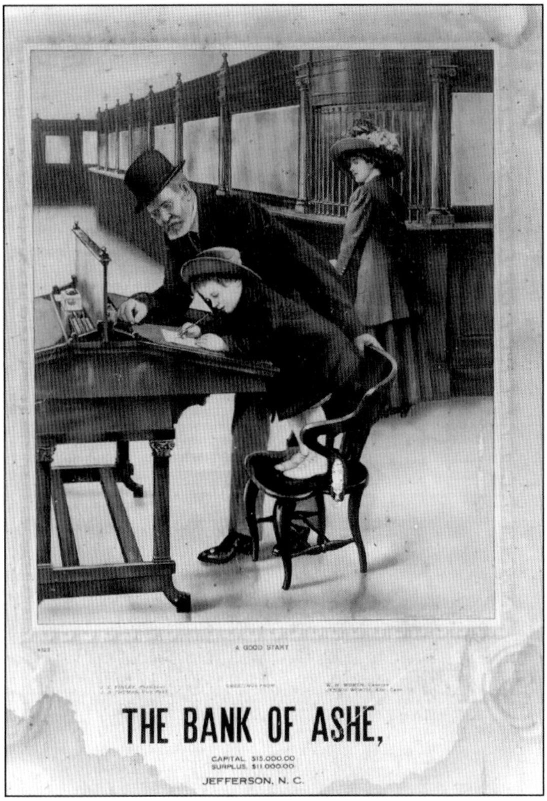

BANK OF ASHE. This early 1900s advertisement attracted customers to one of Ashe County's earliest banks.

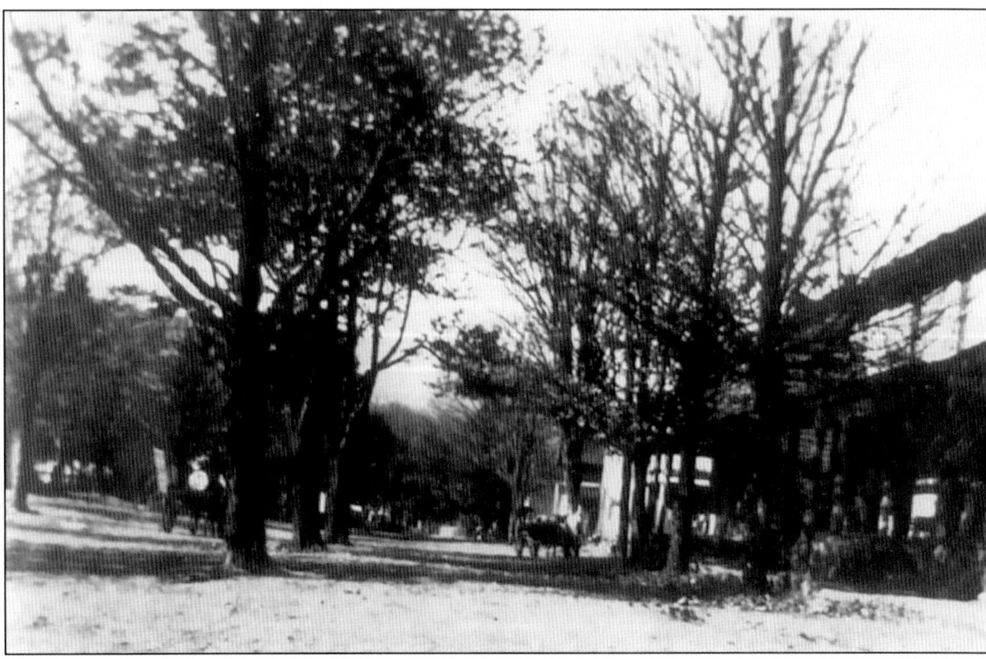

CHERRY TREES ON MAIN STREET. The main street in Jefferson will soon be ablaze with cherry blossoms in 1900.

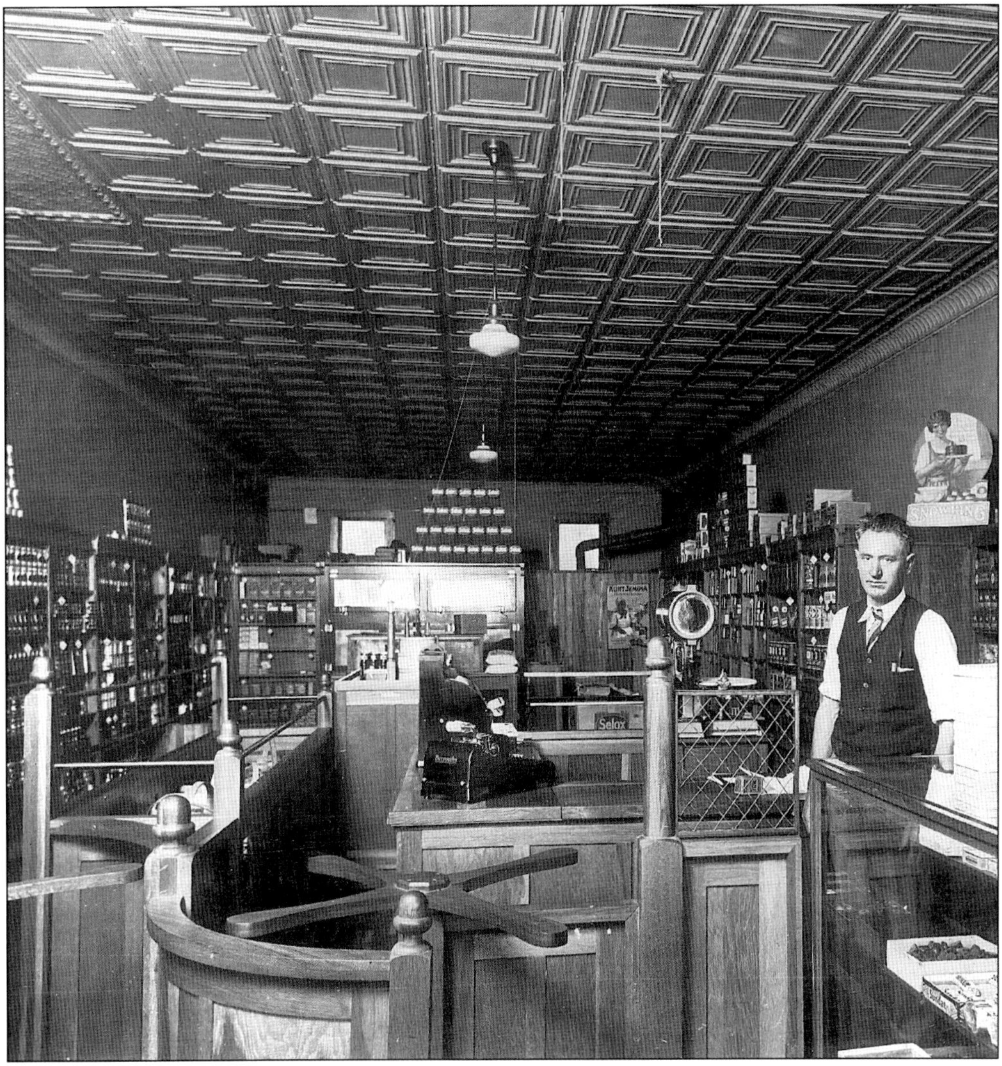

FRED RAY'S GROCERY. Note the beautiful tin ceiling in Fred Ray's grocery store. This was a very prosperous store in the 1900s.

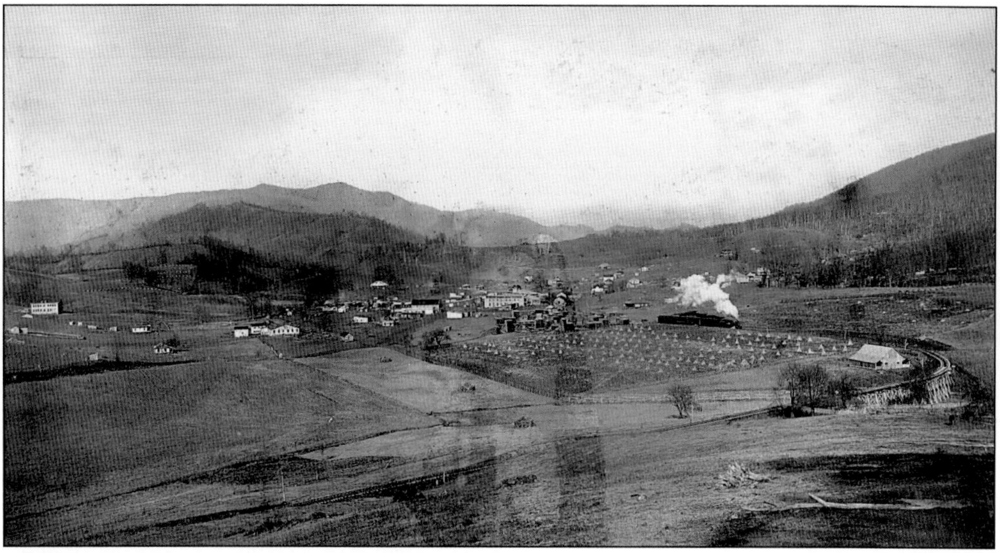

Bird's-eye View of West Jefferson. W.J. Hardware can be seen against the background of Paddy Mountain.

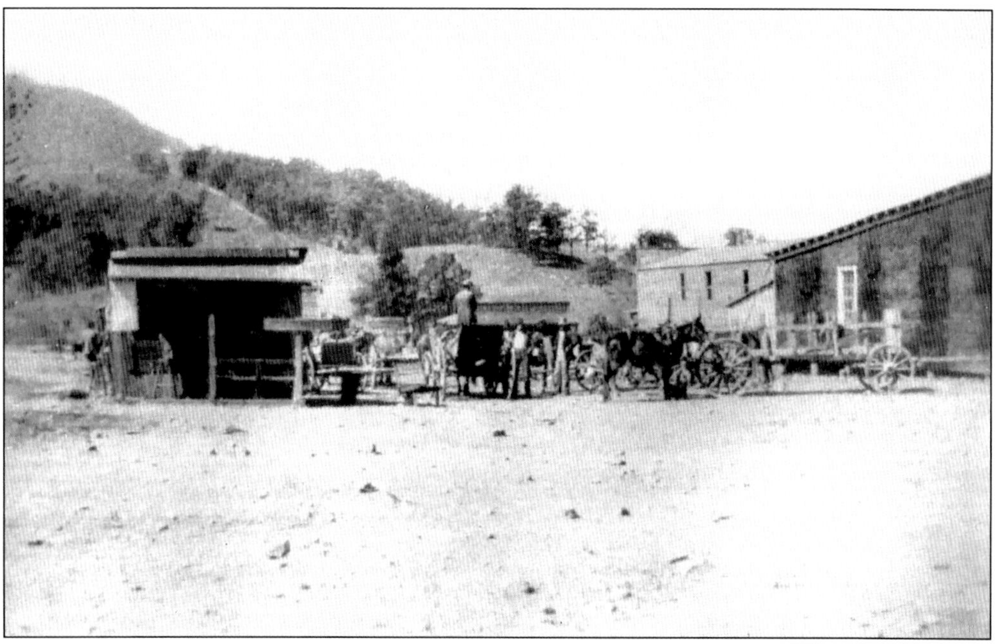

Wagon Yard in West Jefferson, c. 1918. This repair facility was on Third Avenue North between the Dr Pepper bottling plant and the present Burgess Furniture.

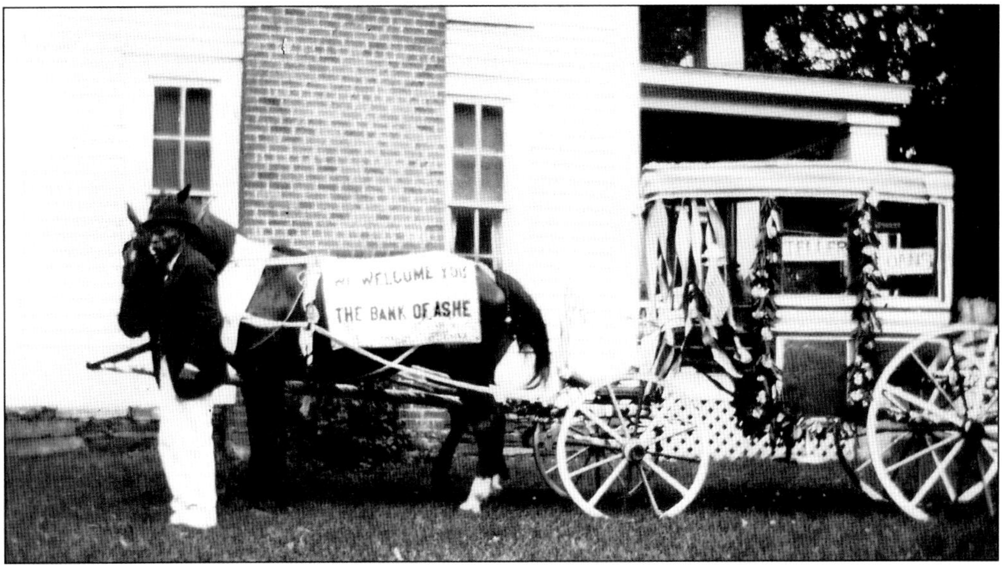

Alex the Wagon Master. The Bank of Ashe used this decorated buggy for promotions and publicity.

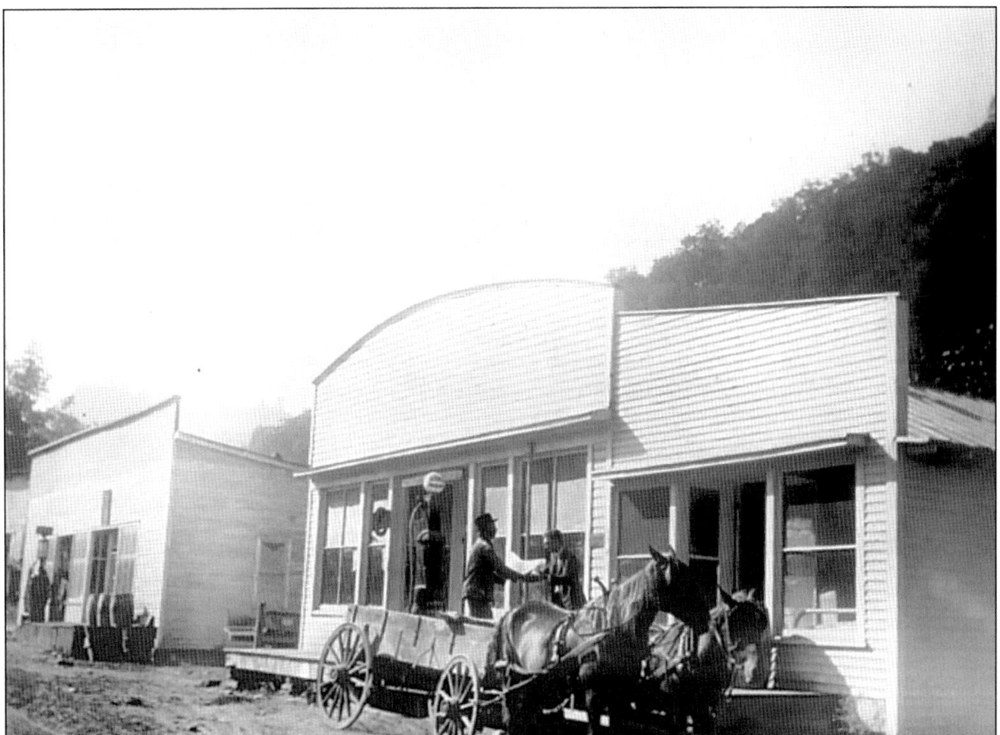

The Yates Store in Warrensville. This was a busy and prosperous store during the early 1900s. Much of the business was conducted on a barter system.

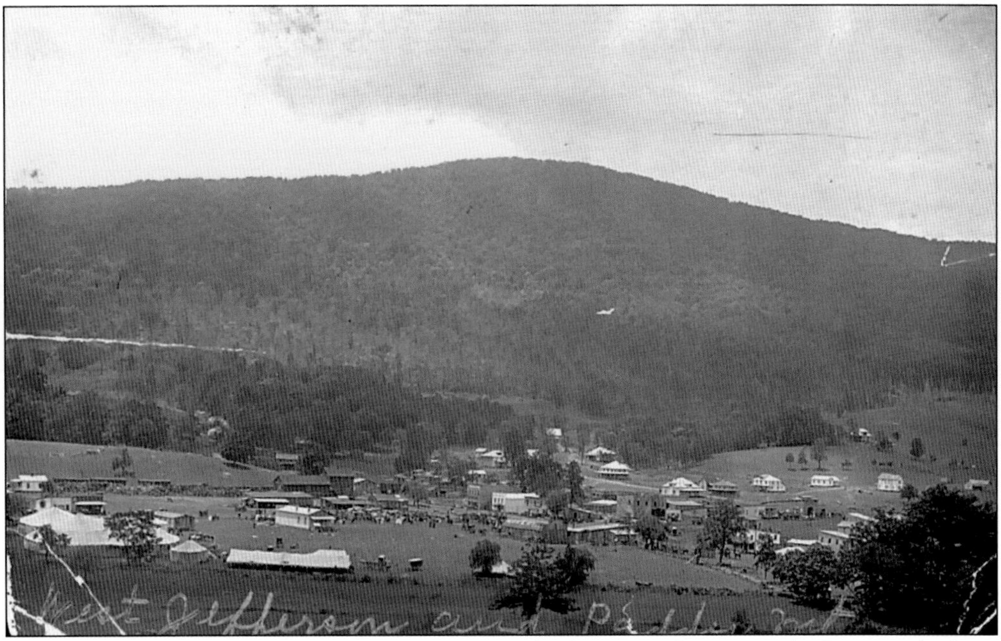

WEST JEFFERSON VIEW. Paddy Mountain cast its shadow over the town, which was only three years old in 1910, the year this photo was taken.

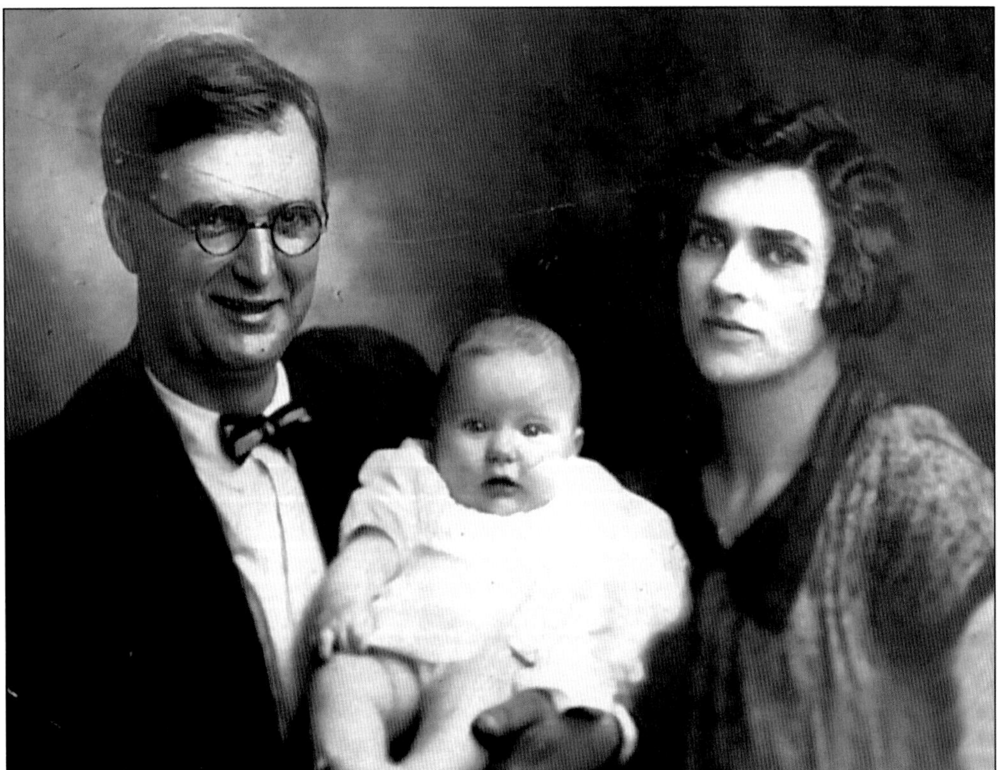

THE JOHNSONS OF WARRENSVILLE. Shown here are Gordon and Claudia Johnson with their daughter Lucille in 1919.

MEDICAL CORPSMAN SGT. IRA T. JOHNSTON. Sgt. Ira T. Johnston served during World War I. He later practiced law in Jefferson and represented Ashe County in both the State House and the Senate.

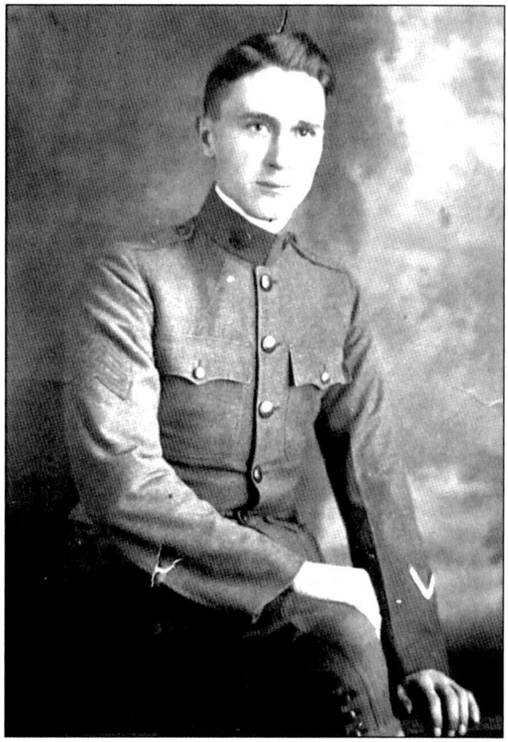

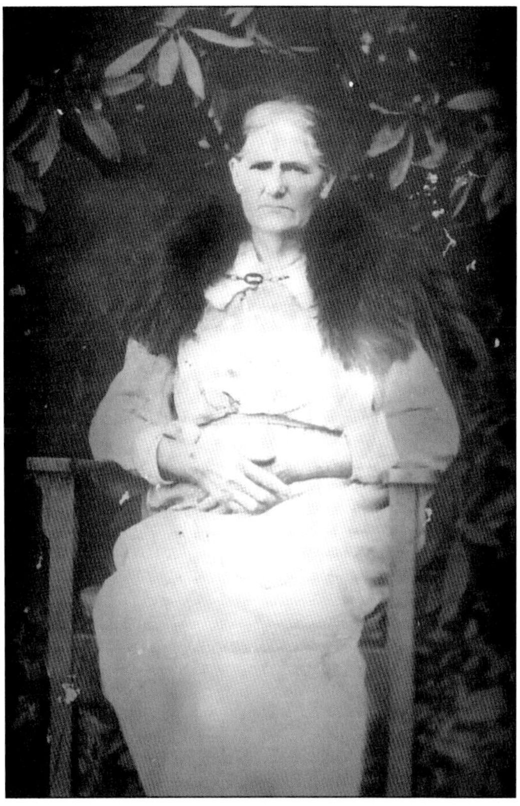

AMERICA HOUCK. This photograph of America was taken c. 1922. She was the mother of H.R. and Reddie Houck and a resident of the Old Bristol community.

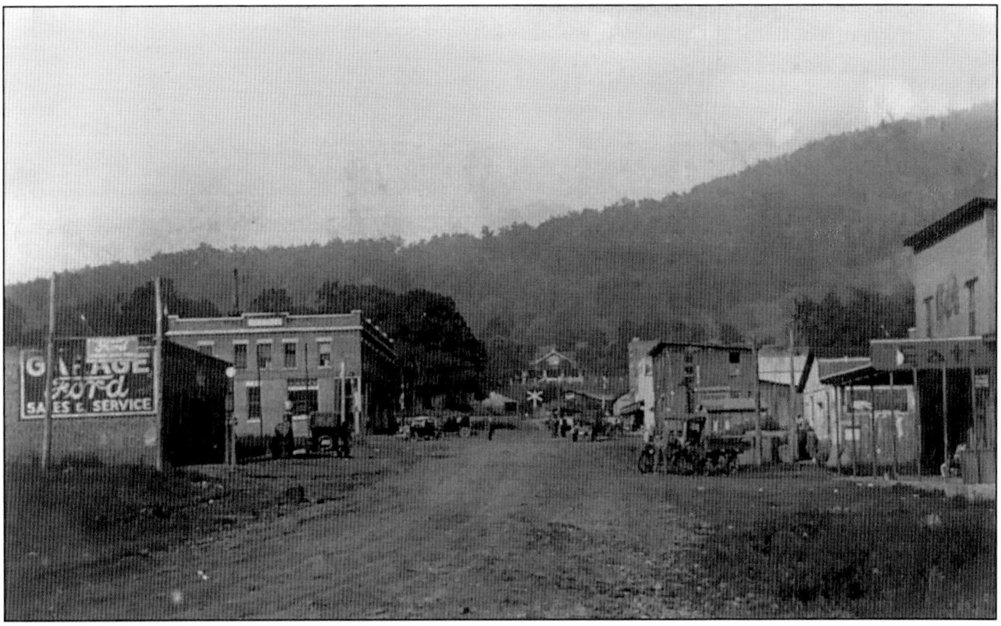

EARLY 1928 PHOTOGRAPH OF WEST JEFFERSON. The R.C. Barr home can be seen in the background of this early photograph. The Ford Garage is pictured on the right.

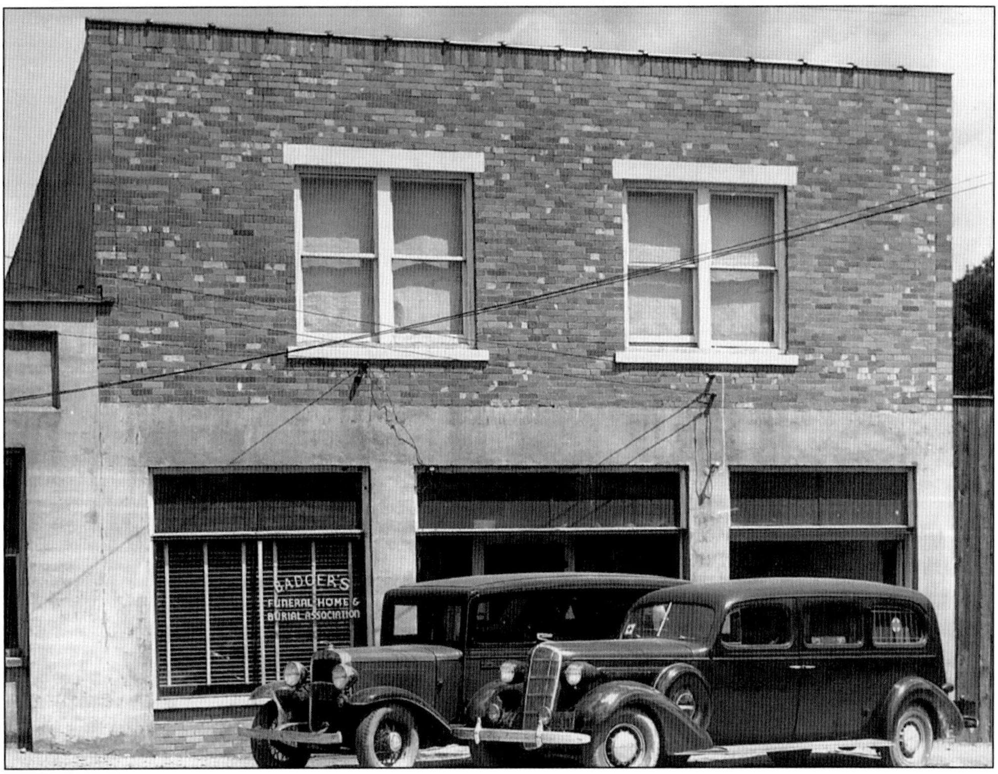

BADGER FUNERAL HOME. Guy and Roy Badger of West Jefferson founded Badger Funeral Home in West Jefferson. An ambulance and hearse are pictured in front of the funeral home. The Essex hearse was the first motorized funeral vehicle in Ashe County.

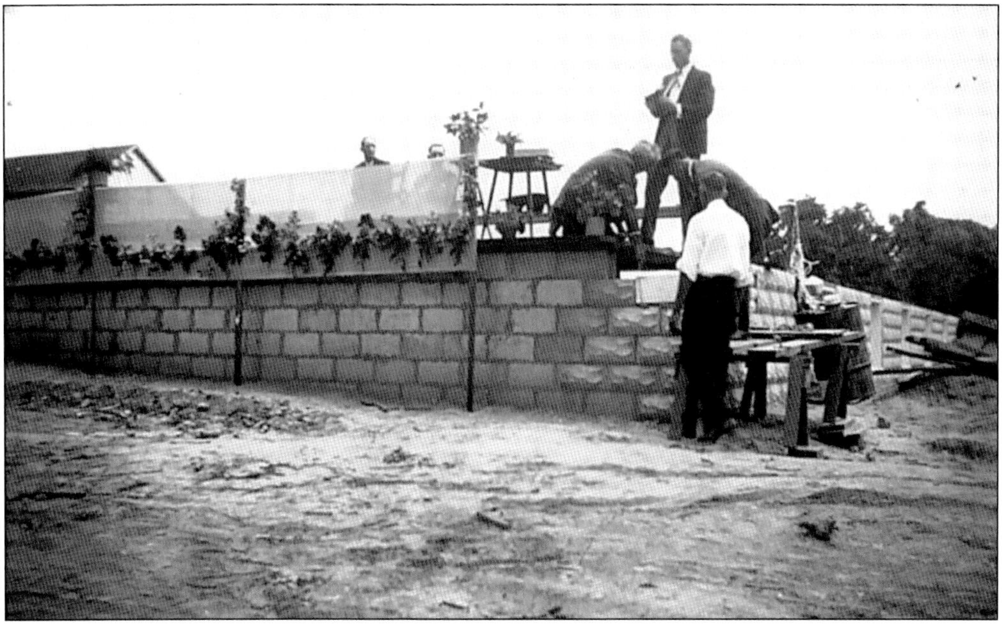

Baptists Lay the Cornerstone. In 1929, the cornerstone was set at the West Jefferson First Baptist Church. The Rev. Coy Blackburn reads scripture during the service.

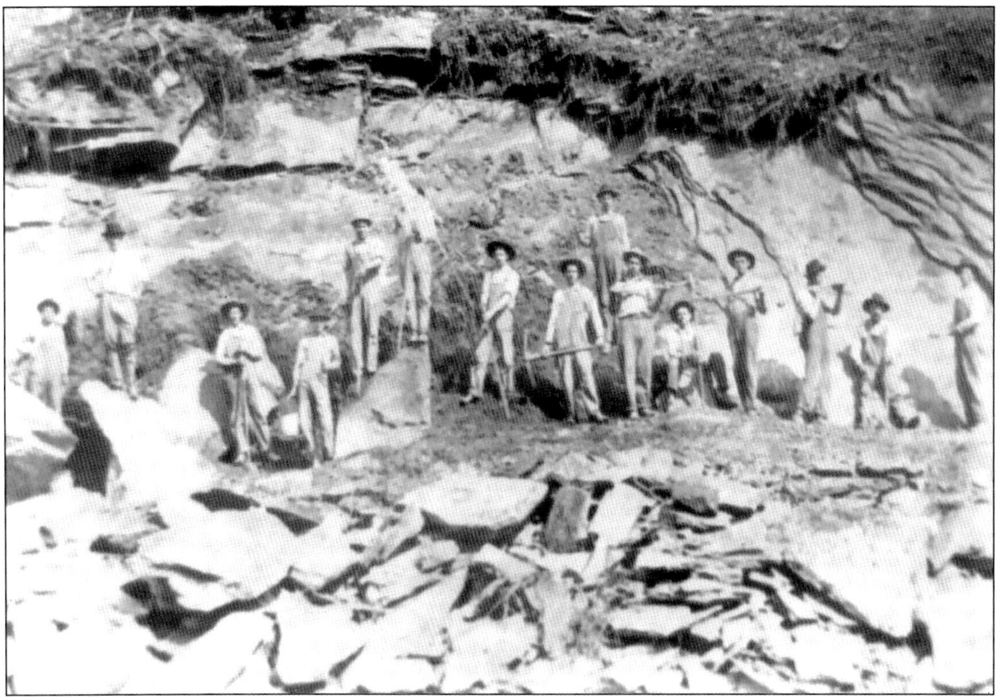

Mandatory Road Work at Devil's Stairs. From the early 1800s, roadwork was of the utmost importance in the county. A law was passed in 1806 that named overseers to specific sections of road along with a work team. This photo shows roadwork at Devil's Stairs above Warrensville.

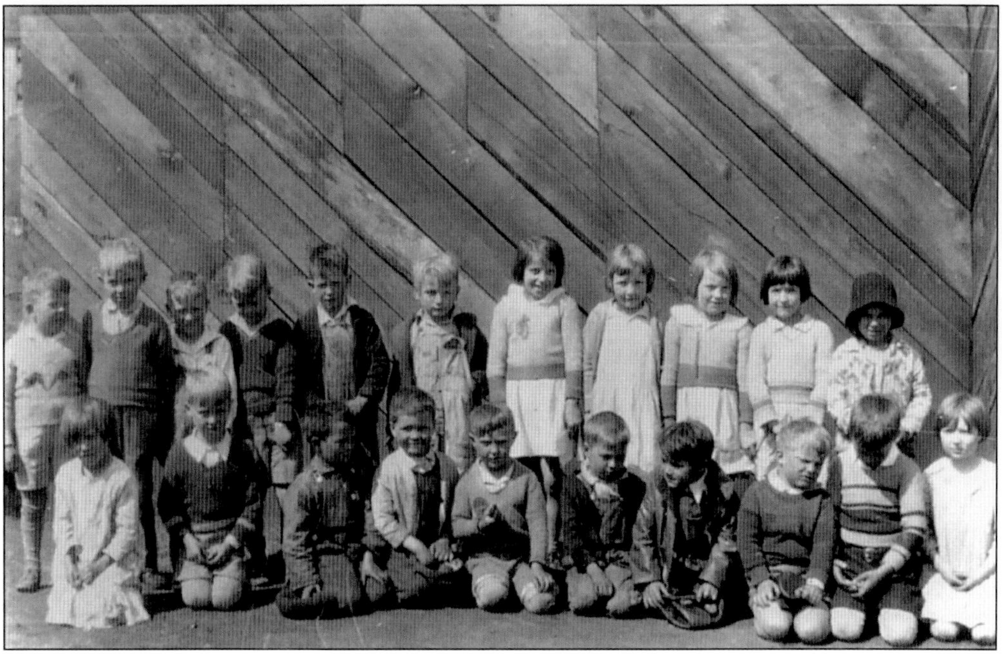

THE WEST JEFFERSON ELEMENTARY SCHOOL. Pictured is West Jefferson Elementary School's first-grade class of 1932.

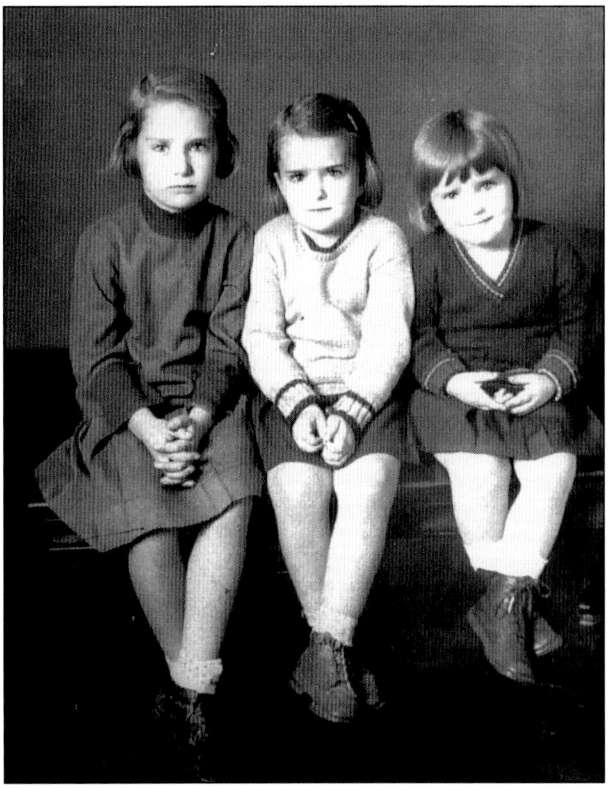

THE JOHNSON CHILDREN OF WARRENSVILLE. Pictured in this 1930 photograph are three of Gordon and Claudia Johnson's seven children. Pictured from left to right are Mary Lynn Richards, Marguerite (Dede) Hunter, and Francis Eleanor (Sammie) Scally.

GREAT-GRANDFATHER AND GREAT-GRANDSON. In this 1938 photograph taken in Warrensville, William Howard Jones of Warrensville holds young Sam Shumate's hand.

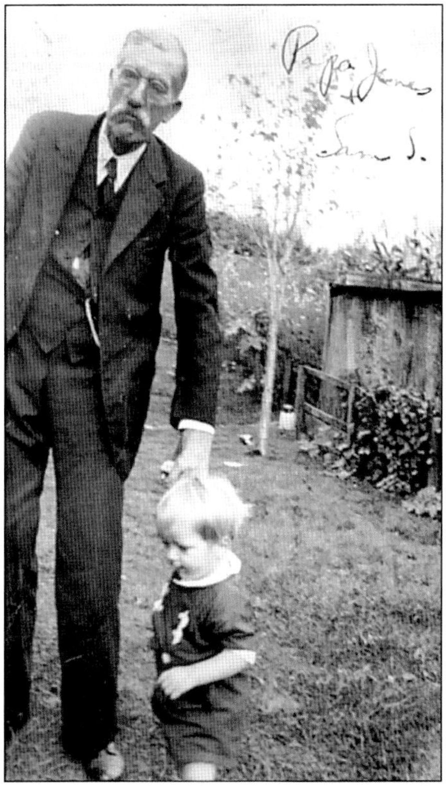

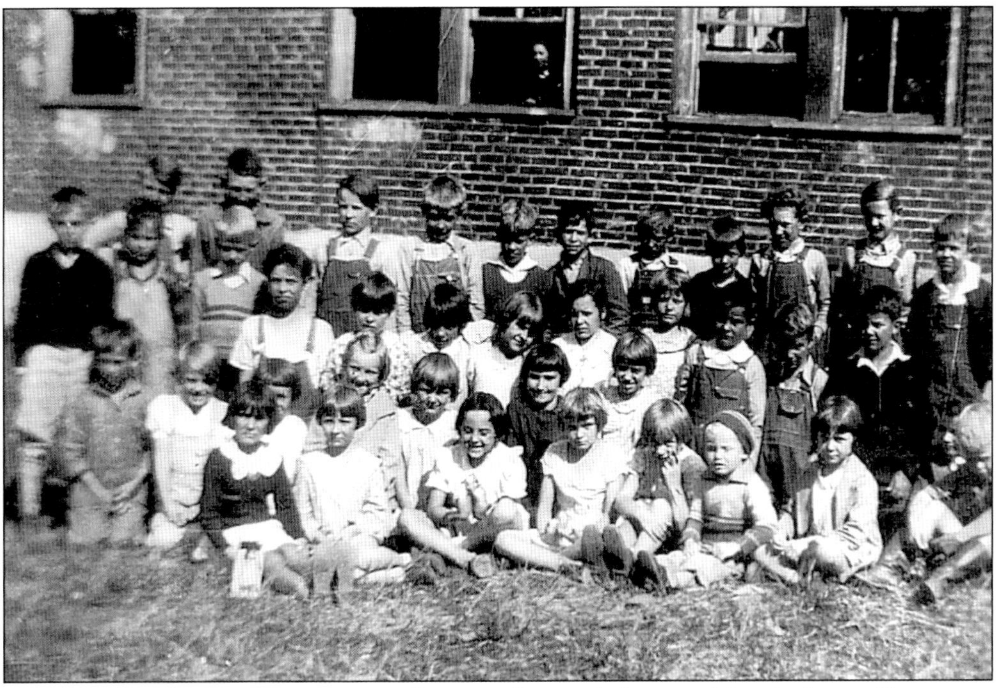

THE WEST JEFFERSON ELEMENTARY SCHOOL. Pictured above is West Jefferson Elementary School's second-grade class of 1933.

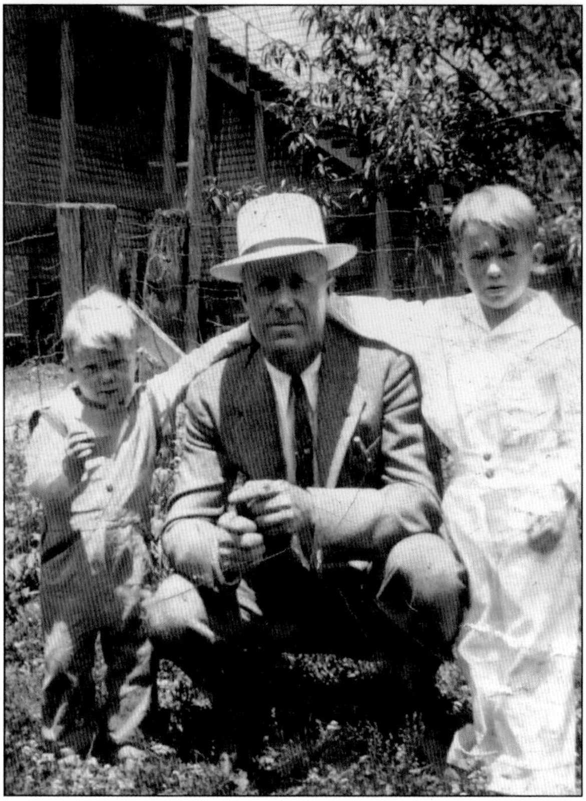

H.R. HOUCK AND SONS. Heggie R. Houck was born in the old Bristol Community where he grew up with his mother on their farm, which is presently Ashe Park. This picture is from the summer of 1934 and photographed from left to right are John R. Houck, H.R. Houck, and Edward H. Houck.

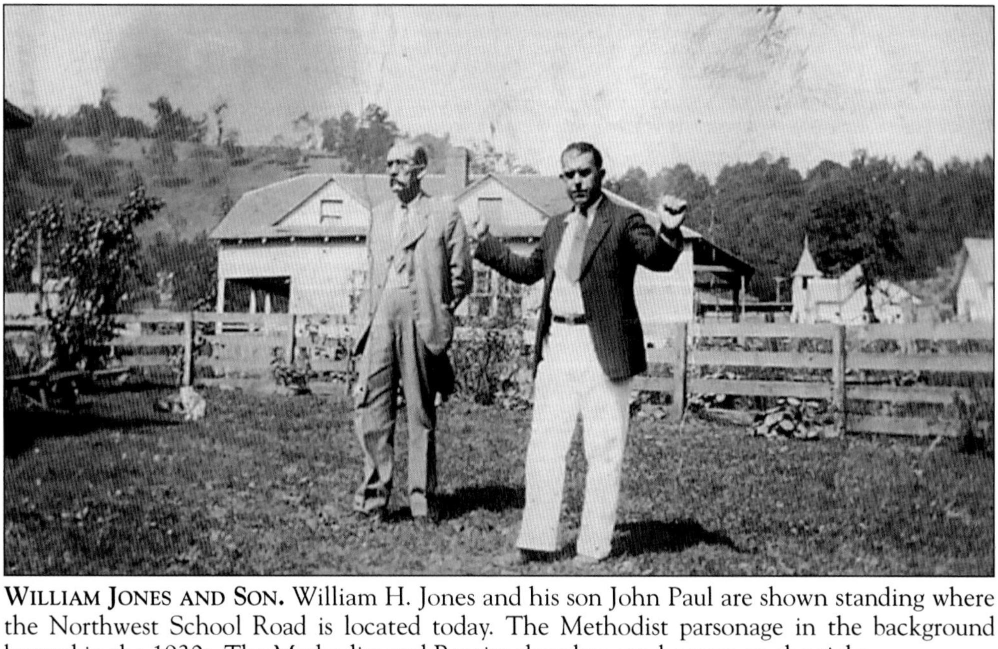

WILLIAM JONES AND SON. William H. Jones and his son John Paul are shown standing where the Northwest School Road is located today. The Methodist parsonage in the background burned in the 1930s. The Methodist and Baptist churches can be seen on the right.

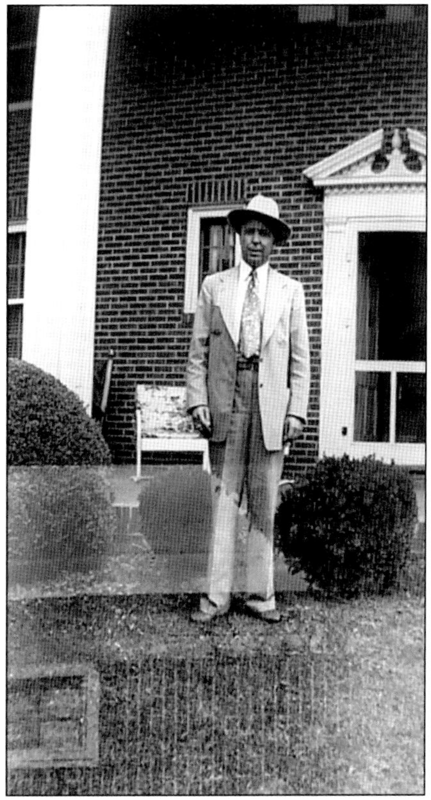

ROBERT G. BARR, 1930. Barr is pictured before his new home on Barr Hill in West Jefferson.

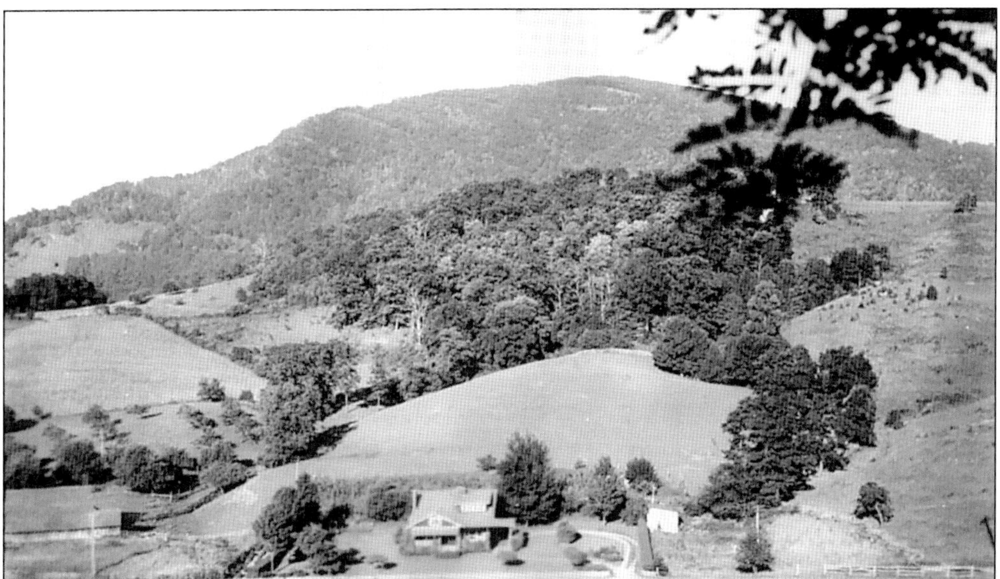

FORMER CARL GRAYBEAL HOME. Graybeal was the former mayor and county sheriff of West Jefferson. In this *c.* 1930s photograph, Mount Jefferson rises above the road that later became the four-lane road connecting West Jefferson to Jefferson.

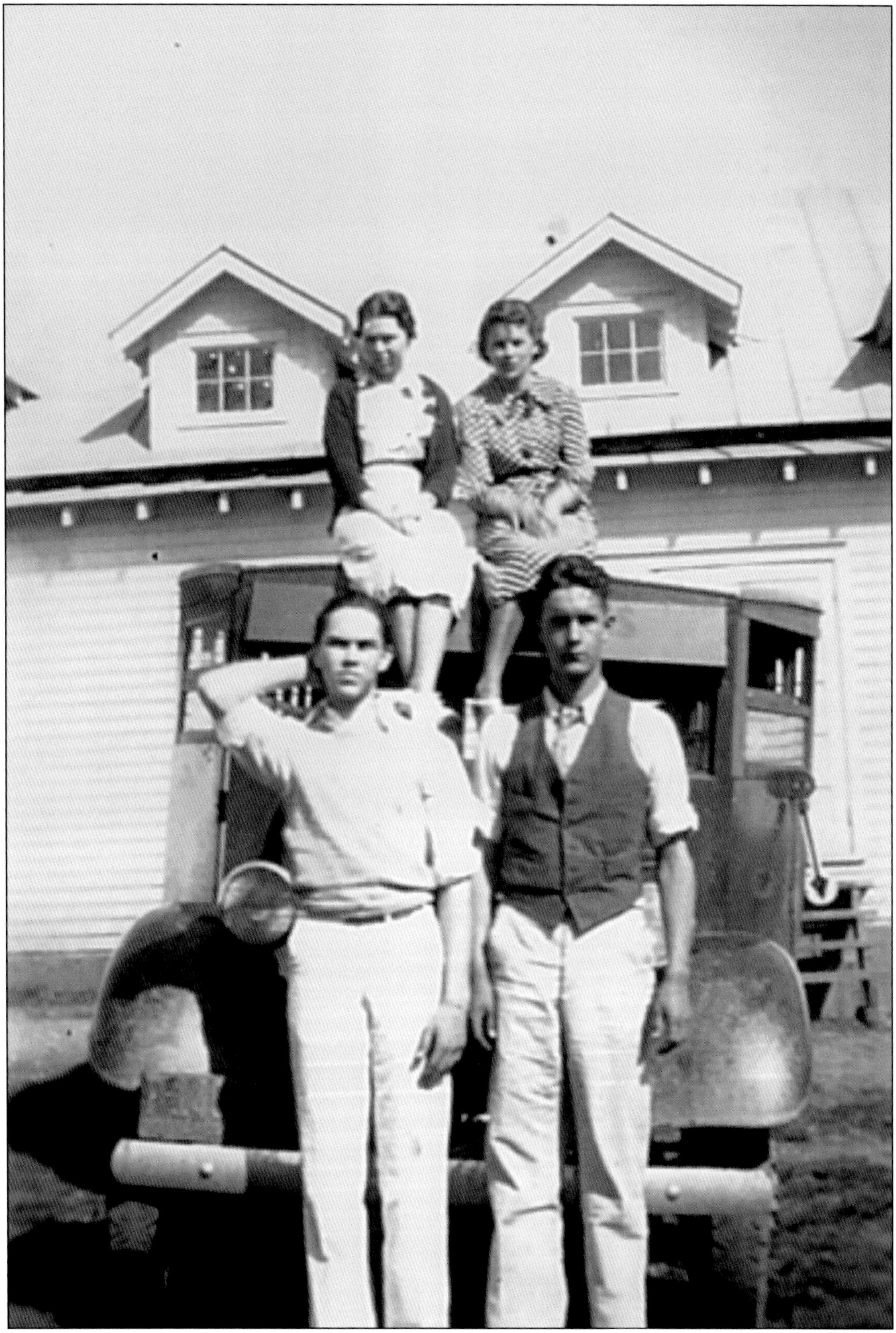

STUDENTS AT JEFFERSON SCHOOL IN 1937. This school was originally the Jefferson Academy. Tom and Mary Carolyn Price are shown on the left.

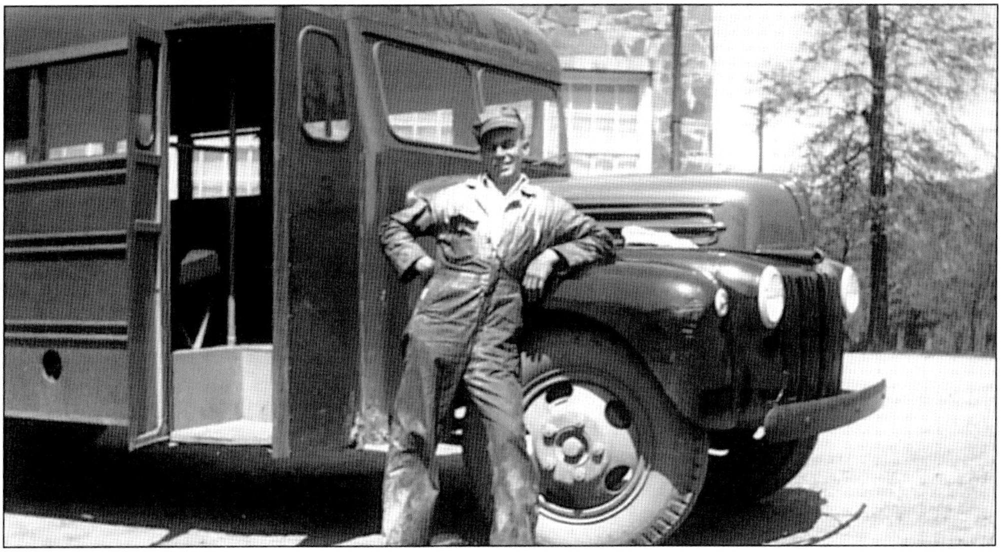

He Kept the Buses Running. Harry Koontz was the main mechanic at the Ashe County School garage in the 1930s.

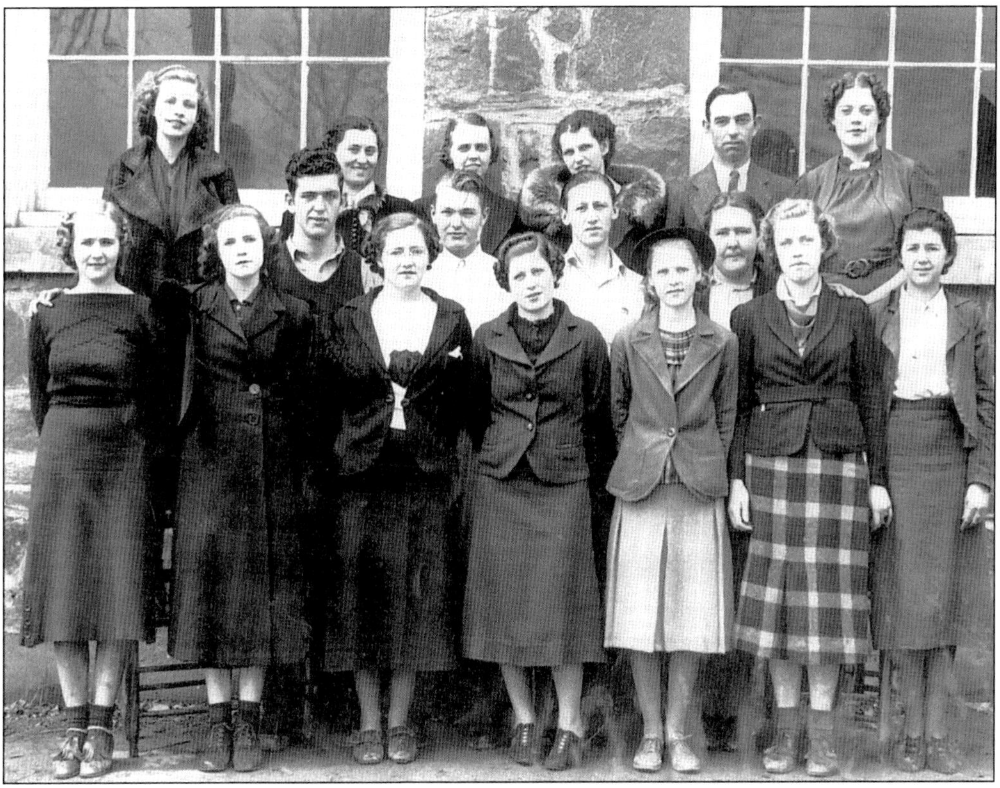

Jefferson High School's 1938 Graduating Class. Pictured from left to right are (front row) Marjorie Long, Cathleen Stringer, Mabel Weaver, Velma Little, Grace Kelly, and Muriel Farrington; (second row) Wava Farrington, John Gordon Johnson, Paul Morphew, Earl Lewis, Jessee Cockerham, Josephine Blevins, and Hazel Bare; (third row) faculty members Florence Calhoun, Mrs. E.D. Barr, Miss Ruth Allen Worth, and Principal G.B. Price.

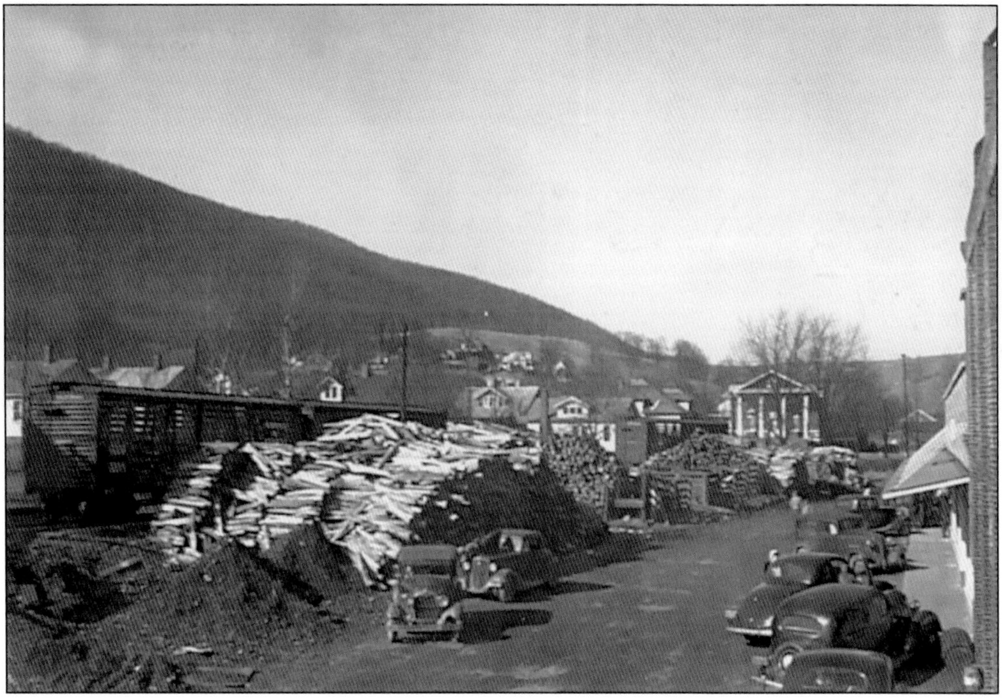

Railroad Avenue or the Back Street in West Jefferson. The First Baptist Church is visible in the background.

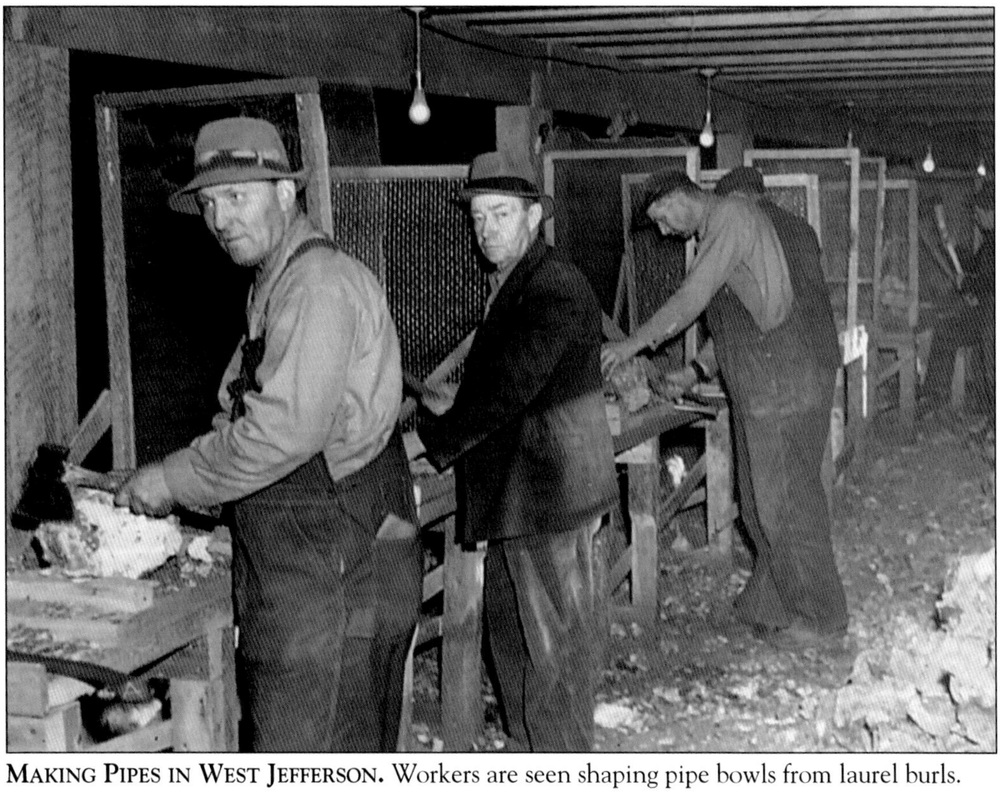

Making Pipes in West Jefferson. Workers are seen shaping pipe bowls from laurel burls.

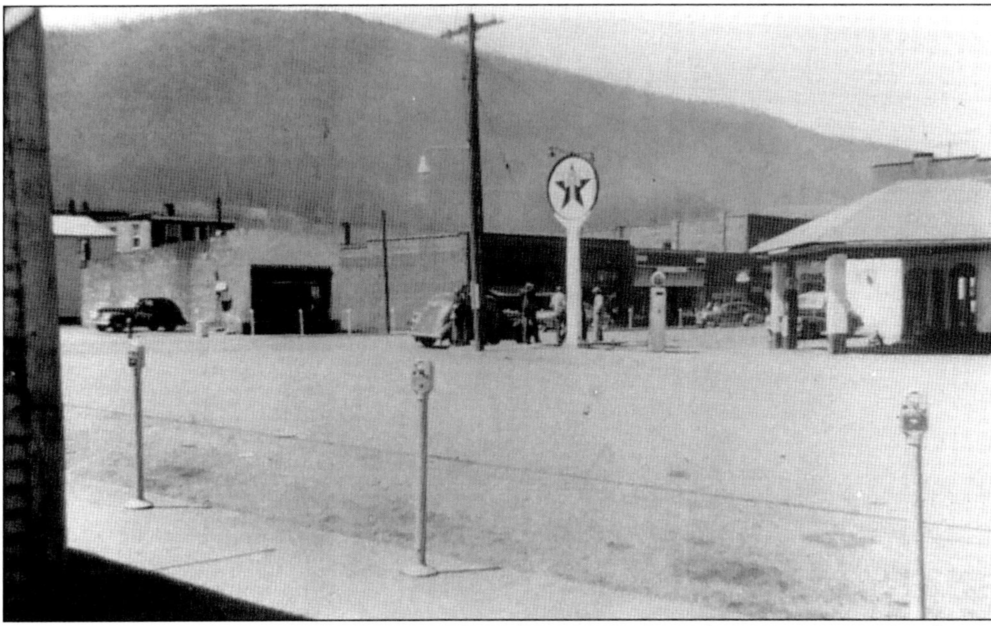

PARKING METERS. Parking meters, located at the intersection of Main Street and Jefferson Avenue in West Jefferson, are visible in this photograph. Parking meters became a source of income in the 1930s and 1940s. The gas station stands in the present location of McNeill's Department Store.

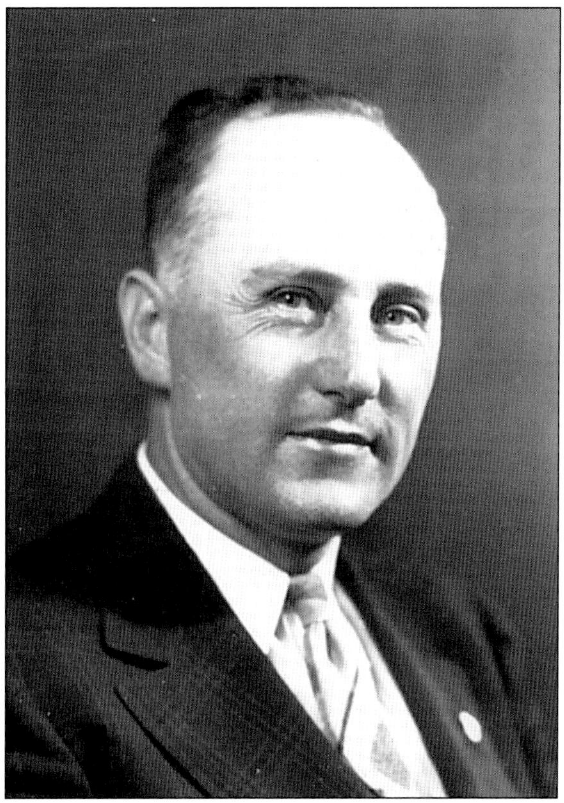

WEST JEFFERSON ENTREPRENEUR. Everett O. Woodie, pictured c. 1940, formed the first transportation company in Ashe County. His business grew to include over 200 buses in Western North Carolina, Tennessee, and Virginia.

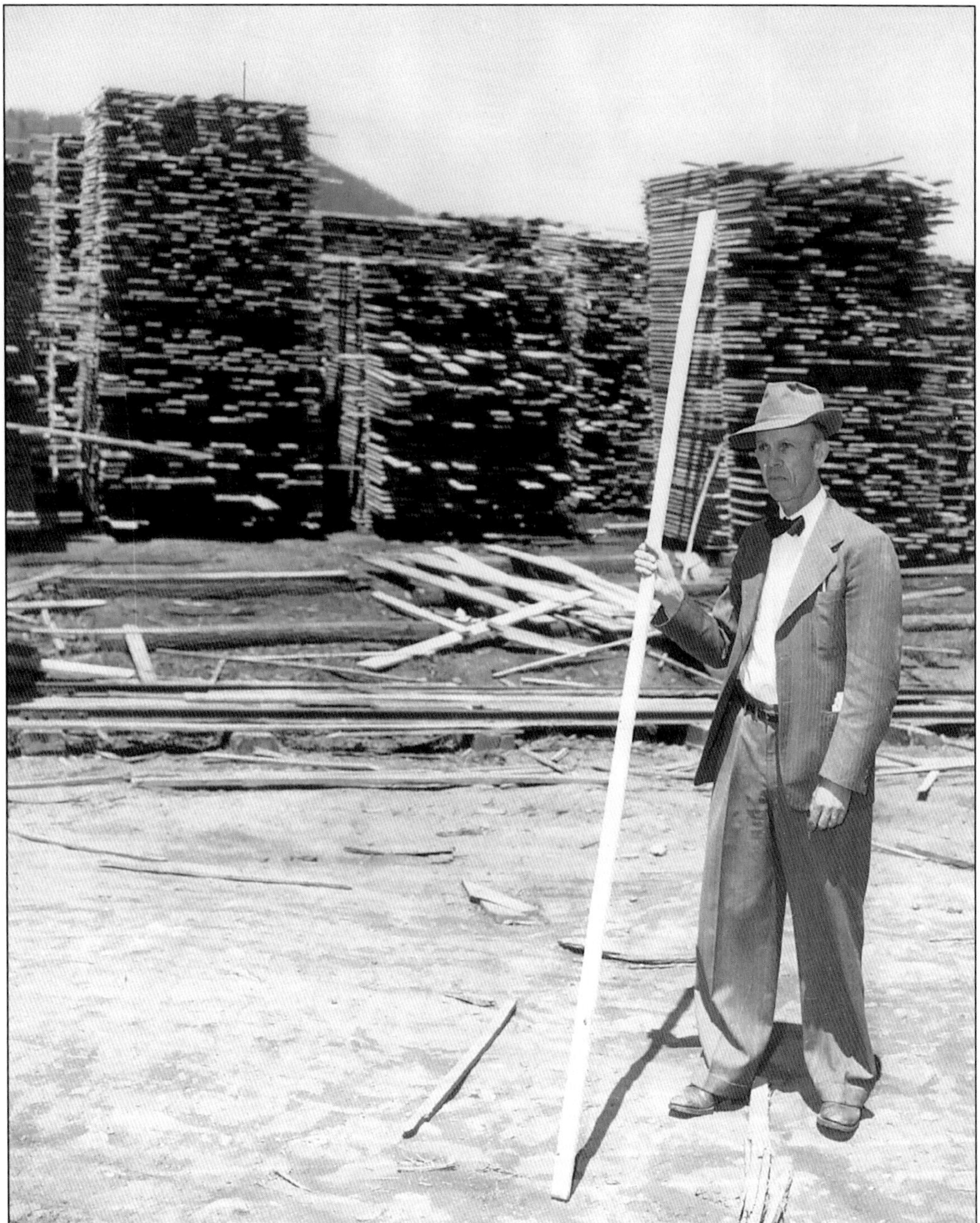

WADE E. VANNOY IN HIS LUMBERYARD. These stacks of lumber were used in Mr. Vannoy's successful flooring plant in West Jefferson, which was started in 1935.

GRADUATE AND FRIENDS. Mascots Frank Colvard and Beverly Little celebrate with West Jefferson High School graduate Vivian Johnson in the early 1940s.

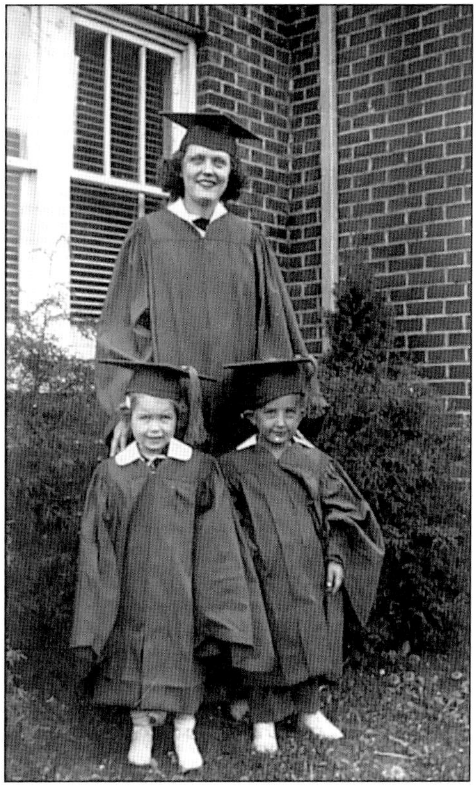

NEW ADDITIONS TO THE JEFFERSON SCHOOL. The original Jefferson School was constructed in the mid-1930s through the WPA program. These additions were made in the mid-1940s.

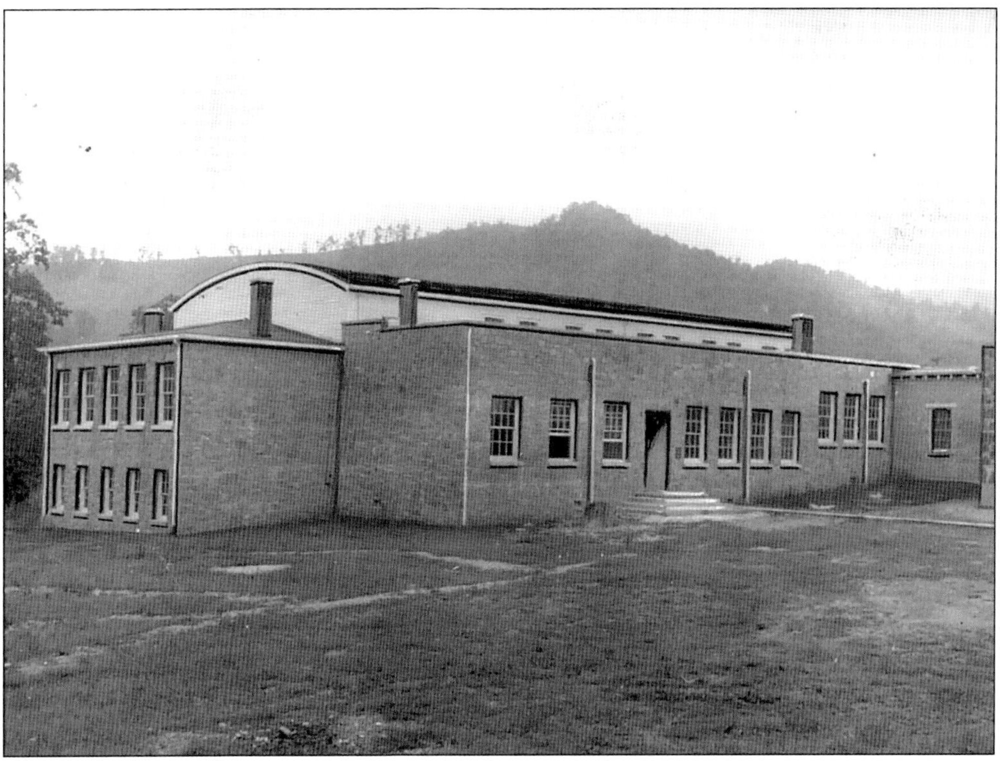

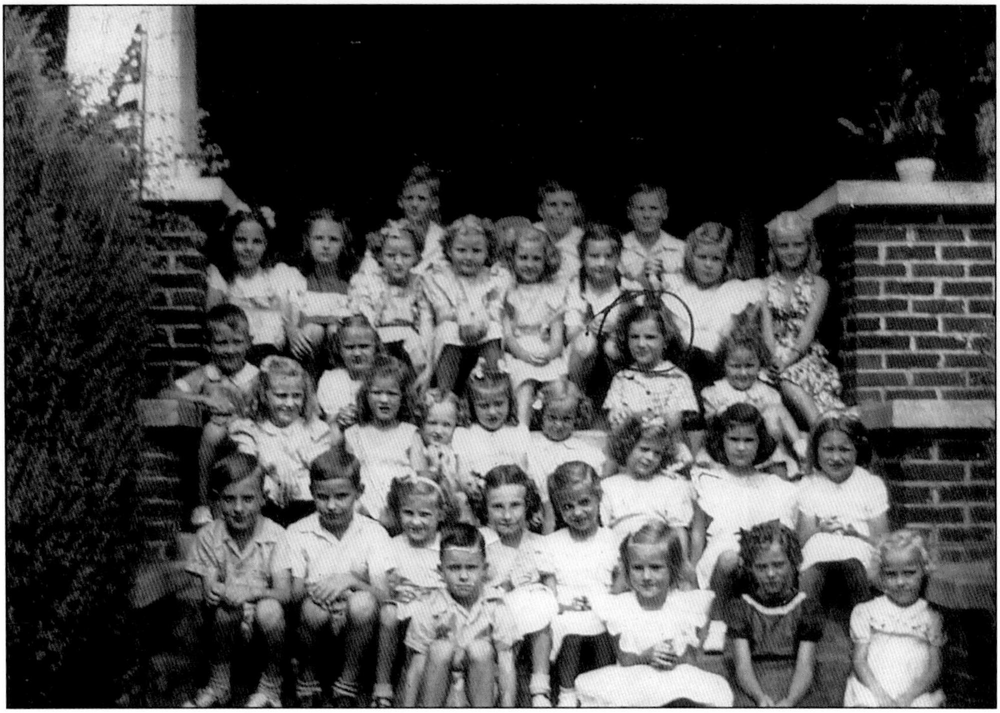

HAPPY BIRTHDAY FOR STELLA WILLIAMS ANDERSON. Many friends joined the birthday celebration in 1943 at the Anderson home.

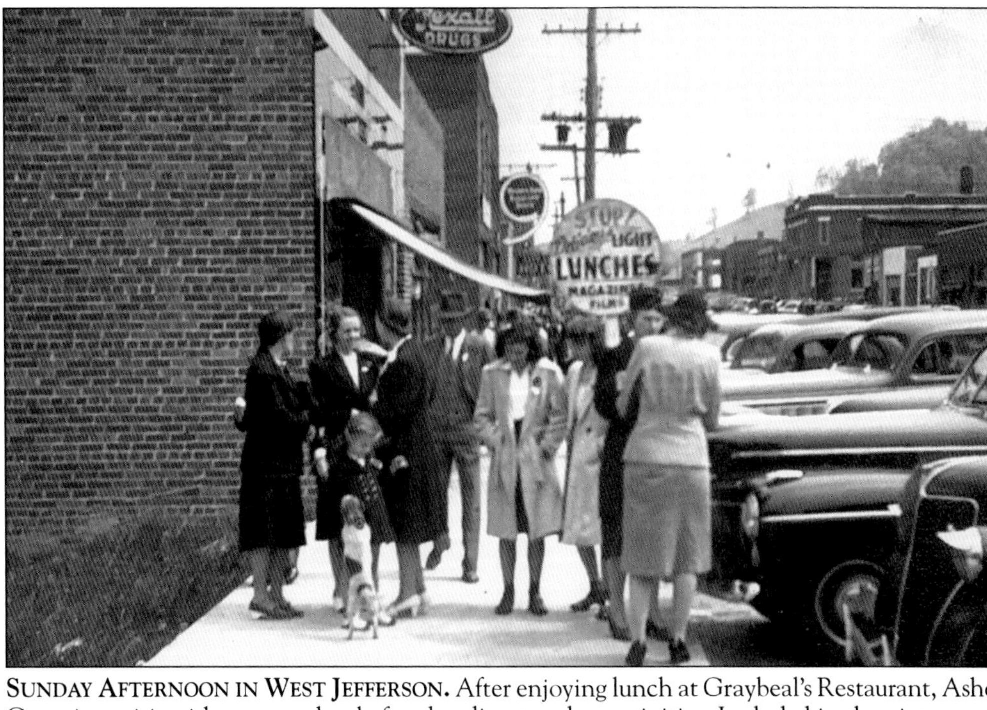

SUNDAY AFTERNOON IN WEST JEFFERSON. After enjoying lunch at Graybeal's Restaurant, Ashe Countians visit with one another before heading to other activities. Included in the picture are Edith and Betsy Barr, Rena L. Colvard, Mary Belle Vannoy, and Wick Vannoy.

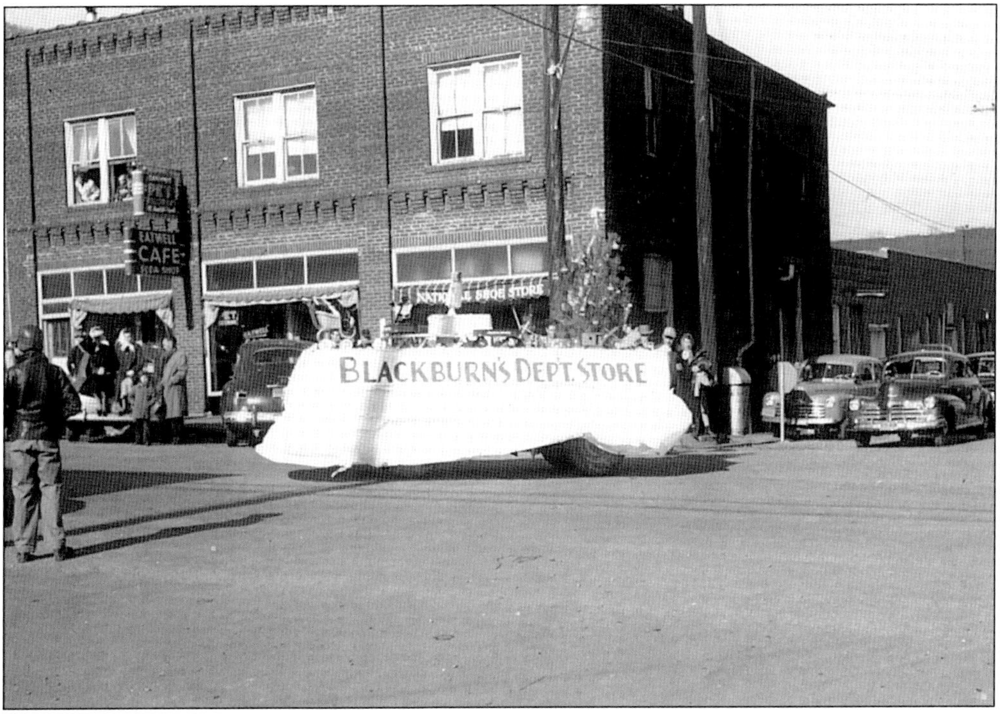

The Parade Moves Out. Blackburn's Department Store's float proceeds up Main Street in this c. 1940 Christmas parade.

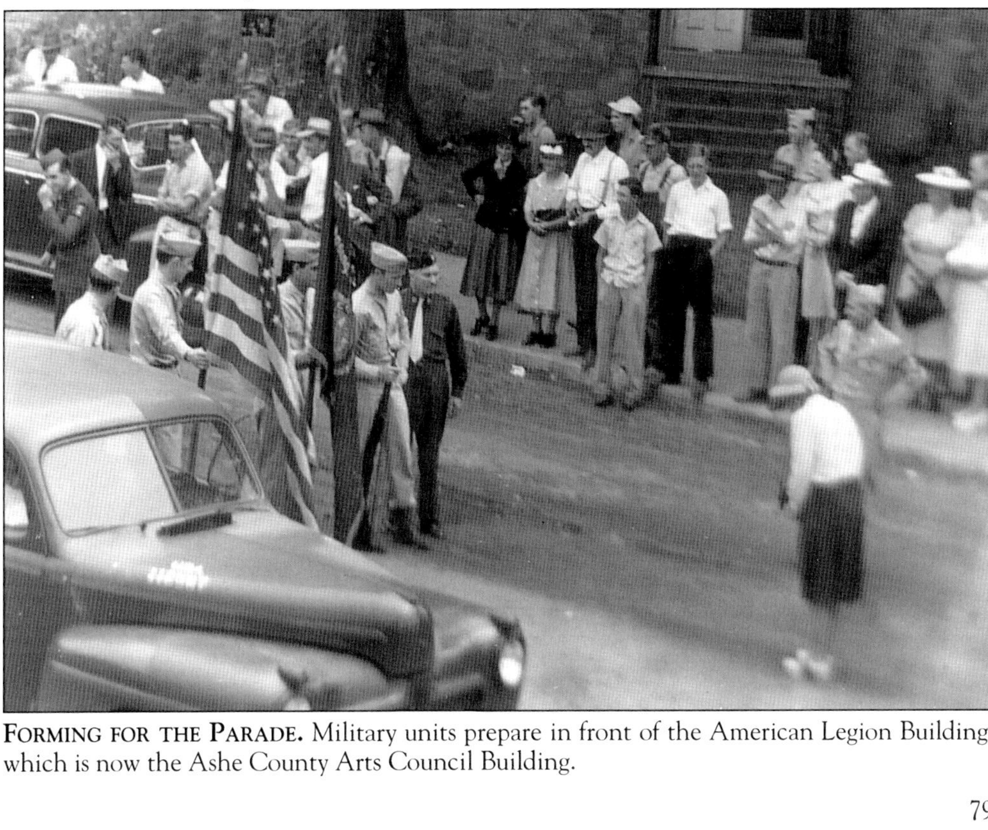

Forming for the Parade. Military units prepare in front of the American Legion Building, which is now the Ashe County Arts Council Building.

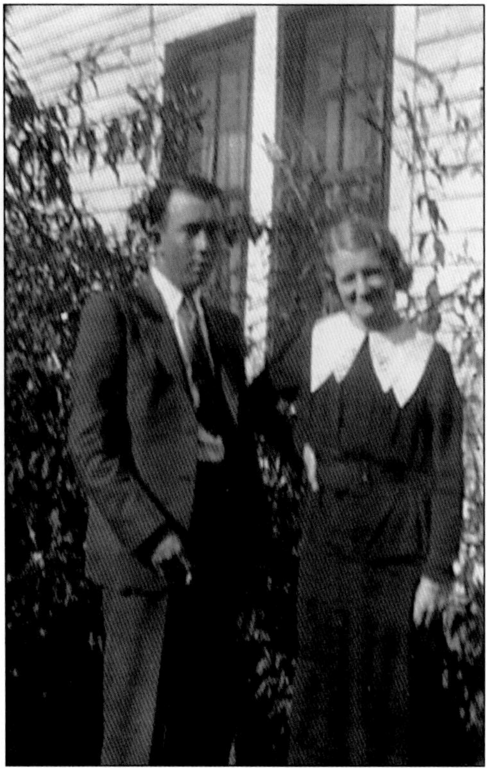

SUE AND CARL F. COLVARD. Mr. Colvard was a prominent businessman in Ashe County. This 1940 picture was taken at the Colvard home in West Jefferson.

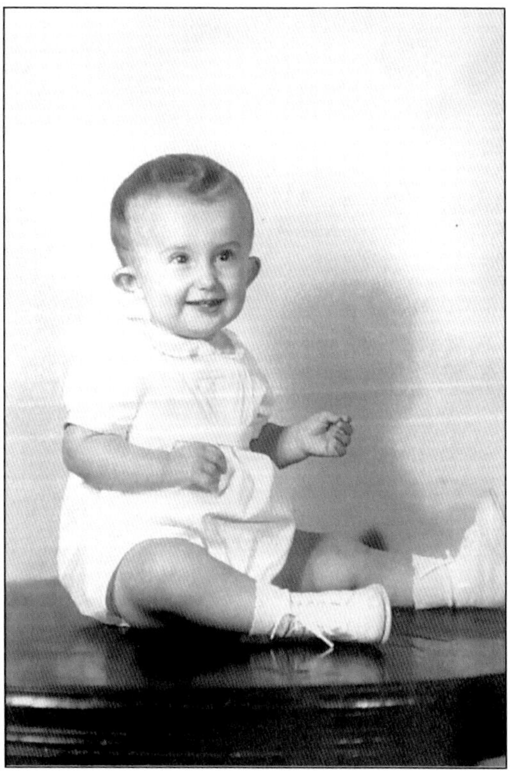

FRANK COLVARD, 1941. Frank Colvard is the son of Sue and Carl F. Colvard. He followed in his father's footsteps, becoming a civic-minded businessman.

ASHE COUNTY HISTORIAN. Lt. Col. Arthur Fletcher's legacy to Ashe County is his book *Ashe County: A History* published in 1963. Though not a resident, he had his roots in Ashe County. He lived at Little Phoenix Lodge during the 1950s while working on his history.

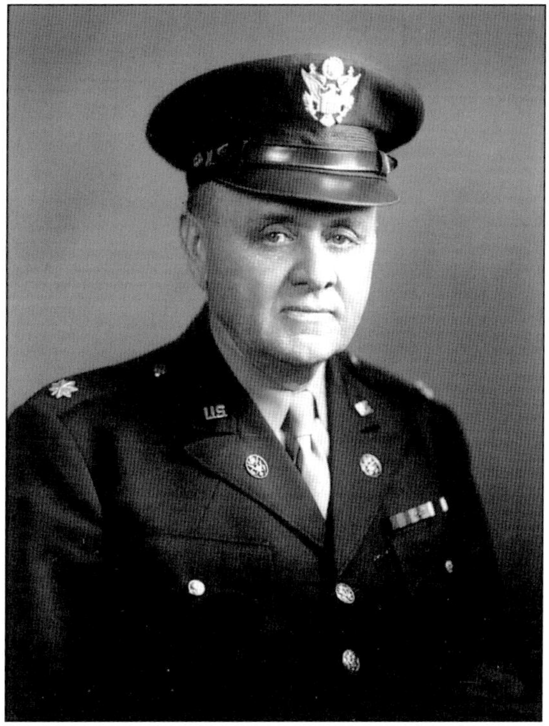

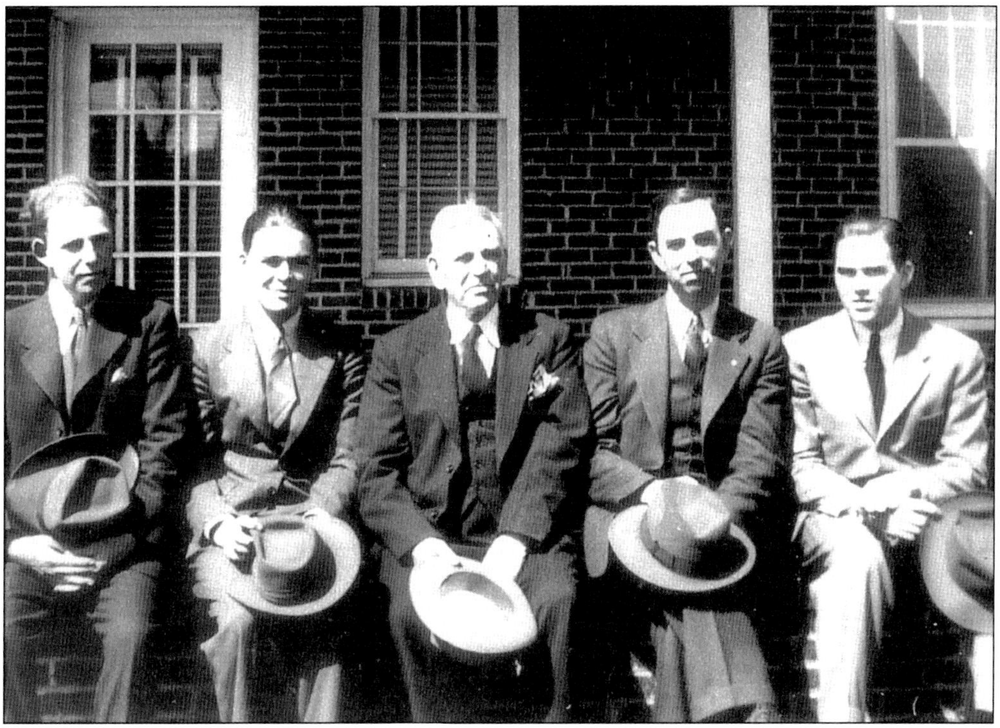

THE PRICE FAMILY. These five brothers all became prominent businessmen. Pictured in this 1948 photograph are, from left to right, Todd, Joe, Avery, Gywn, and Tom Price.

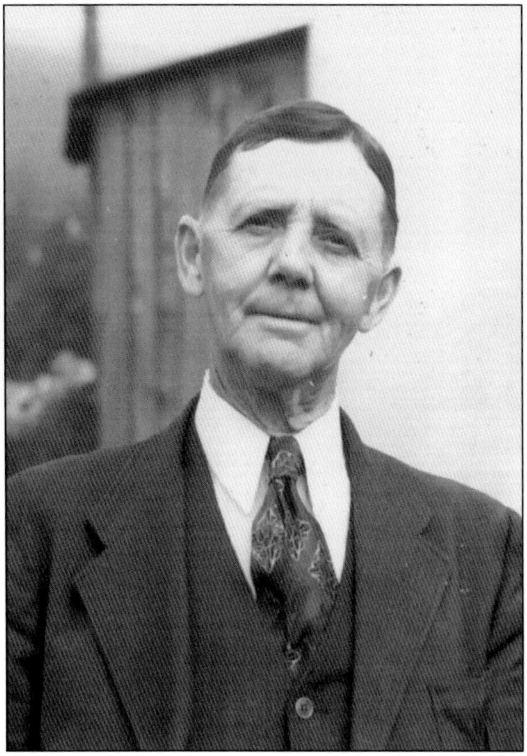

F.B. JONES. Jones lived in several different parts of the county and operated a general store and a gristmill. After moving to West Jefferson in 1917, he managed a mercantile business in partnership with Elihue McNeill and was postmaster for 12 years. He was mayor of West Jefferson during the 1940s.

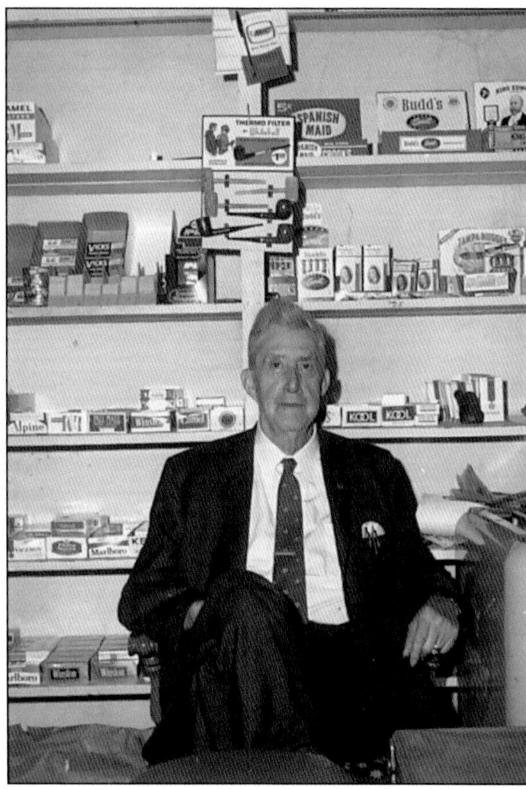

WEST JEFFERSON MERCHANT. Frank H. Colvard owned a successful general merchandise store. He took an interest in the community's youth.

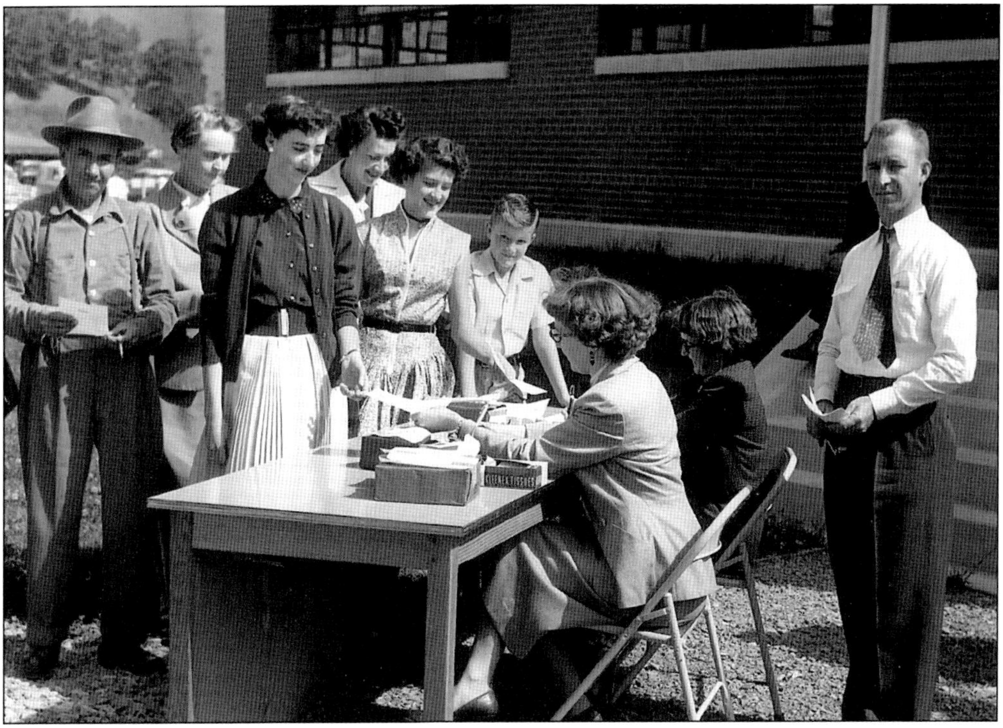

OPEN HOUSE AT SPRAGUE ELECTRIC. Registering guests at the 1954 open house are, from left to right, Clarice Wiles Weaver and Clara Shepherd Barker. Standing behind them is Gilmer Bledsoe, who is preparing to take visitors on a tour of the plant.

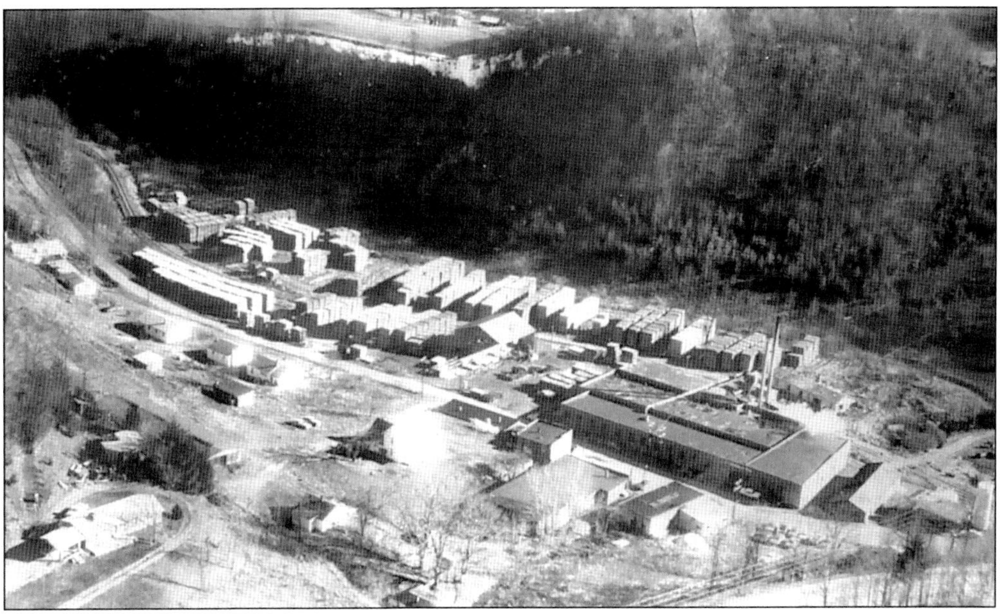

OAK FLOORING PLANT, WEST JEFFERSON. This plant was located off the present four-lane street below Reeves Photography Store. This is the newer of the two plants, the first one having burned in 1956. It handled and processed six million feet of lumber annually, providing farmers a market for their timber.

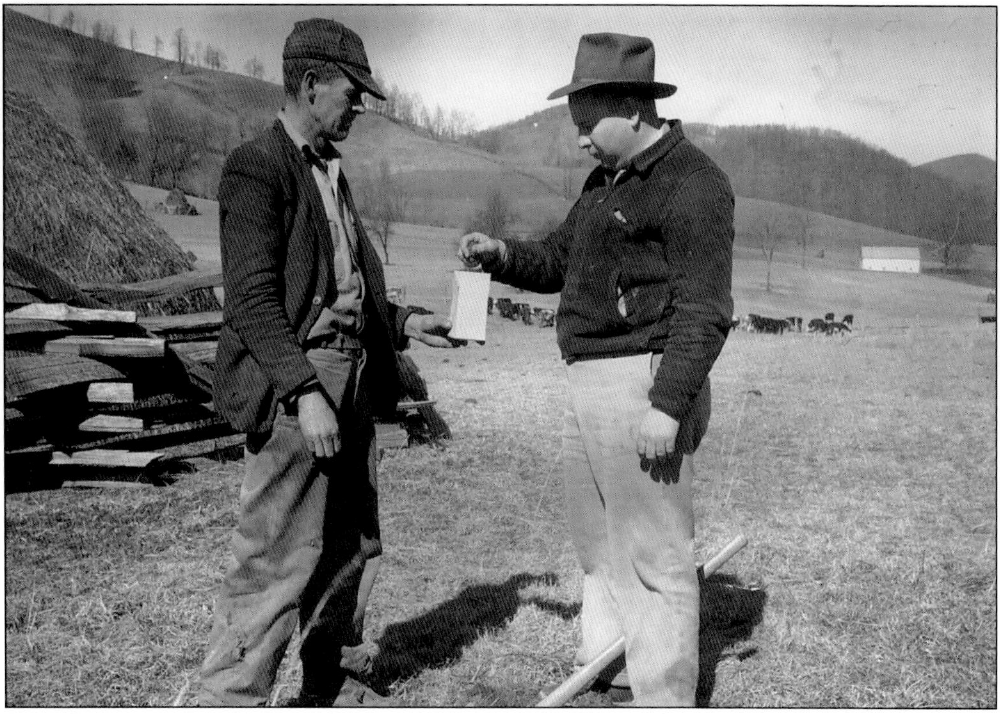

Soil Conservation Agent Jim McLaurin. McLaurin is shown here getting soil samples from the Ray farm near West Jefferson.

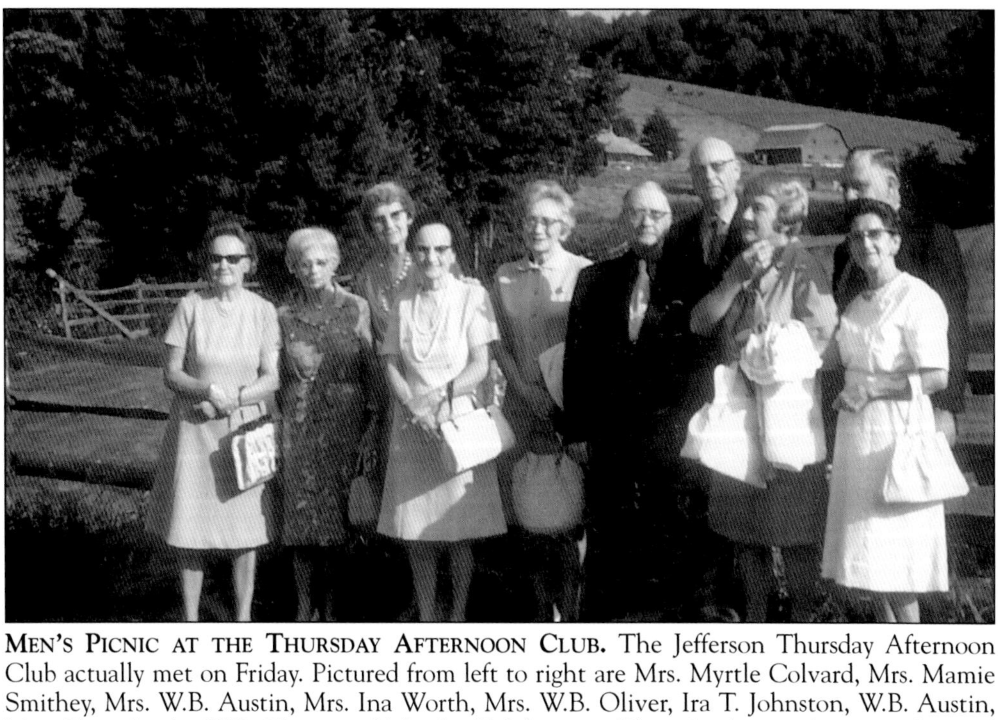

Men's Picnic at the Thursday Afternoon Club. The Jefferson Thursday Afternoon Club actually met on Friday. Pictured from left to right are Mrs. Myrtle Colvard, Mrs. Mamie Smithey, Mrs. W.B. Austin, Mrs. Ina Worth, Mrs. W.B. Oliver, Ira T. Johnston, W.B. Austin, Mrs. Glenn Little, W.B. Oliver, and Mrs. Ira T. Johnston. Glenn Little was also a member and he probably took this photograph.

HEART MOTHER OF THE YEAR, 1955. Nancy Kenickell Johnston accepts her award from the North Carolina Heart Association in recognition of her exceptional efforts on behalf of the association.

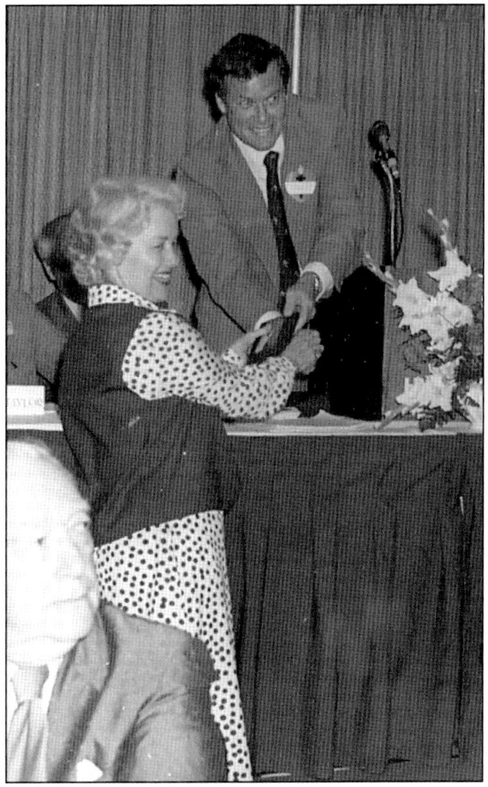

GRADUATING CLASS, 1952. This class was the next-to-last graduating class from West Jefferson High School before it consolidated with Beaver Creek in 1954.

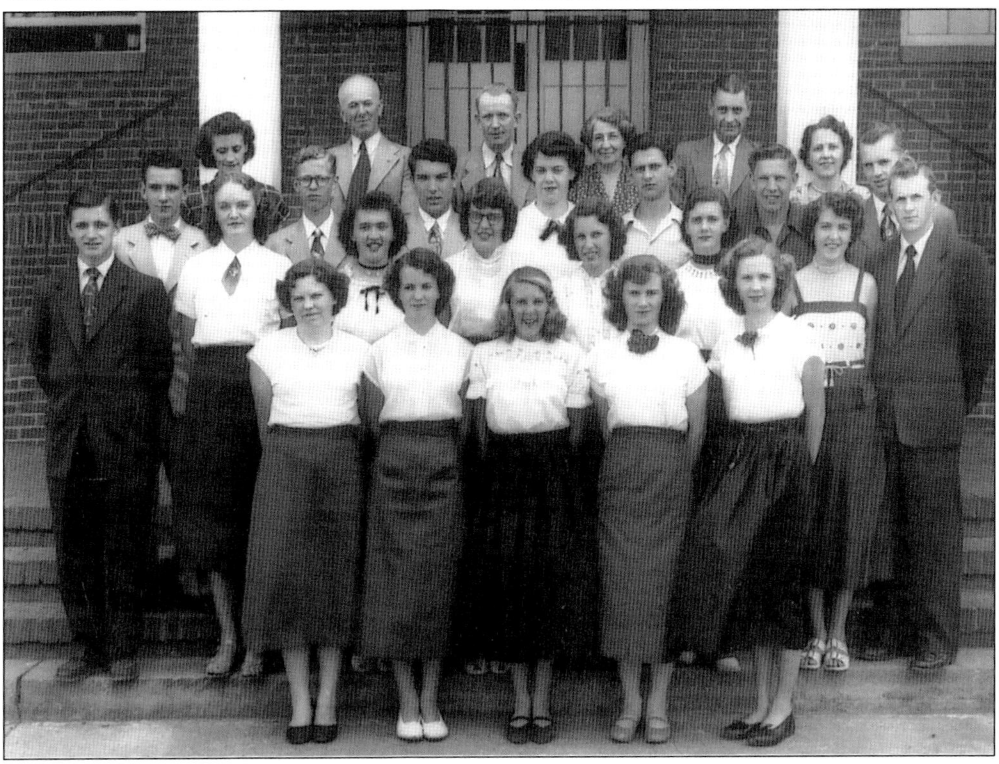

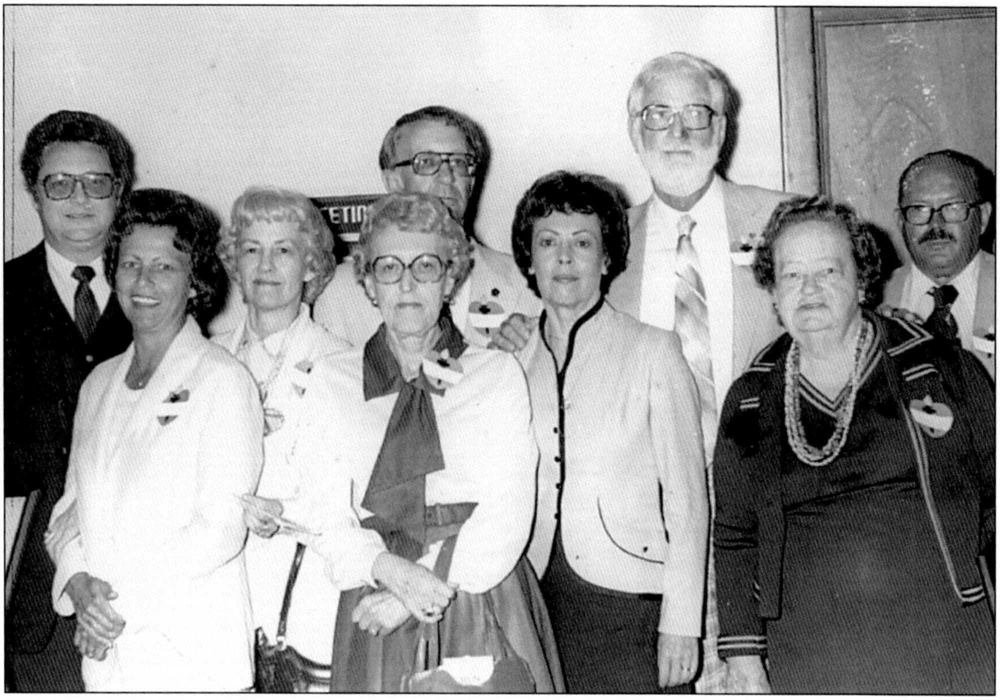

NORTH CAROLINA HEART ASSOCIATION RECOGNIZES ASHE COUNTIANS. Pictured from left to right are Jan and Lucy Caddell, Nancy Johnston, Ruth Shepherd, Jack Miller, Evelyn and Roy Freeman, Stella Anderson, and Bob McNeill.

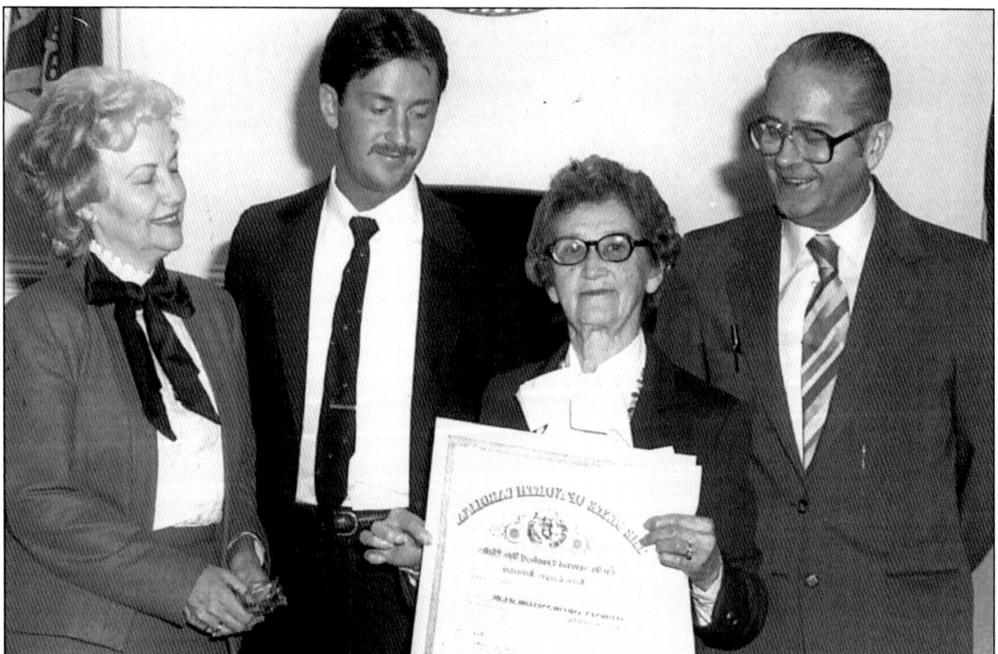

A THIRD GENERATION BECOMES AN ATTORNEY. John C. Johnston's family looks on with pride at his swearing-in ceremony. Included in the picture are his grandmother, Mrs. Ira T. Johnston, and his parents, Mr. and Mrs. Thomas S. Johnston.

"MISS" CLAUDIA JOHNSON. Claudia Johnson's 73rd birthday was celebrated at her Warrensville home in this photo. Her beauty shop in West Jefferson was known for its slogan: "The best of care for my ladies' hair."

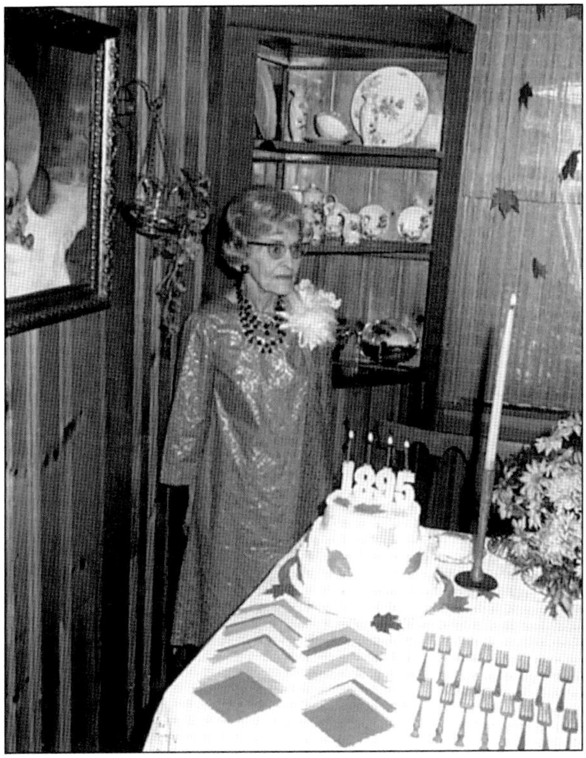

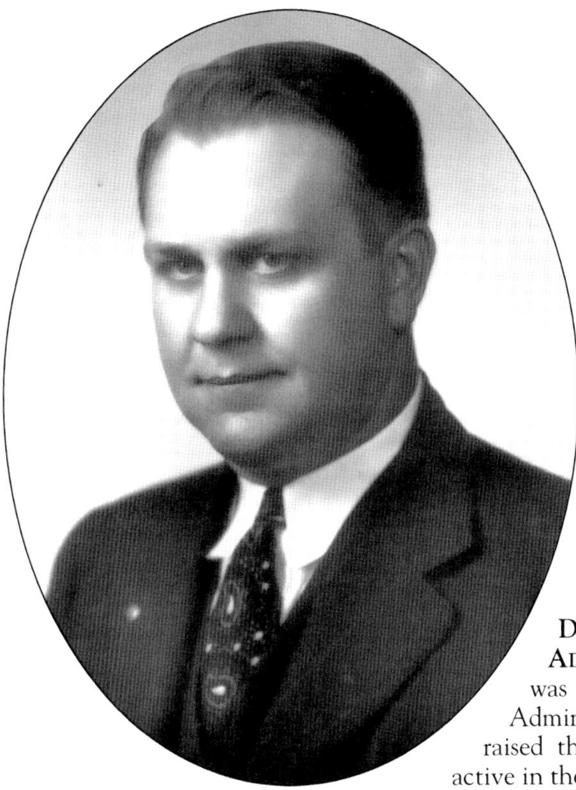

DIRECTOR OF THE FARMERS' HOME ADMINISTRATION. William Bryan Oliver was the director of the Farmers' Home Administration for 34 years. He and his wife raised their family in Jefferson and were very active in their church and community.

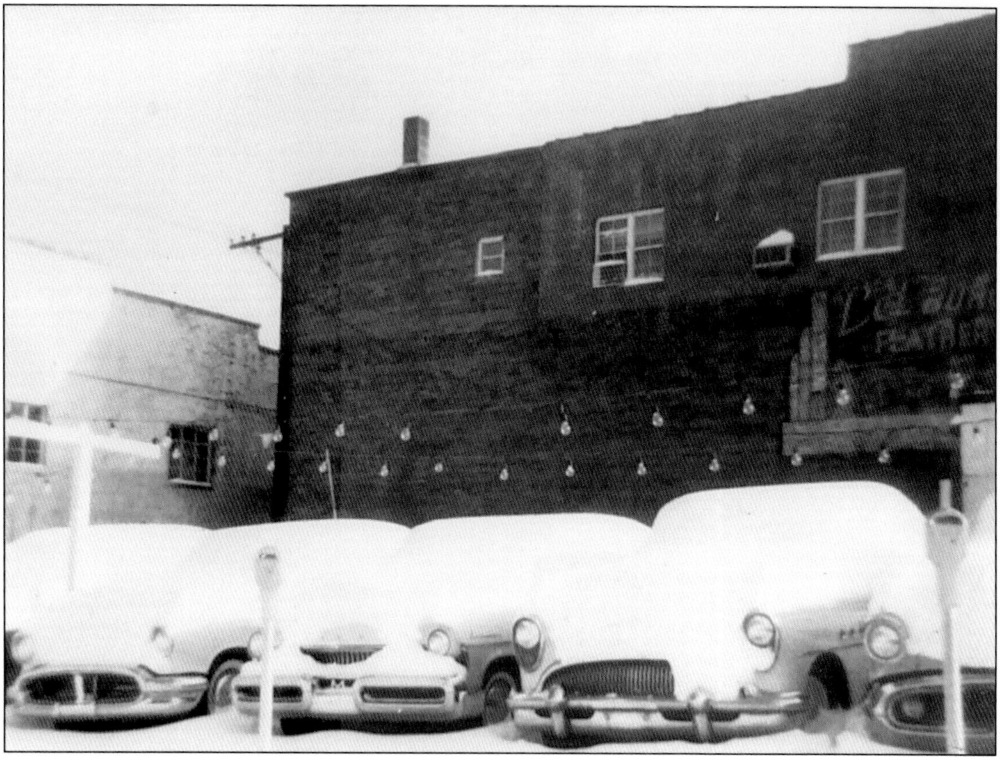

SNOW FALL, 1960. Cars at the corner of Main Street and Jefferson Avenue are covered with snow in this 1960 photo.

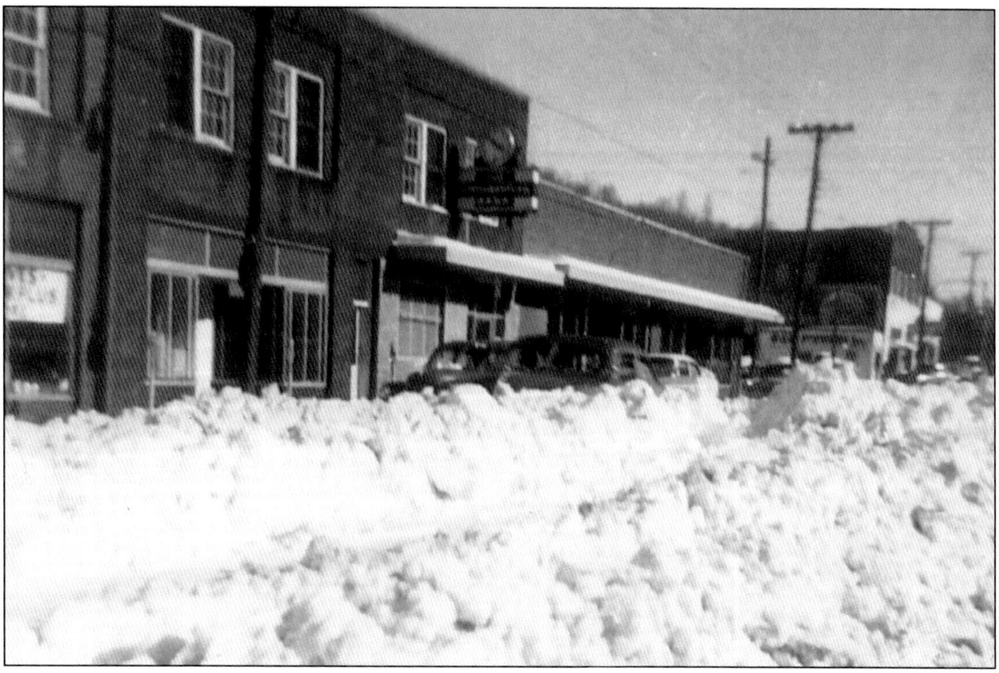

WEST JEFFERSON SNOWBOUND. Traffic moves slowly along Jefferson Avenue after the plows finally cleared two lanes. The snow is piled in the center of the street.

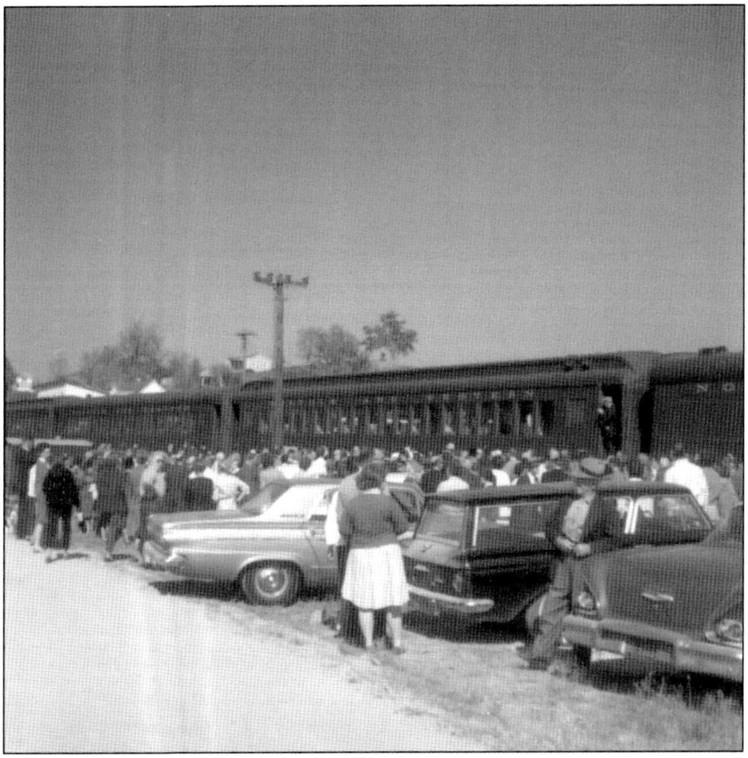

THE VIRGINIA CREEPER'S LAST RUN. Pictured above are passengers boarding the train for a last, special trip in 1963.

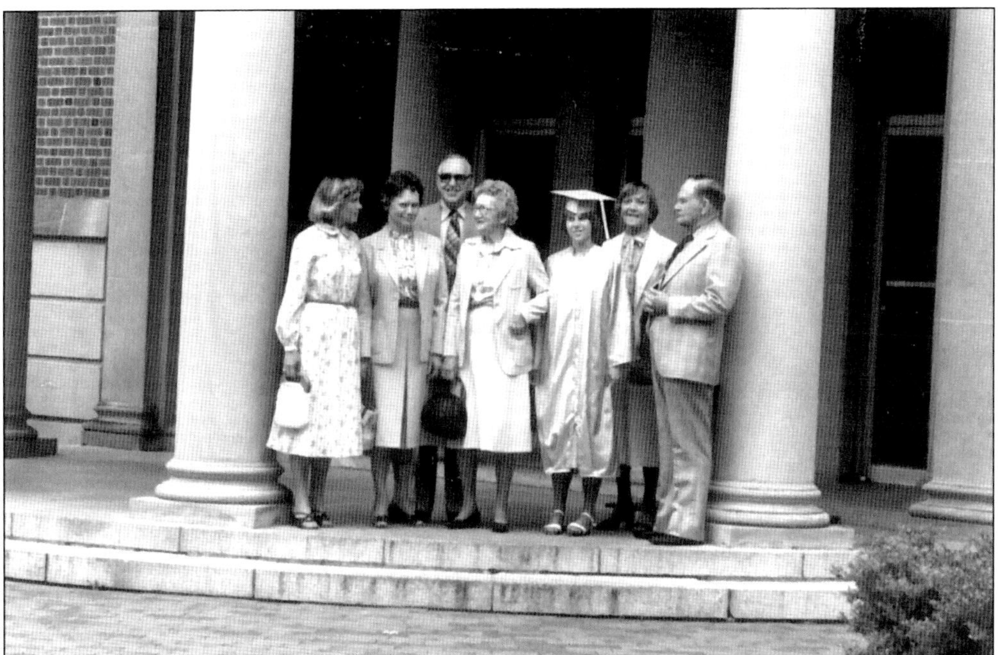

CATHY COCKERHAM LIPPARD GRADUATES. Three generations gathered for Cathy Cockerham Lippard's 1978 graduation from the University of North Carolina. Pictured from left to right are her aunt Billie Huffman, parents Clarene and Tom Cockerham, grandmother Mrs. W.B. Oliver, Cathy Cockerham, aunt Peggy Oliver, and grandfather, W.B. Oliver.

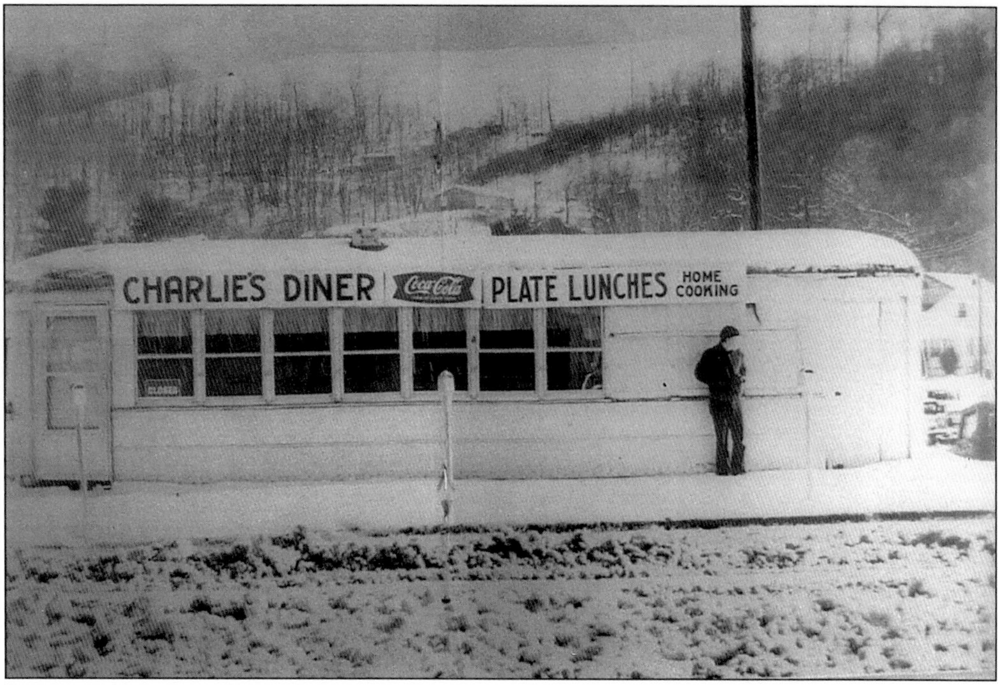

POPULAR DINER IN WEST JEFFERSON, 1950. Problems were solved and news passed on over hamburgers and coffee in Charlie's Diner. The diner, owned and operated by Charlie and Jean Davis, was located next to the present Ashe Federal Savings and Loan.

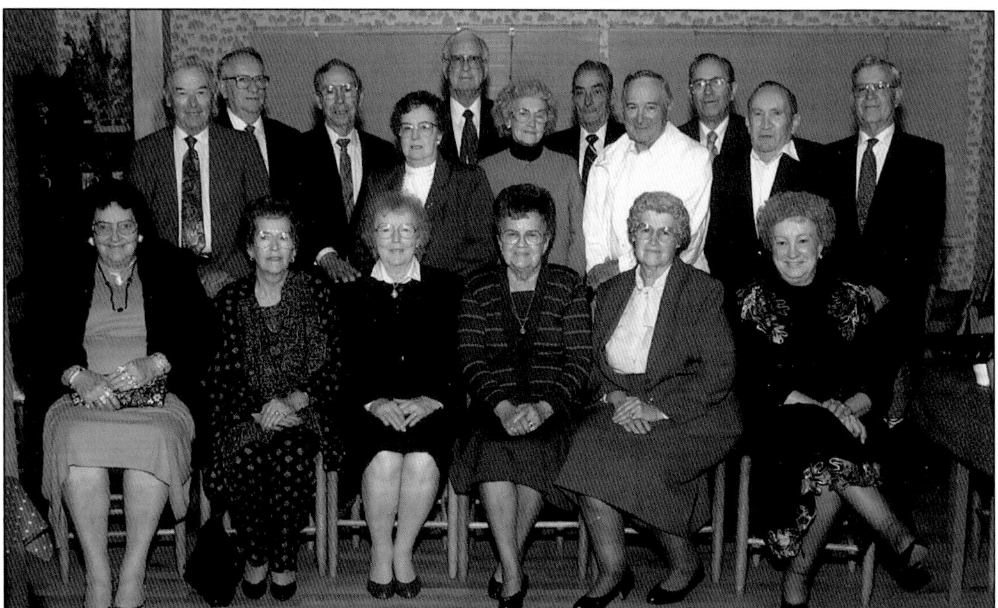

REUNION OF JEFFERSON CLASS OF 1941. Pictured from left to right are the following: (front row) Virginia March Penry, Alice Weaver Bare, Margaret Woodie Bare, Nona Bell Mullis Frazier, Burl Dollar Jones, and Faye Wilcox Dancy; (second row) Eddie Woodie, Leonard Bare, Burley Bare, Virginia Miller Wagoner, Dr. Roy Freeman, Ozella Rash Duncan, James A. Badger, W. Parks Colvard, Thomas S. Johnston, Joe P. Worth, and Pat Caudill.

A Male Offspring at Last, 1971. J. Leet Vannoy of West Jefferson is enjoying a special time with his third child, Neil Vannoy.

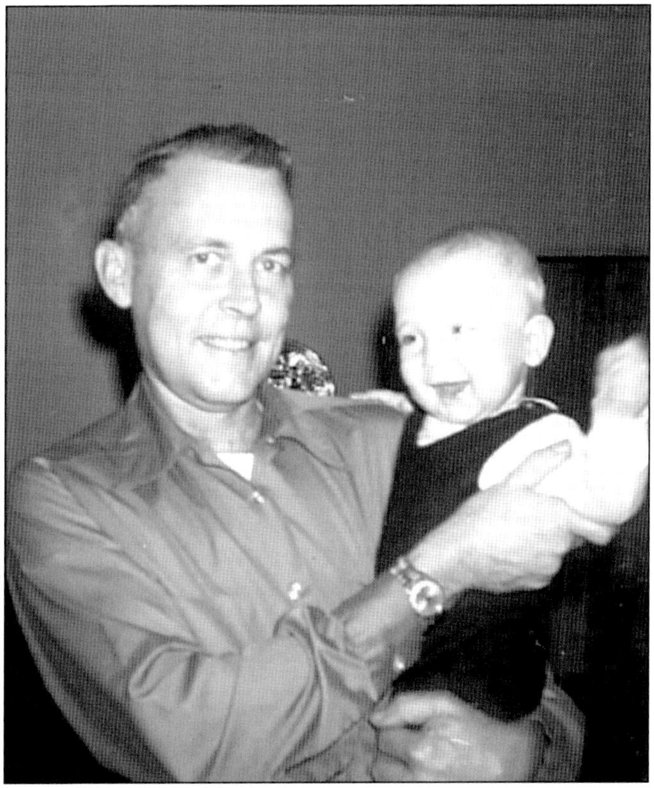

James K. Vannoy and Aunt Sue Colvard. In 1977, James K. Vannoy (1950–1978) visited with his aunt Sue Colvard during the Christmas season. He was a gifted organist, librarian, and educator.

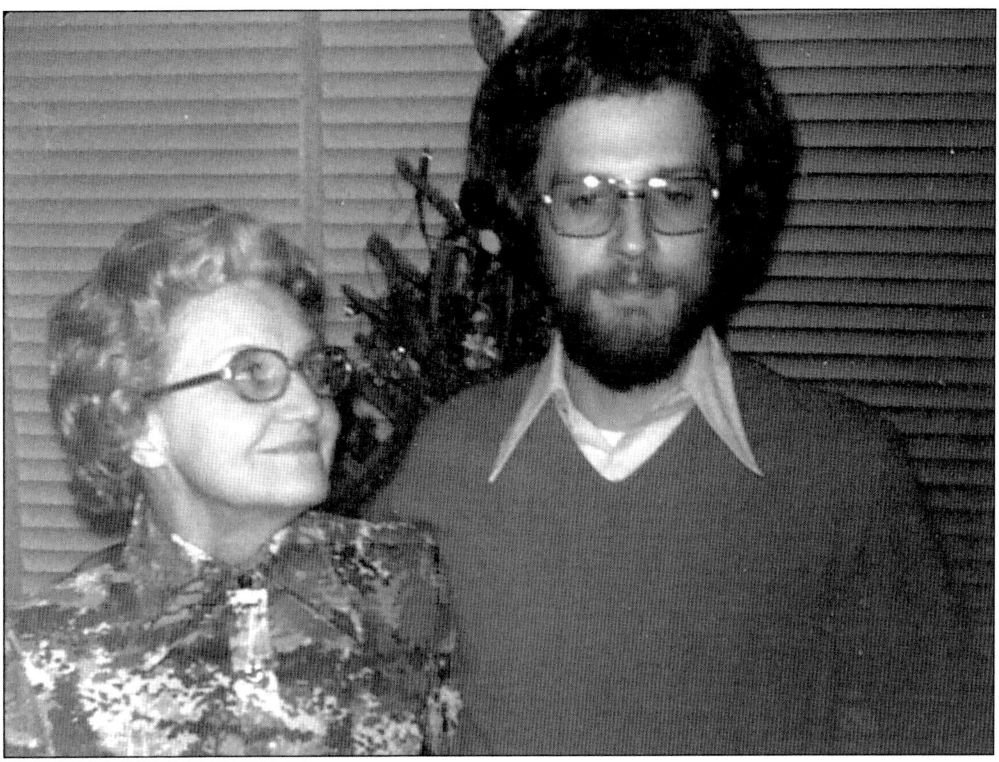

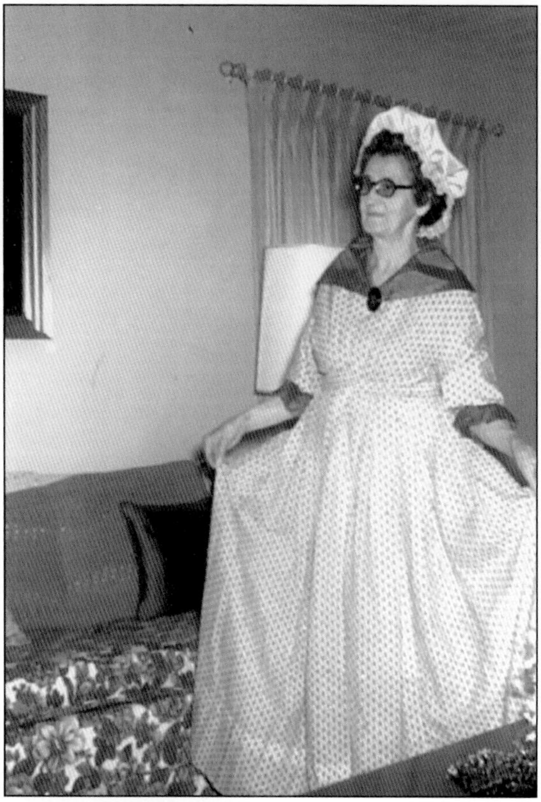

CELEBRATING THE BI-CENTENNIAL. Mrs. Ira T. Johnston models a dress made from the same pattern as a dress once worn by her grandmother.

ROBERT G. BARR WELCOMES FRIENDS. Robert G. Barr invites his friends to join him at his home in 1981. Visiting with Mr. Barr, from left to right, are Wade E. Vannoy Jr., Mr. Barr, Gov. Robert Scott, and Bill Williams of Middlesex, North Carolina.

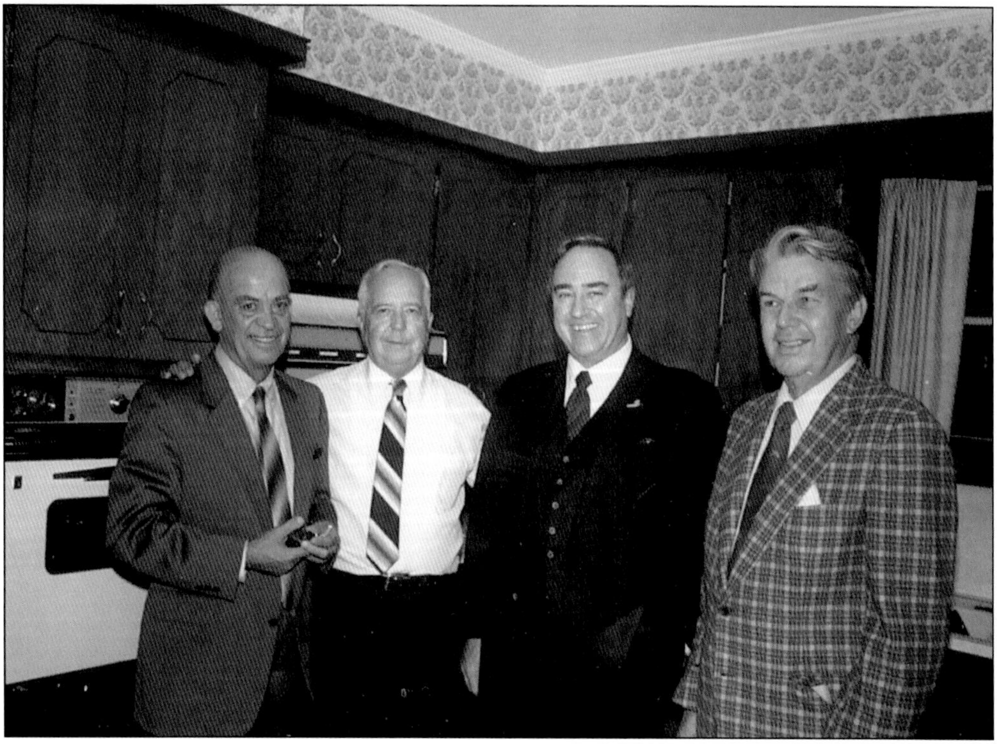

Four

Crests on the Oceans of Mountains

Black Mountain to Smethport

Nature placed several of the tallest crests in Ashe County's "ocean of mountains," the area located between Black Mountain in the southwest and Smethport in the center of the county. The major crests in this area are the three "Bs" (Bluff, Buck, and Bald Mountains) and Three Top Mountain. They tower over the neighboring valleys, supplying recreation, legendary tales, and a unique combination of geology, hydrology, and ecology.

The valley lying between Three Top and Bluff Mountain has long been a major artery into the county. Before white settlers found this mountainous region, Native Americans hunting buffalo herds followed them along Buffalo Creek. The farmers and herders who followed Native Americans into the region found thick forest and open "balds" friendly to herding, logging, and farming.

Always dominating the landscape were the mountains, particularly Bluff Mountain with its unusual mixture of flora and wildlife. The underlying rock is rich in minerals, which support many threatened species: bobcats, tiny bog turtles, red Gray's lilies, spreading avens, and Heller's blazing star. From the 5,100-foot peak, a dramatic waterfall drops into a pristine cove forest of 200- to 300-year-old white and northern red oaks and sugar maples.

These mountains have long been a place for locals to picnic, hike, and live. Mountaineers still talk about old man Perkins who lived on the Bluff. The story is told that one day Mr. Perkins was looking into a pool of water up on the Bluff when he saw a reflection so terrifying, he ran down the mountain. He told everyone about the horrifying sight and said that if he lived seven days, he would tell them what he had seen. Mr. Perkins died on the evening of the sixth day. It is said that no one has lived on Bluff Mountain since.

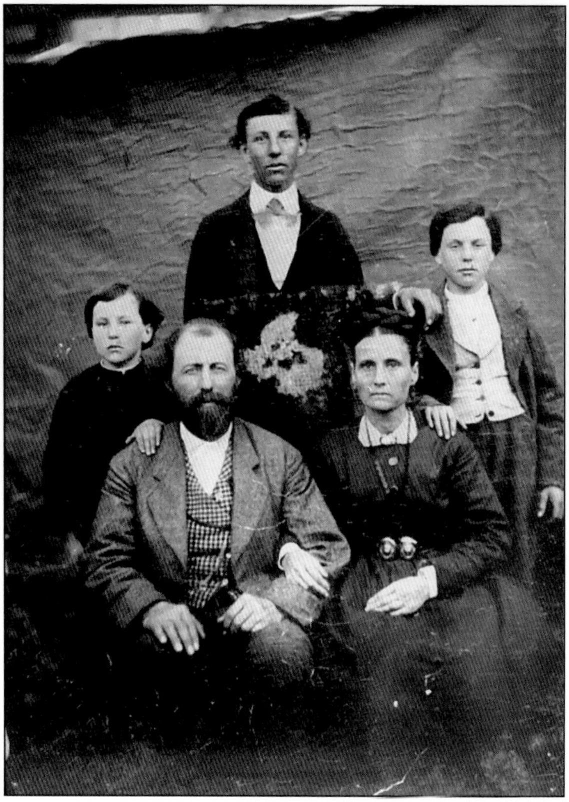

THE RAY FAMILY OF THE BUFFALO COMMUNITY. This portrait, taken around 1800, showcases Frank Ray, Elbert Ray, Thomas Ray, Hilton Ray, and Mary Ann Ray.

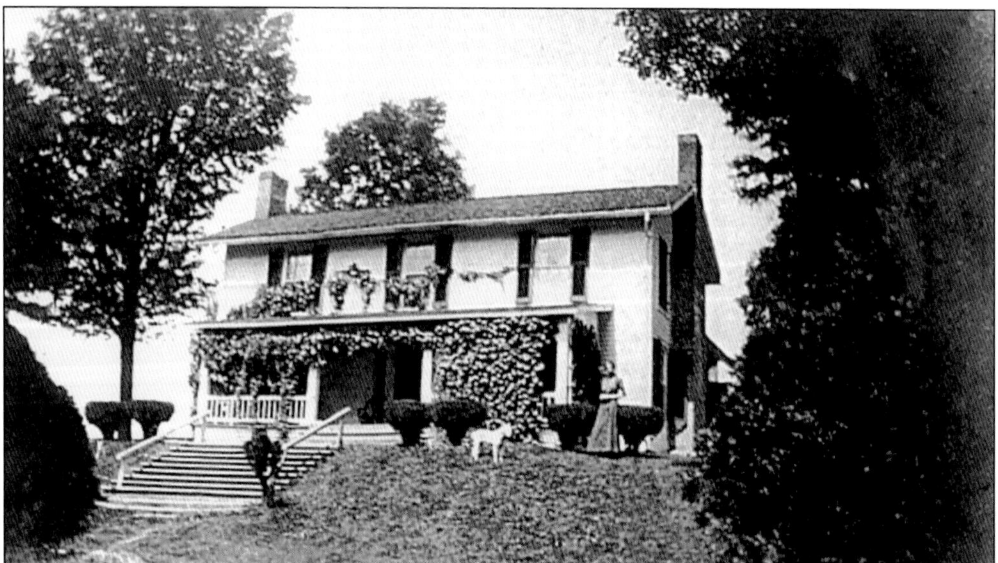

W.H. HAMILTON HOME IN THE 1880S. This is a photograph of the original Hamilton Home on Beaver Creek School Road.

PIONEER WIFE THEODOSIA HAMILTON. Theodosia Elvira Horton Hamilton was the wife of George Hamilton I of Beaver Creek. They were the first Hamiltons to move into Ashe County.

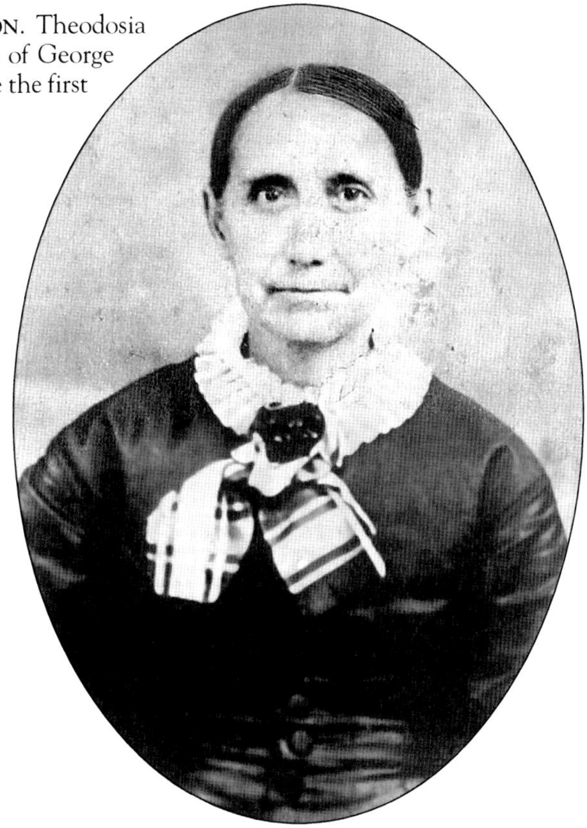

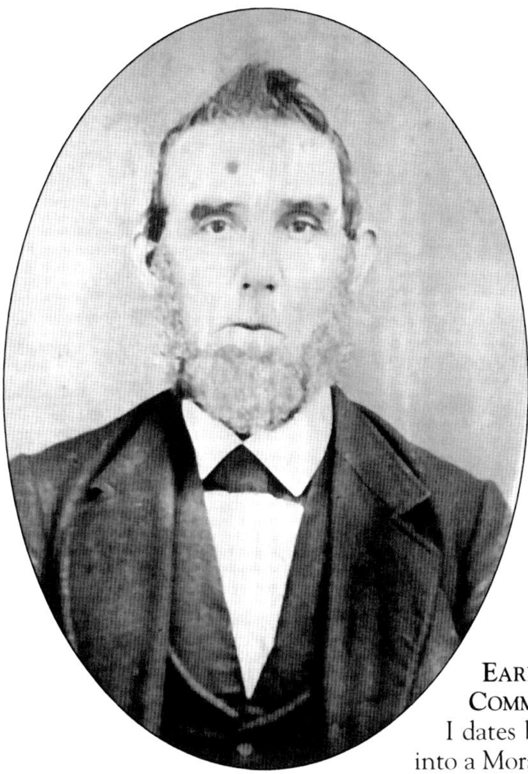

EARLY SETTLER OF THE BEAVER CREEK COMMUNITY. This portrait of George Hamilton I dates back to the early 1800s. Hamilton was born into a Moravian family.

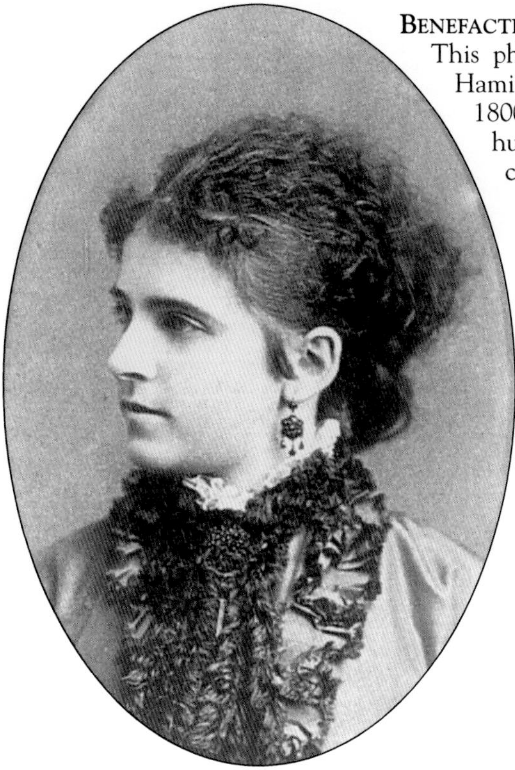

Benefactress of St. Mary's Episcopal Church. This photo of Laura Hamilton, the wife of Rufus Hamilton, was taken sometime in the late 1800s. Laura Agathe Hamilton influenced her husband to donate land to build St. Mary's church, the first Episcopal church in Ashe County. In 1974, Ben Long painted his first fresco at St. Mary's.

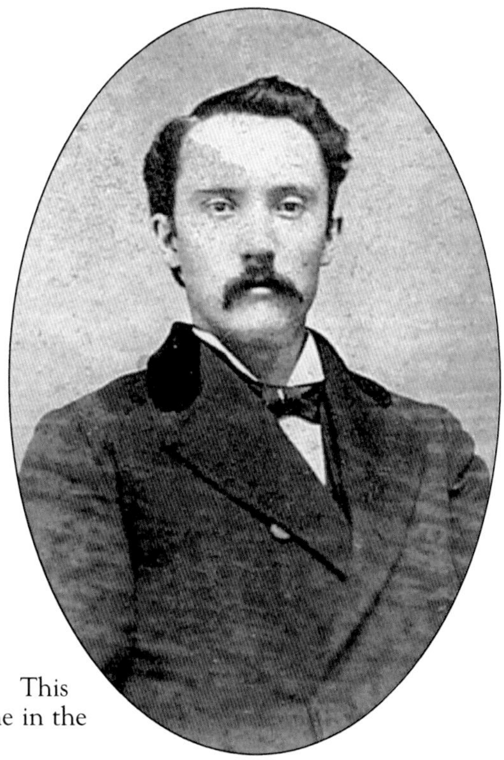

Prominent Citizen of Beaver Creek. This portrait of Rufus Hamilton was taken sometime in the late 1800s.

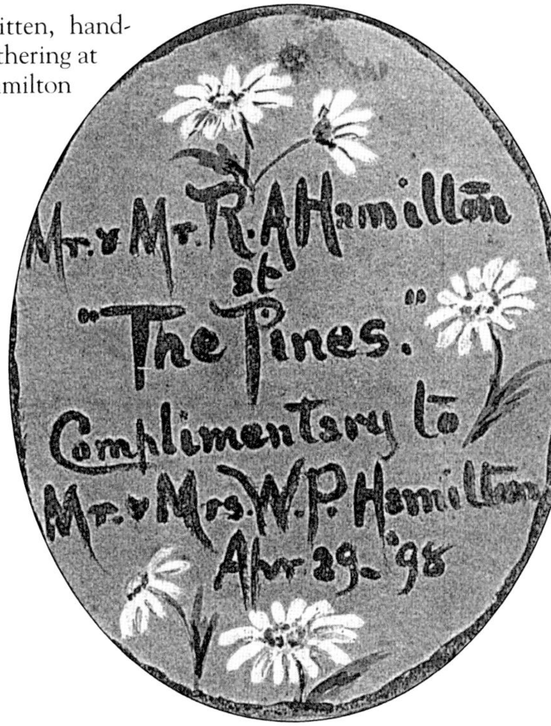

PARTY AT THE PINES. This handwritten, hand-decorated invitation was for an 1898 gathering at the home of Rufus and Laura Agathe Hamilton in Beaver Creek.

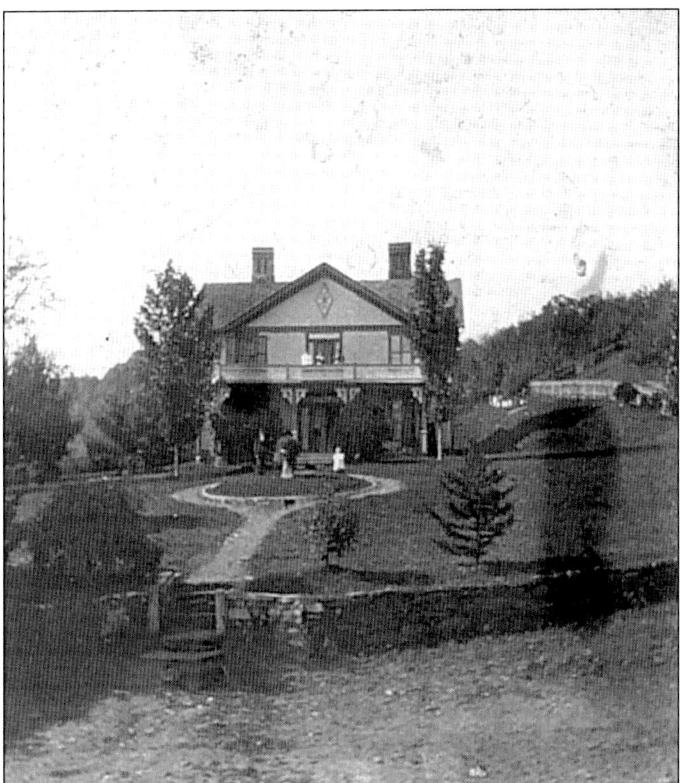

THE RUFUS HAMILTON HOME IN BEAVER CREEK. This photograph of the Hamilton home was taken in the 1890s. The home was known as "The Pines" while the Hamiltons lived there. The house still stands, but is now referred to as the Dr. Cicero Gambill House.

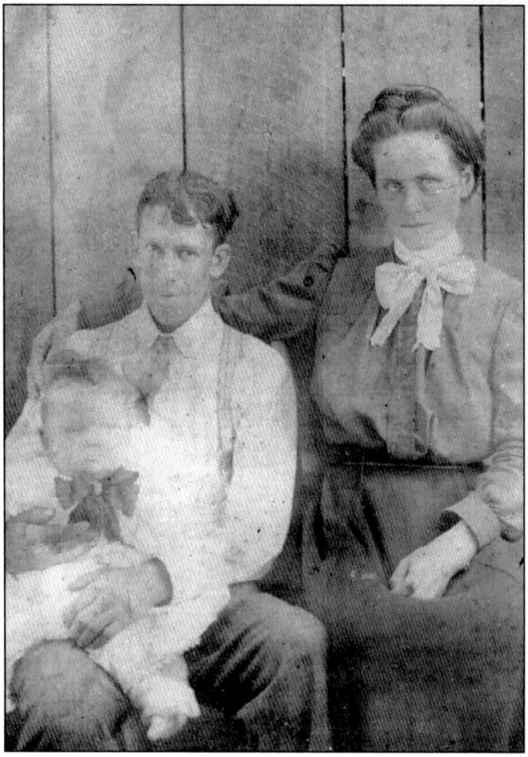

Proud Parents of the Buffalo Community. This is a 1911 portrait of Tom and Nellie Lewis Holman holding their son Rob.

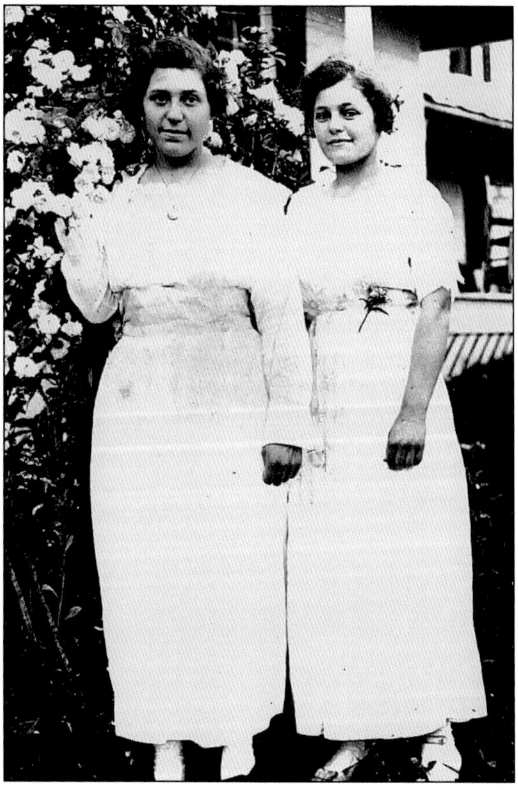

Beaver Creek Sisters. Pictured from left to right are Zora Alice Williams (Colvard) and Mamie Williams (Goodman).

JOHN HOUCK, 1912. The well-dressed young man is John Houck, son of Arthur and Myrtle Houck, and later husband of Connie Marie Dickson.

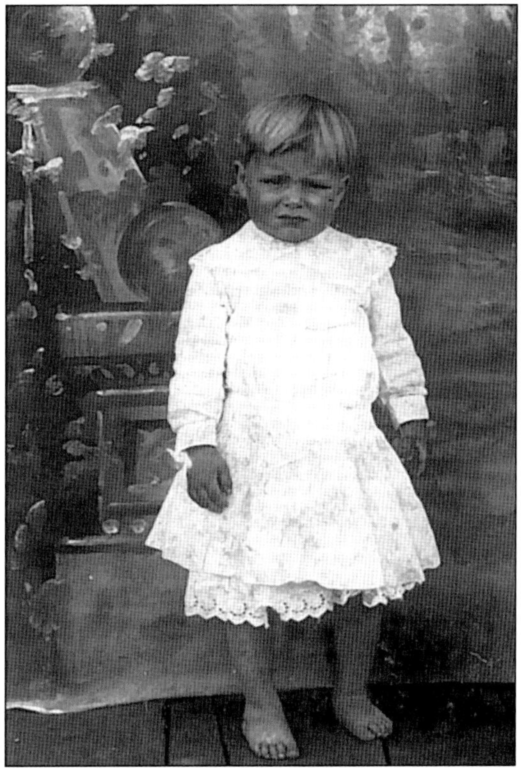

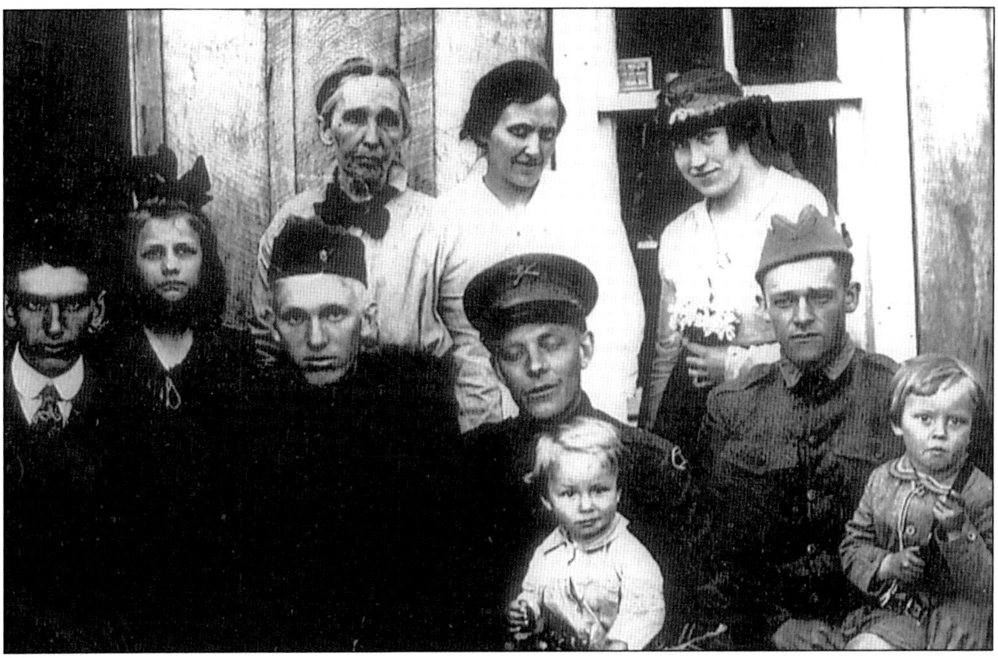

SERVICE TO THEIR COUNTRY. Pictured from left to right are the following: (seated) Gurna Houck, Jesse Houck, Charles "Jack" Houck holding Gabrielle Black, and Clyde Gentry holding Roscoe Black; (standing) Flossie Miller, Jane Houck Gentry, Gertie Gentry Black, and Hilda Houck.

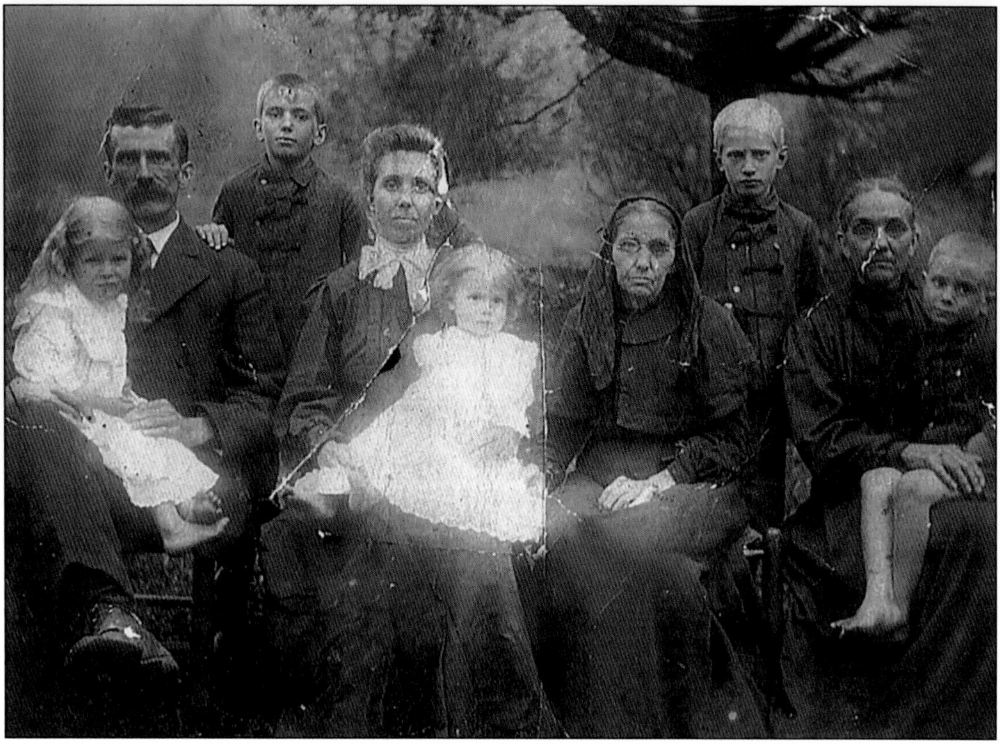

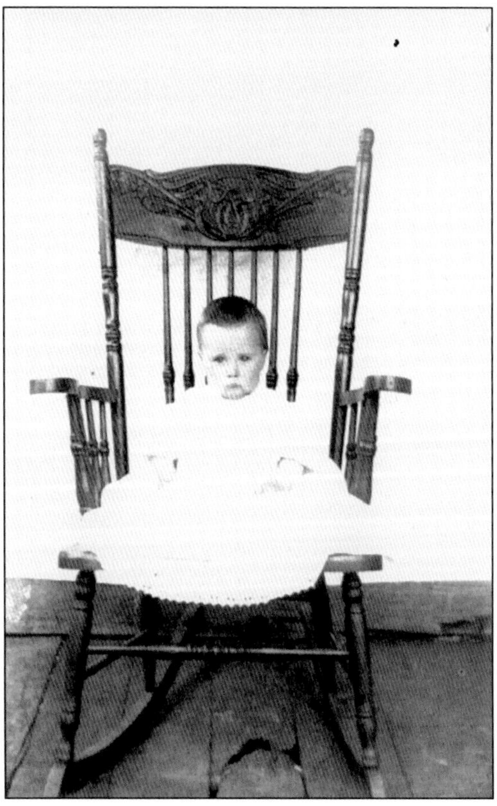

PROMINENT FAMILY MAN. This 1908 photo shows Arthur Jacob Houck, Sunday School Superintendent of Bethany United Methodist Church and a lumberman. He and his wife reared 11 children. Pictured from left to right are Arthur Jacob Houck holding Anne Houck, Gurna Park Houck, Myrtle Nevada (Edwards) holding Mary McCorkle Houck, Nancy McCorkle Houck, Jesse Ellis Houck, and Harriet "Addie" Houck holding George Fielder Houck.

WALTER RALEIGH HOWELL, C. 1910. Walter was the son of William Lee Howell of the Fleetwood Community.

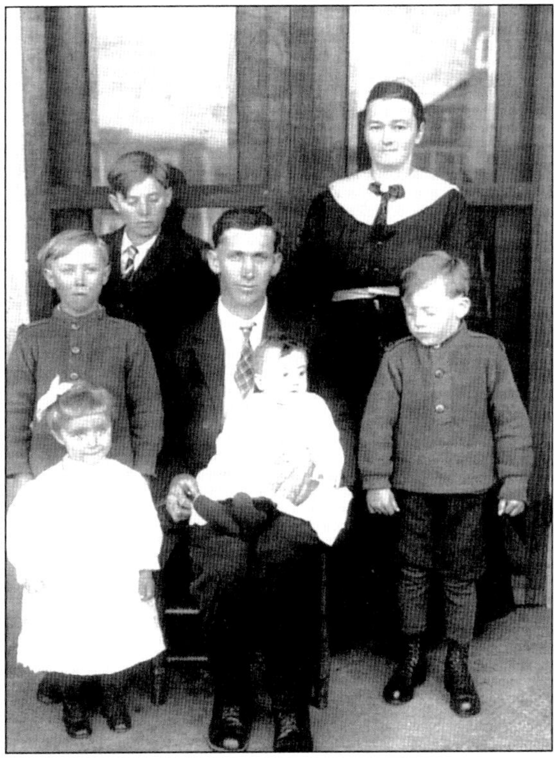

William Lee Howell Family. Pictured left to right are (front left standing) Lizzie Howell; (second row) Joe Neal Howell, William Lee Howell (seated) holding Willie Blair Howell, and Woodrow Wilson Howell; (back row) Walter Raleigh Howell and Sarah Fanny Howell. This photo was taken *c.* 1920.

A Baldwin Home , c. 1916. Myrtle Houck poses with her children, Anne, Mary, Lillis, Bruce, and John, before the home she owned with her husband Arthur Jacob Houck.

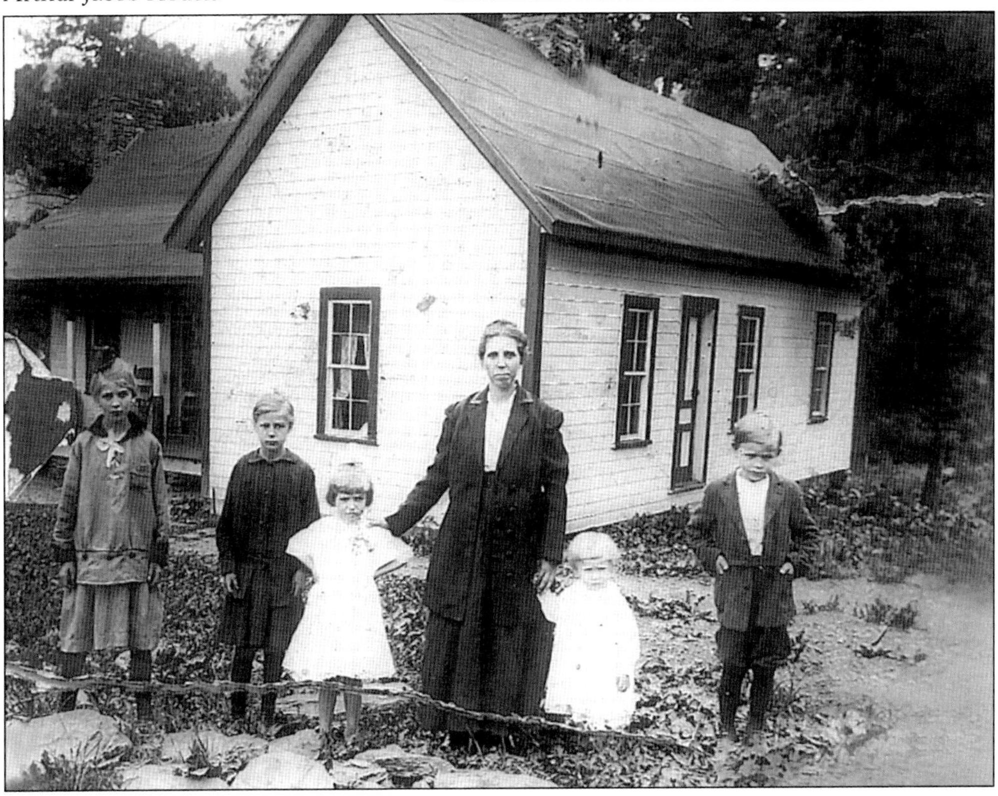

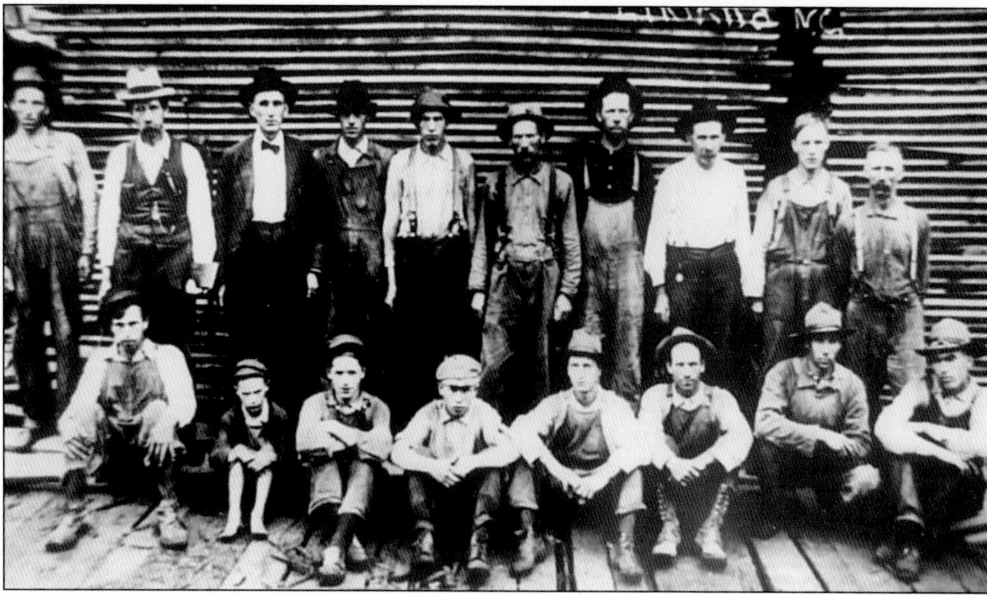

J. WALKER WRIGHT LUMBER COMPANY OF ELKLAND. The advent of the railroad led to the wholesale cutting of hardwood timber, which now had a way to get to market. Because Elkland was on the Virginia Creeper line, it became a major collection point for lumber sawn from local trees. This left the hills and forests denuded until reforestation efforts of the 1950s and 1960s.

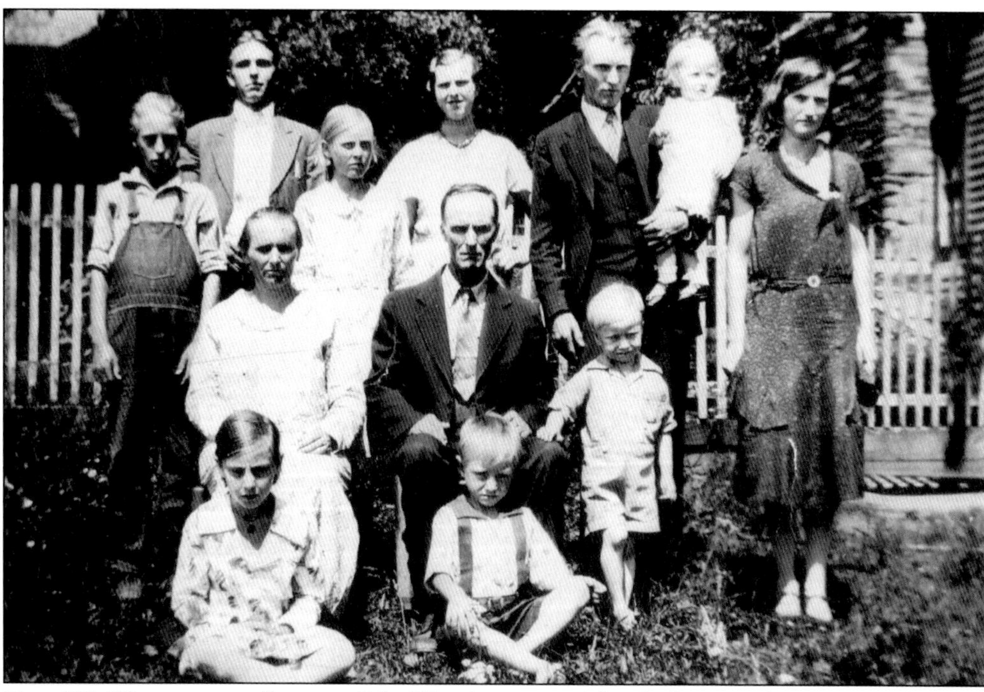

THE C.L.WINEBARGER FAMILY. C.L. Winebarger paid local photographer Nettie Pharr 10¢ to take this portrait of his family in 1932. Pictured from left to right are the following: (seated) Minnie Miller Winebarger and Cyrus Larkin Winebarger; (children in front) Aulcie and Earl Winebarger; (standing) Worth, Charlie, Ada, and Zora Winebarger, Walter Marvin Winebarger, and his wife Pansy Lyalls Winebarger, with their children Thelma and Carl.

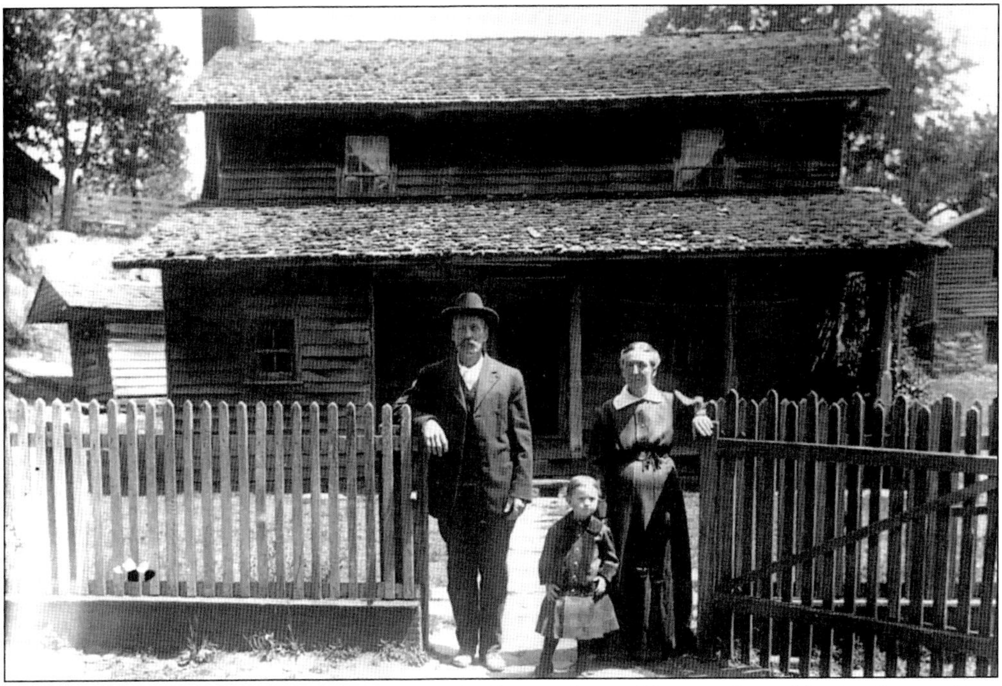

THE ORIGINAL JAMES RAY HOME, 1914. Pictured are Thomas Ray, Hettie Brown Ray, and daughter Elizabeth Ray Graybeal. The picture was taken before rooms were added to accommodate a growing family.

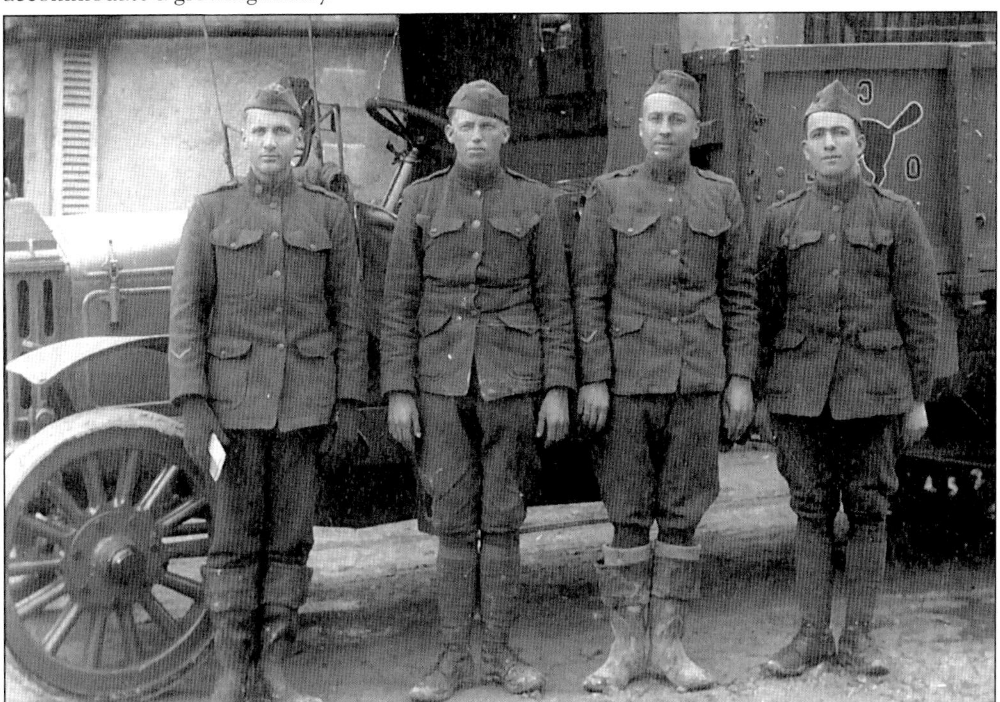

COMRADES IN ARMS, 1918. Bower H. Duncan (right) was a former teacher and principal of West Jefferson High School. Duncan also served as superintendent of schools for Ashe County.

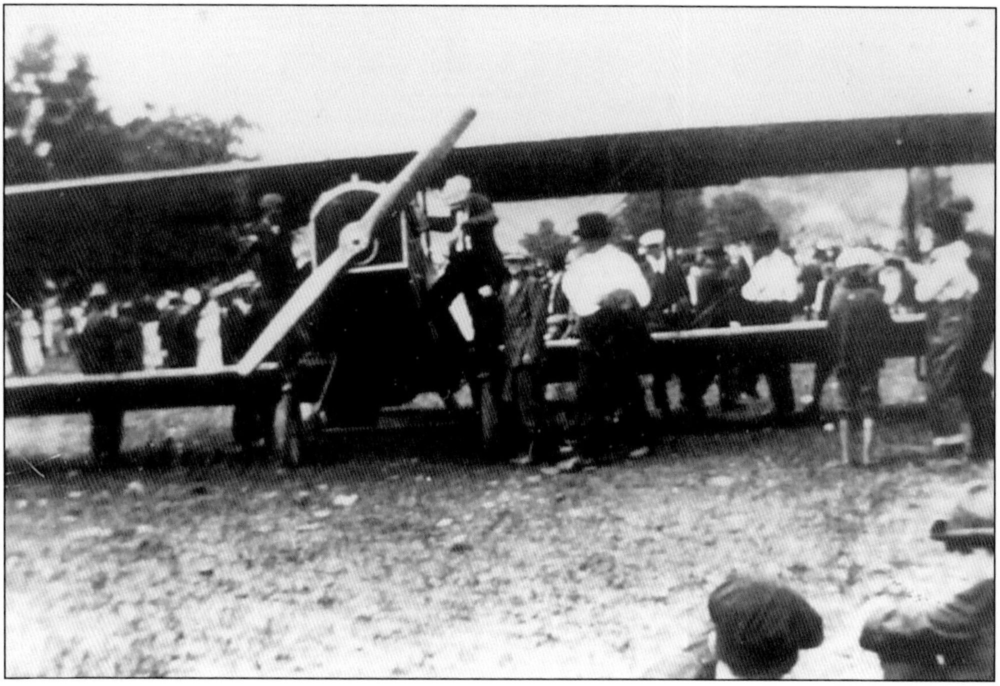

AIRPLANES IN ASHE COUNTY IN THE 1920S. This picture is believed to be a snapshot taken of the first airplane to ever land in Ashe County. Airplane landings were rare in Ashe County.

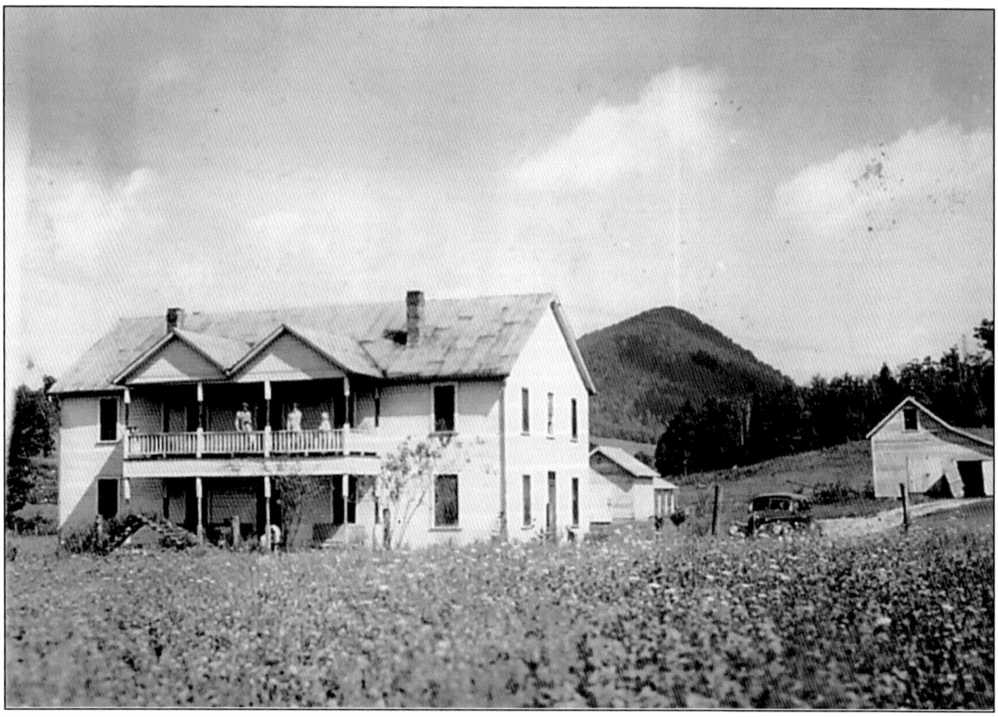

ASHE COUNTY HOME. Before social services existed, the Ashe County Home located in Beaver Creek provided for its poor. In order to feed themselves and each other, residents of the home were required to grow and tend crops and livestock on the land surrounding the home.

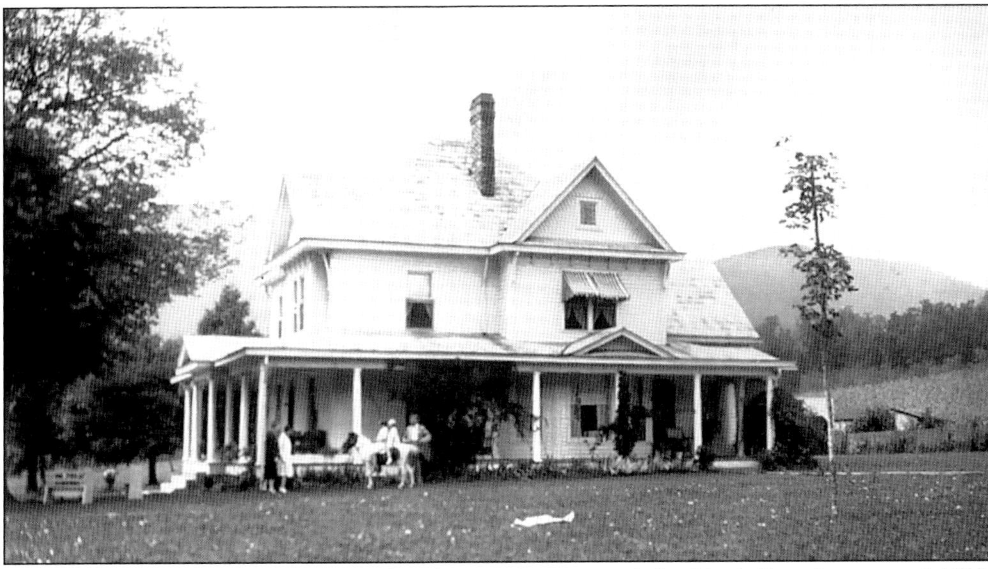

EARLY TOURIST DESTINATION. Fred and Lessie Ray opened the Black Bear Inn around 1927. The inn was named after "The Black Bear Trail" (currently Highway 194), a scenic route for tourists between Quebec and the Florida Keys. The Black Bear Inn was known for its good food and hospitality. It was one of the finest places to stay in Ashe County. It is now being restored by Bill Colvard.

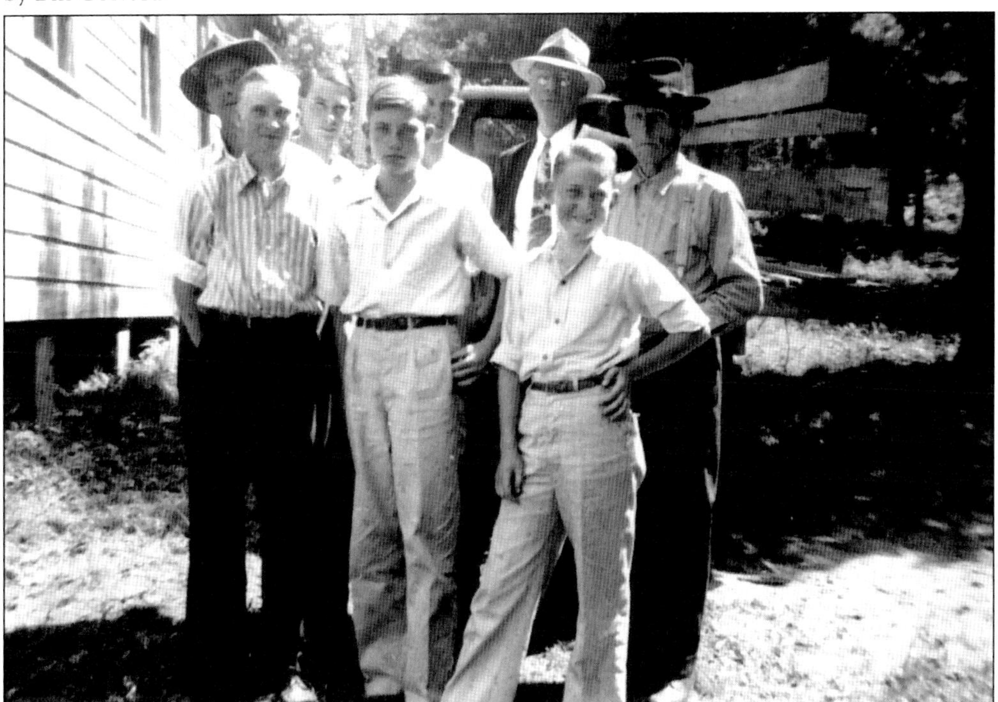

SUNDAY AFTER CHURCH. Standing beside the recently constructed Mt. Olive Baptist Church are, from left to right, the following: (front row) Carl Winebarger, Jack Surber, and Earl Church; (back row) Freeman Sheets, Fred Perry, Clarence Dillard, Levi Greene, and Henry Miller.

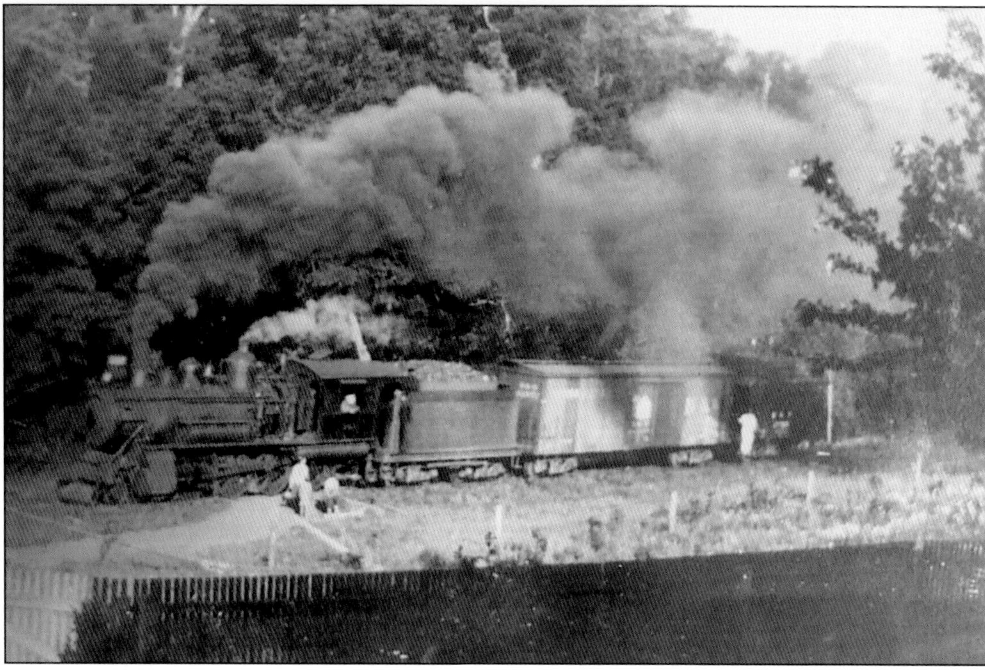

The Virginia Creeper Leaving Todd. Throughout the 1920s, the Norfolk and Western Railroad ran a daily train from Abingdon, Virginia, to Todd, North Carolina. The train transported both passengers and freight.

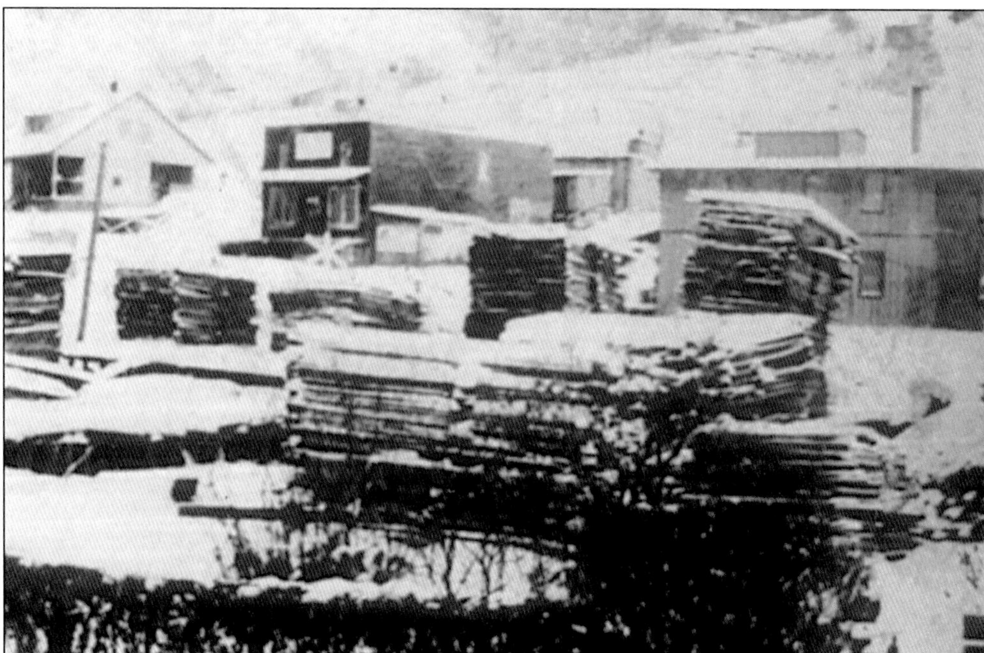

Early View of the Todd General Store. This photo, taken in the 1930s, shows the store before the present A-line roof was added. The home of Walter Cook, the store's owner, is shown in the background on the left. A mill was located to the right of the store; its upper floor was used to store dried herbs awaiting pickup by the Virginia Creeper train.

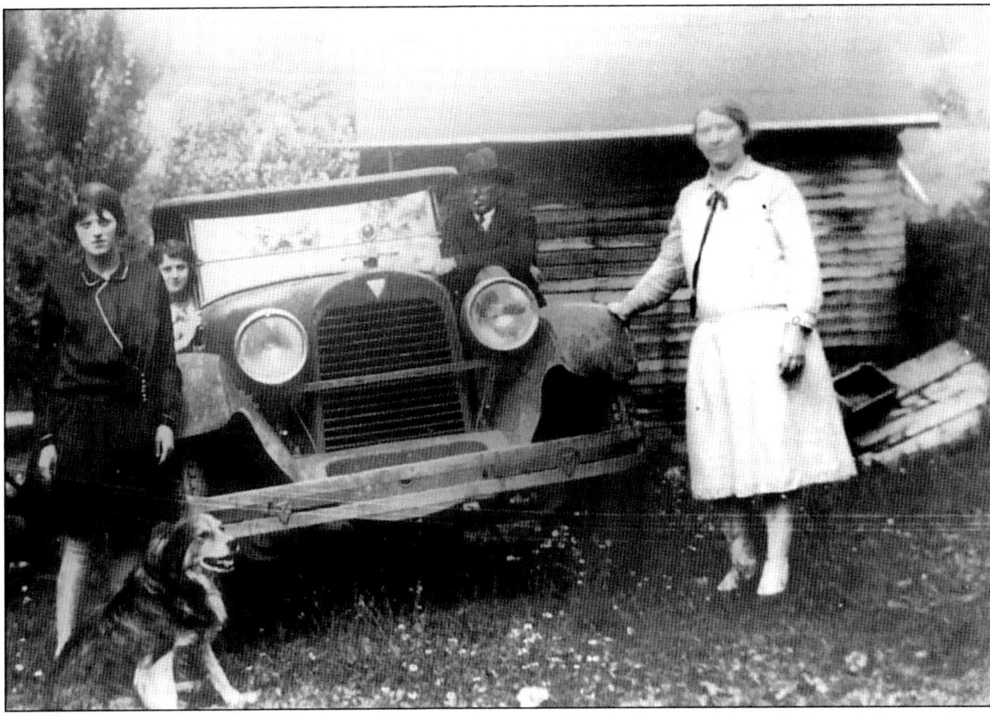

Sunday Outing in the Buffalo Community, c. 1930. Pictured from left to right are Ilene Hodgson Rash, Elizabeth Ray Graybeal, Dwight Hodgson, and Jennie Graybeal Hodgson.

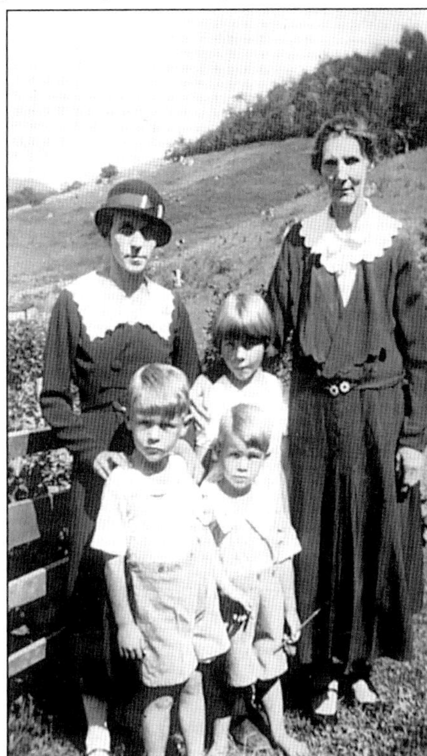

A Lazy Summer Afternoon. Pictured in 1930 from left to right are the following: (front row) Wayne Killen and Grover Killen; (back row) Effie Powell, Viola Killen, and Ann Killen.

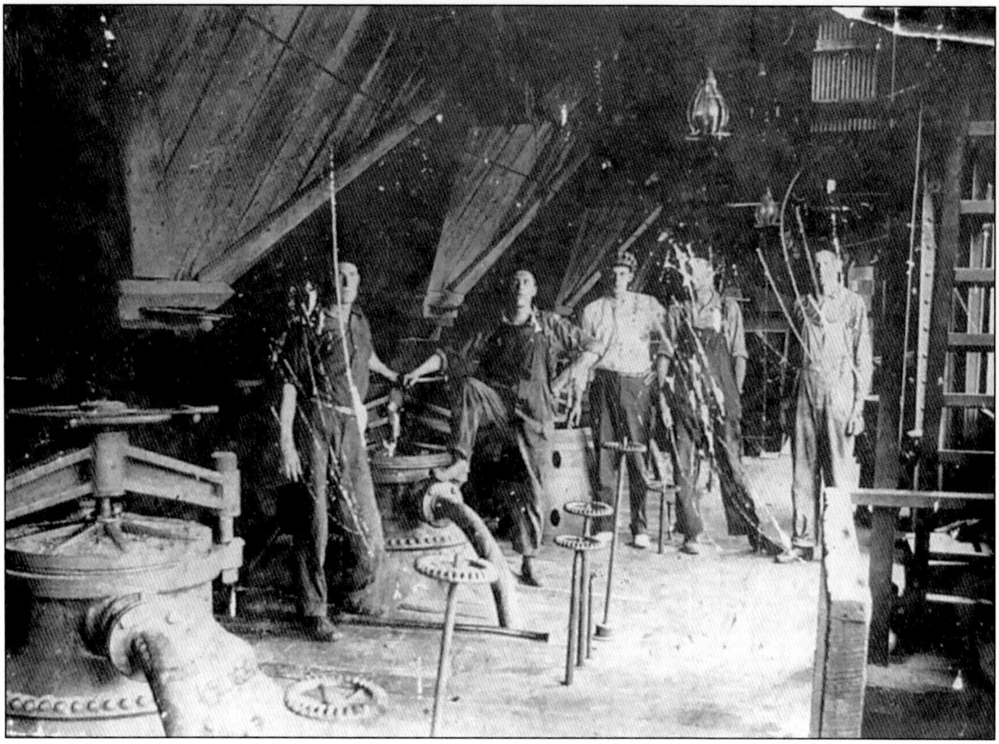

EXTRACTING TANNIC ACID. This photo showcases the interior of the Smethport extract plant, which was one of the leading forces in Ashe County's economy in the 1930s. The tannic acid was extracted from the chestnut trees.

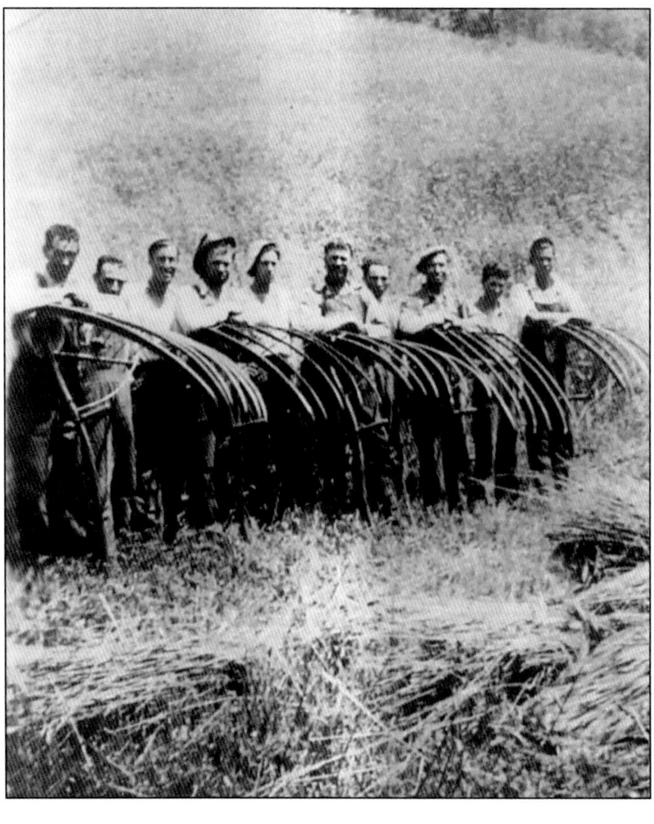

THRESHERS USING AN OAK CRADLE. These men were working on the Joe Kemp farm in the Buffalo community c. 1936.

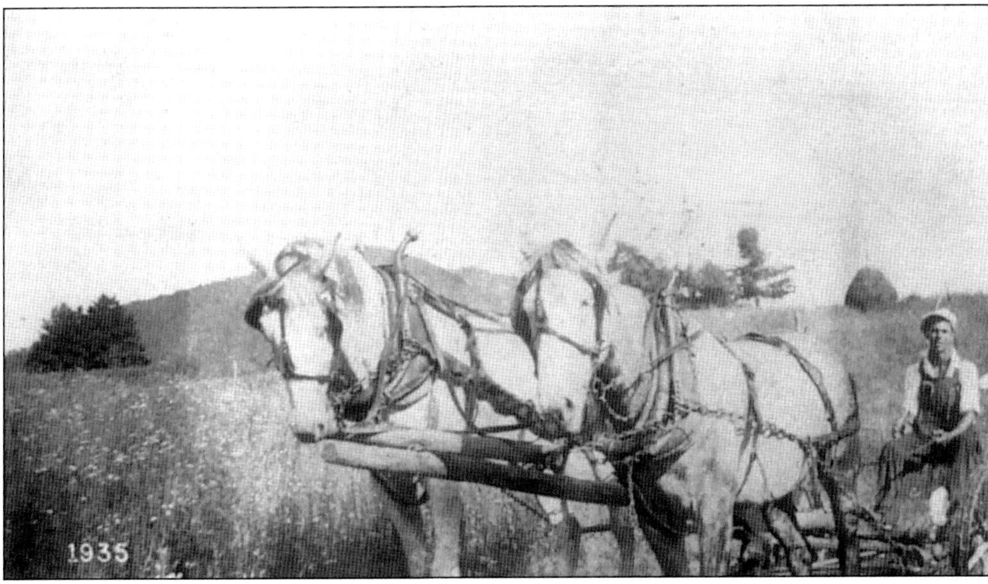

HAY—NECESSARY TO MAINTAIN THE HERDS. Hay was the second vital crop after corn in the early 20th century. The men pictured above were haying on the Joe Kemp farm in the Buffalo community, *c.* 1935.

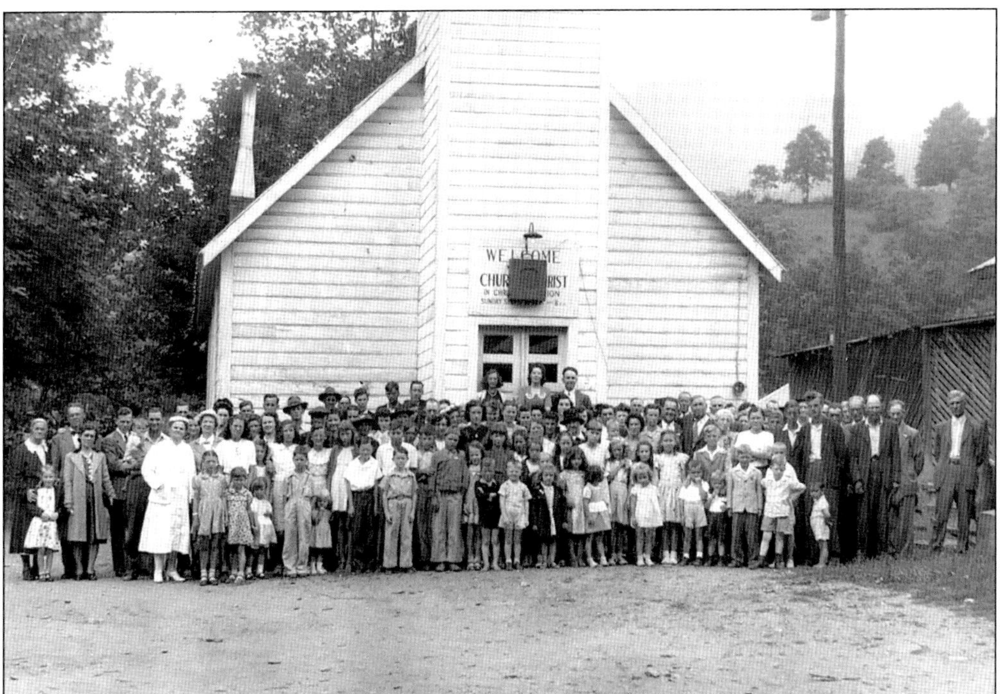

PADDY MOUNTAIN BAPTIST CHURCH. This church was organized in 1936. Floyd Detty was pastor of the church during the 1940s, when this photo was taken. The building was moved in 1980 to its present site on SR 88 and a new sanctuary was added.

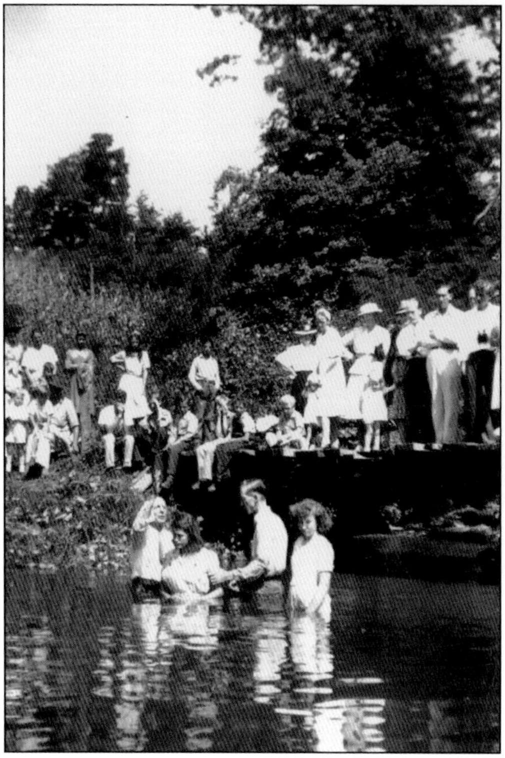

RURAL BAPTISM AT MT. OLIVE BAPTIST CHURCH. The 1940s congregation gathered outdoors for this baptismal service.

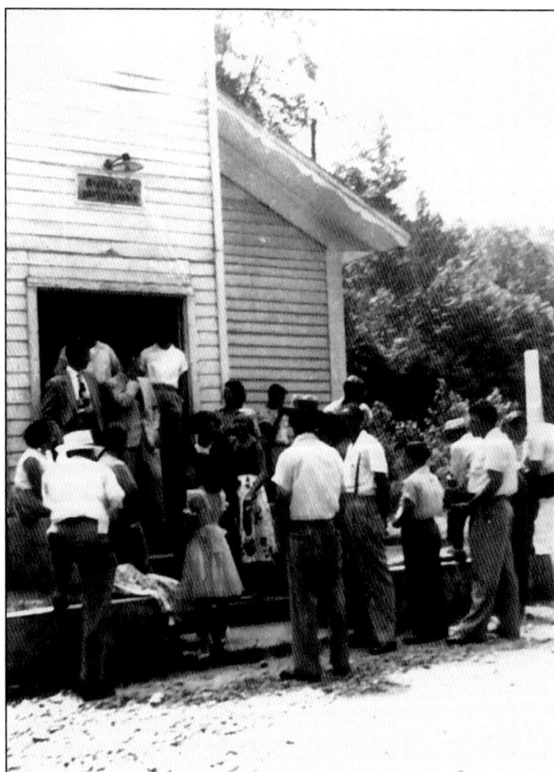

BUFFALO BAPTIST CHURCH, 1940S. Buffalo Baptist Church was organized sometime in 1868 or 1869 in a log schoolhouse near the site of the present church building.

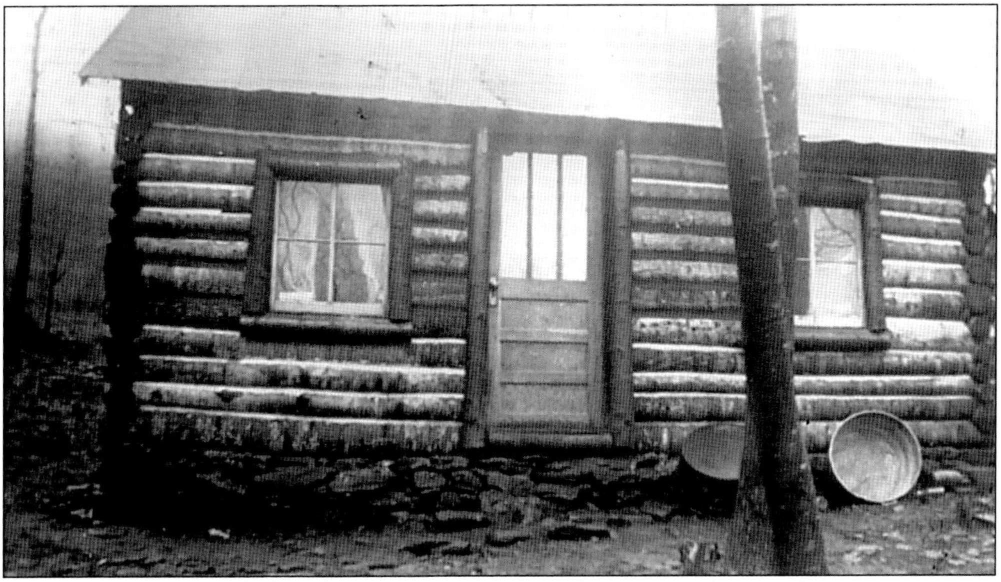

A Home in the Forest. This hand-hewn log cabin was the home of Vance Moretz in the Buffalo community in the 1940s. Ashe County residents relied on the forest for most of their needs.

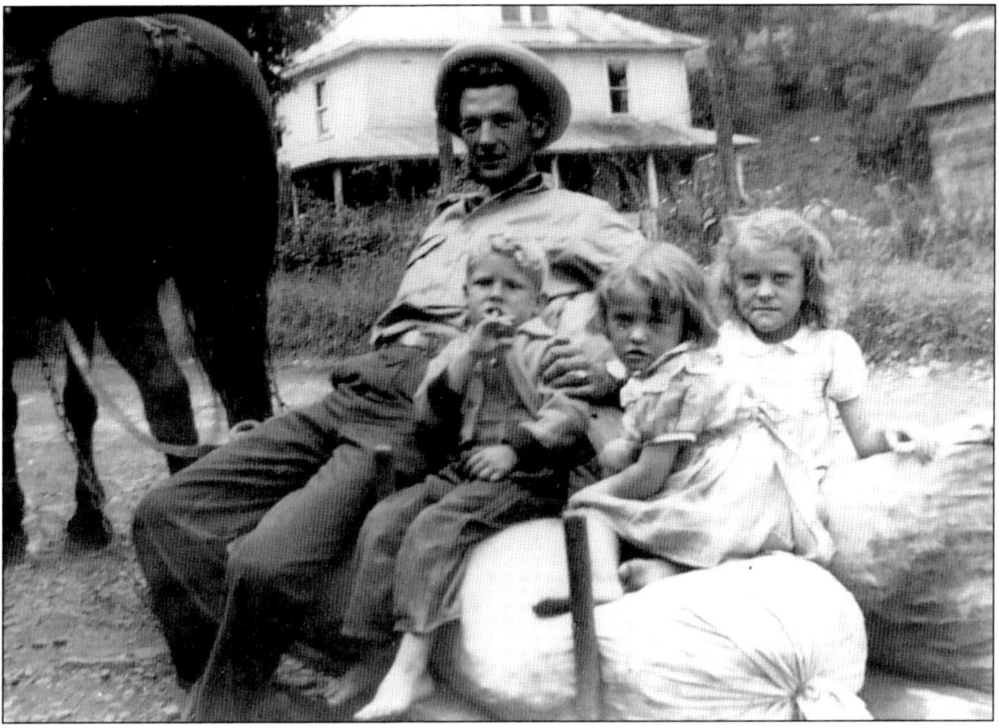

A 1940s Bean Harvest. With the improvement of county roads and the advent of the railroad, beans overshadowed corn as the leading agricultural crop. The first harvest year saw the sale of 100,000 bushels of beans. After a hard day's work, Tine Gentry, Barty Eller, Betty Graybeal Speeker, and Margaret Graybeal Ashby rest on their harvest of fresh green beans on the way to market. The old Graybeal home on Buffalo Road is in the background.

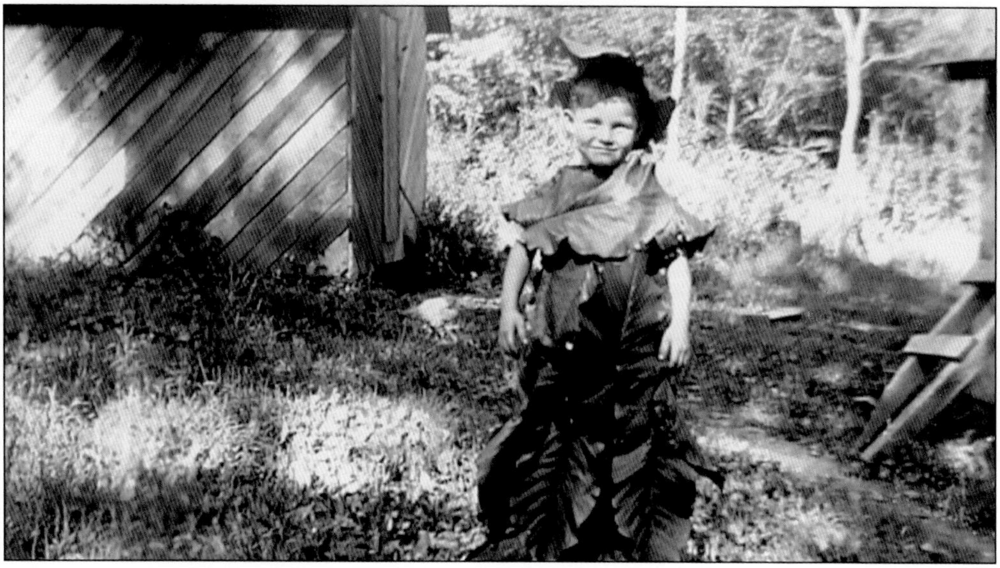

Costume Inspired by Mother Nature. Burl Flannery is covered with leaves from an umbrella magnolia tree. His aunt Viola Moretz pinned them on him.

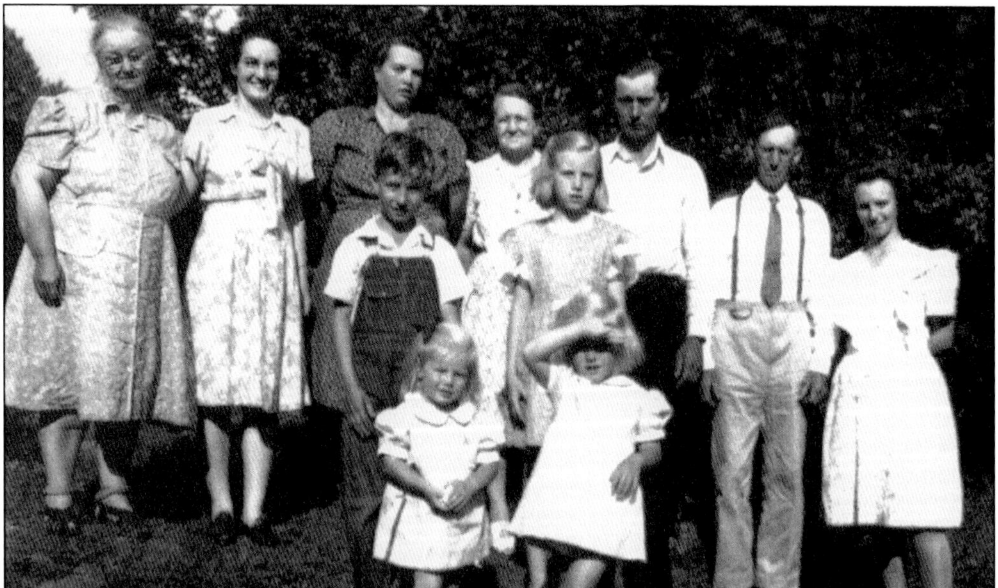

Summer Visit, 1947. Pictured from left to right are the following: (front row) Martha Ann Howell and Wilma Irene Howell; (middle row) Carroll Lee Howell and Willa Inez Howell; (back row) Sarah Fanny Goodman Howell, unidentified, Cleo Alverta Howell, Anna Waddel, Walter Raleigh Howell, William Lee Howell, and Lizzie Howell Fairchild.

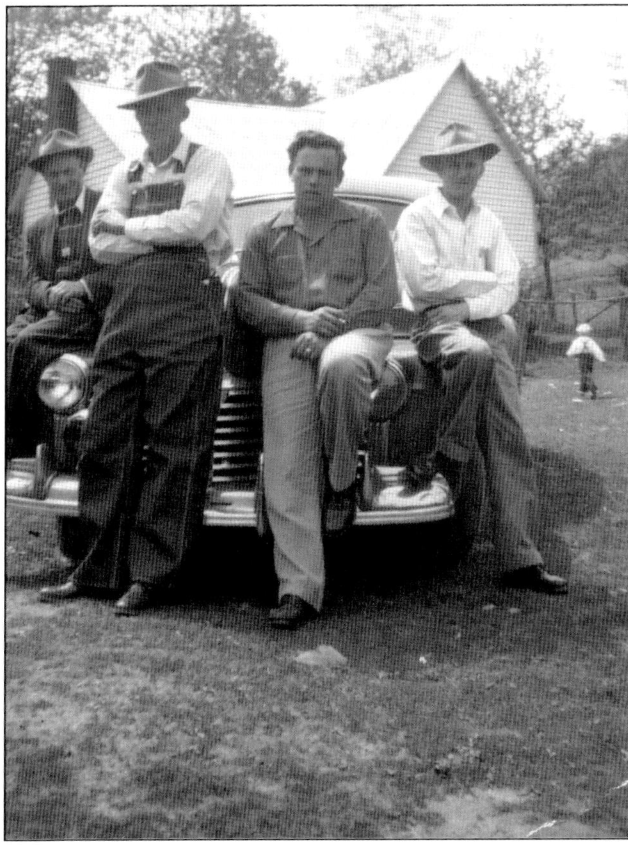

SIGN OF THE TIMES. These gentlemen lean against a 1940s Chevrolet during a visit at Daniel Lyalls's home. Pictured from left to right are Daniel Lyalls, Clint Lyalls, James Duvall, and Carl Winebarger.

NEW HOUSE IN THE OVAL COMMUNITY. Daniel Lyalls and his wife Martha Annie Houck Lyalls pose before the newly completed home of their daughter, Pansy Belle Lyalls Winebarger, and her husband Walter Marvin Winebarger in 1950.

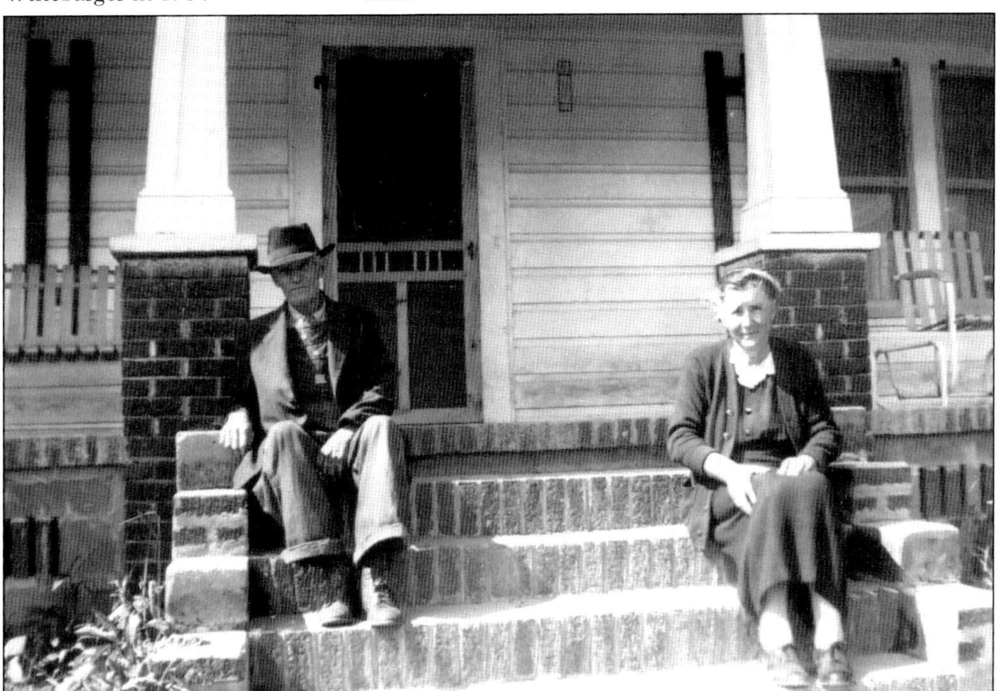

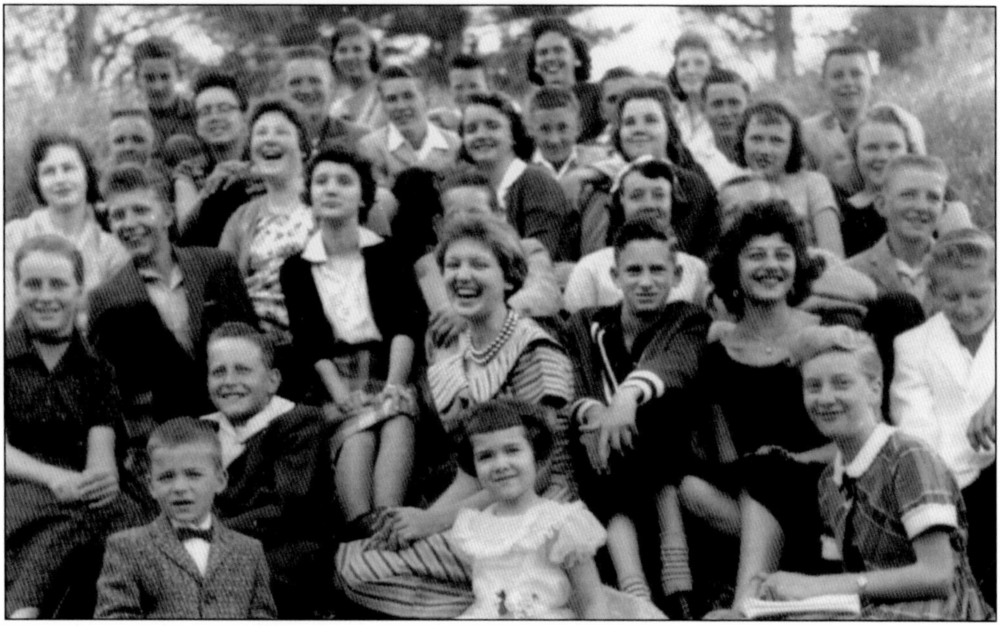

Graduating Class at Fleetwood Elementary School. This photo was taken of the 1959 eighth-grade class. Included in the photograph are mascots Teddy McNeil and Anne Scott along with their teacher Mrs. Imojean Hopper Weaver.

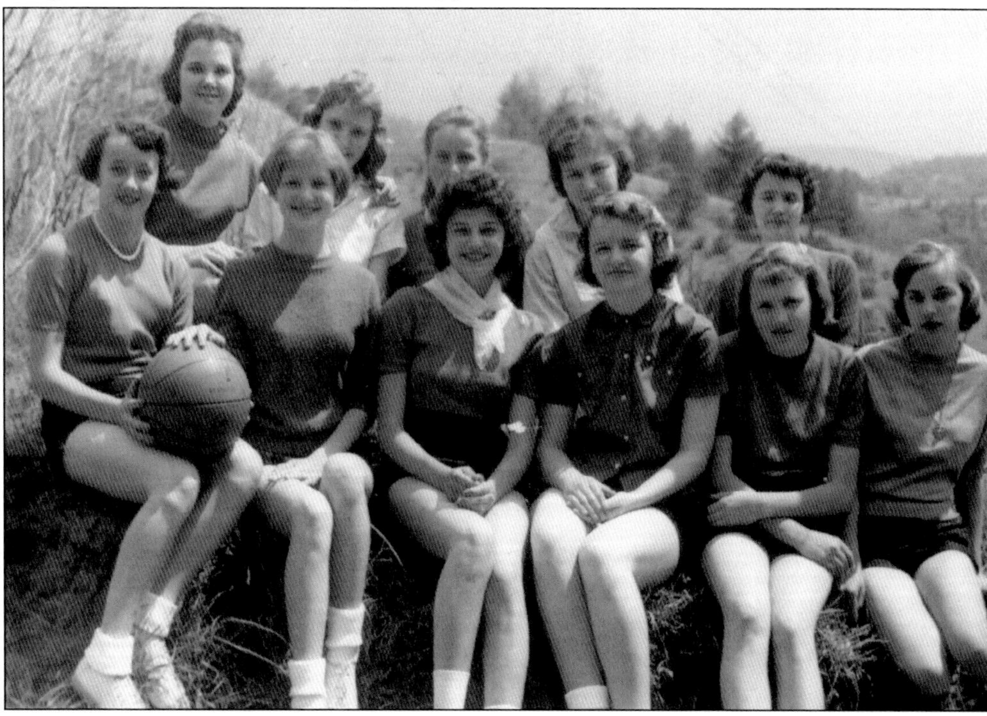

Fleetwood Girls Basketball Team, 1959. Pictured from left to right are the following: (front row) Vivian Church, Janice Church, Irene Church, Mary Anne Kincaid, Barbara Greer, and Shirley Blevins; (back row) Alma Jean Lyalls, Betty June Surber, Reba Woodie, Lola Brooks, and Sylvia Johnston.

PIONEER BUFFALO COMMUNITY FAMILY. Thomas and Elizabeth Graybeal pose for a formal portrait in the 1950s.

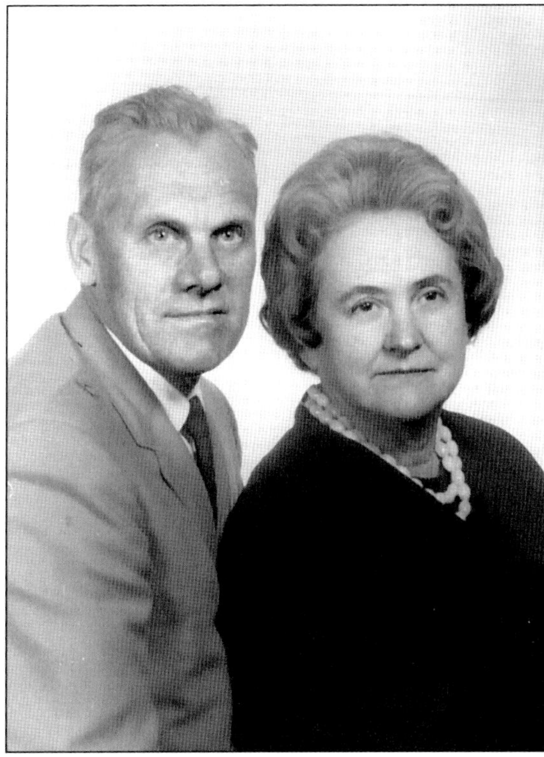

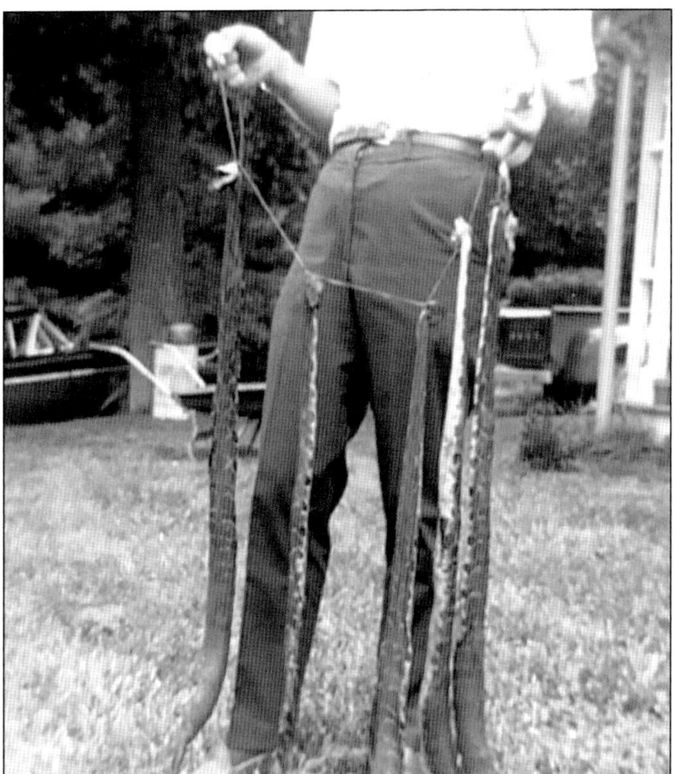

RATTLESNAKE BOUNTY. Grover Killen displays five rattlesnakes killed by his neighbor Paul Trivette in the 1960s. Both men lived in the Buffalo community.

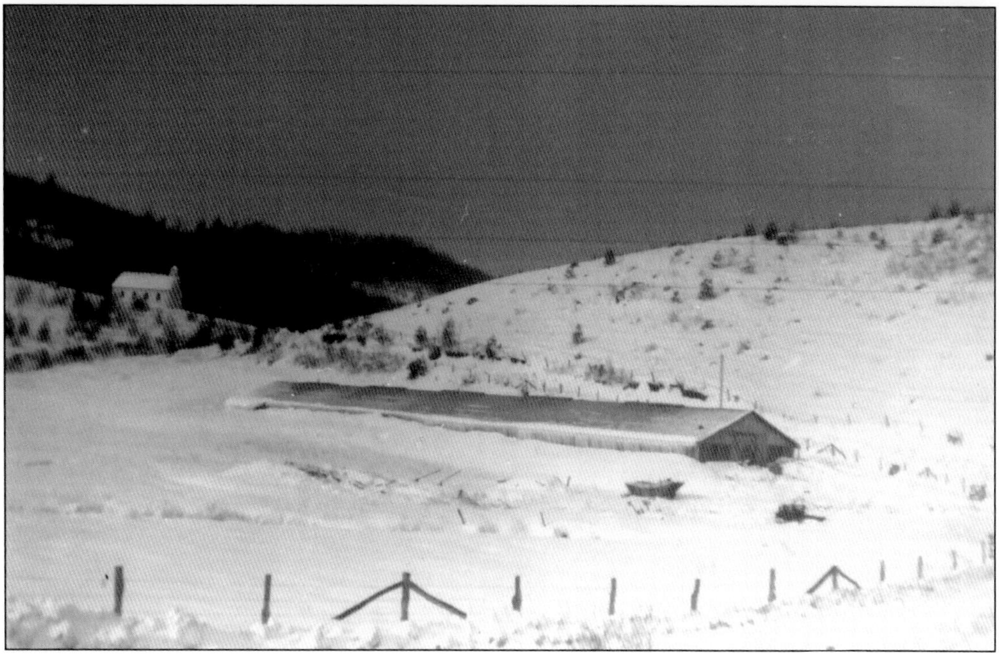

THE BIG SNOW OF 1960. This chicken house in the Oval Community is nearly buried in the snowfall. Chicken houses like this one were a very common sight in Ashe County throughout the 1960s and 1970s. "Raising chickens," first as layers and then later as broilers for the commercial market, became a livelihood as well as an income supplement for Ashe County farmers. A house like this one would contain as many as 10,000 chickens at one time.

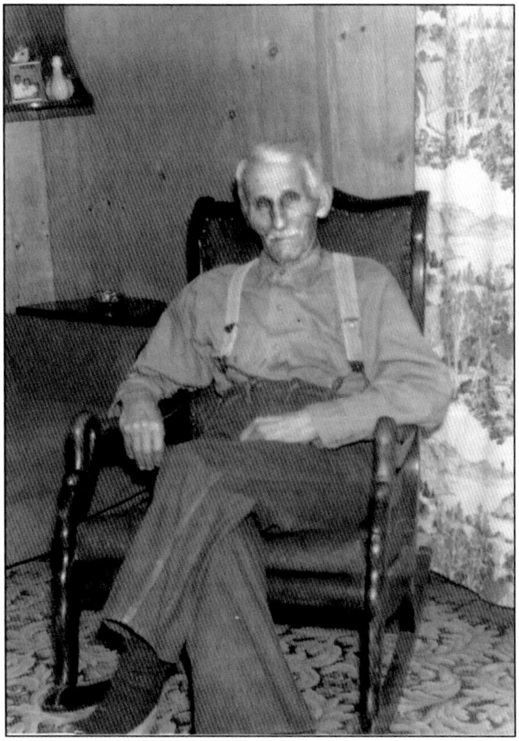

OVAL COMMUNITY ELDER. Henry Miller, pictured here in 1960, lived to be almost 100 years old.

Five

WATER AND THE BOTTOMLANDS

BROWNWOOD TO LAUREL SPRINGS AND SCOTTVILLE

The South Fork of the New River slowly winds northeastward through a more level slice of the plateau. It was water, a necessity of life, which brought early settlers to build communities south of the New River. The fertile bottomlands that flanked the South Fork provided the opportunity to build homes and begin a lifestyle centering on agriculture.

These level fields were easier to cultivate, making it possible for a family to build a dwelling and have a vegetable garden convenient to the homestead. In addition, there was ample grass for grazing livestock and enough room left to grow corn and other grains for winter provisions. The abundance of smaller creeks, streams, and natural springs—all tributaries of the New River—provided families with water for cooking, laundry, personal hygiene, and harness power to grind corn into cornmeal and wheat into flour.

From these bottomlands rose great forests of virgin chestnut timber, which harbored food for both domestic livestock and an abundant variety of wildlife. It was this same timber, which later was harvested for its tannins (extract) and brought the railroad to Ashe County in 1914, giving birth to the bustling town of Todd.

By the 1880s, cattle, sheep, hogs, and chickens were being raised for domestic use as well as for commercial market. Word of the area's abundance of natural resources was spreading. Cowles Stand in Gap Creek (Deep Gap) was recognized as a flourishing center of commerce. Here people bought, sold, or bartered such goods as butter, cheese, lard, beeswax, venison, furs, and ginseng.

Toward the east, copper and iron ore were being mined for commercial markets. The Blue Ridge Parkway designers changed their original planned route through Tennessee to take advantage of the breathtaking views from the edge of the high country plateau. The new plan placed 28 miles of the Parkway through Ashe County.

—By Sherry Winebarger Houck and Ann Winebarger

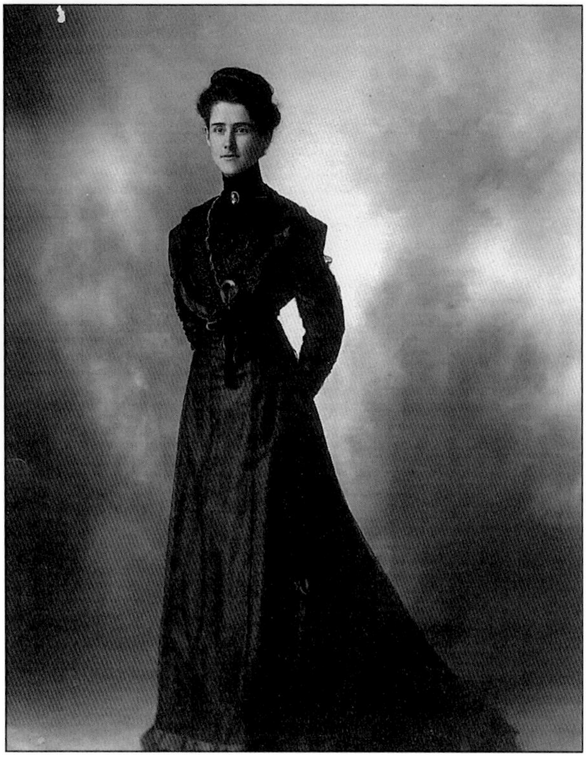

Daughter of an Ashe County Pioneer. The granddaughter of George Hamilton I, Kate Clyde Hamilton Price, pictured in the late 1890s, grew up in Beaver Creek. After she was married, she lived and reared six children in Laurel Springs.

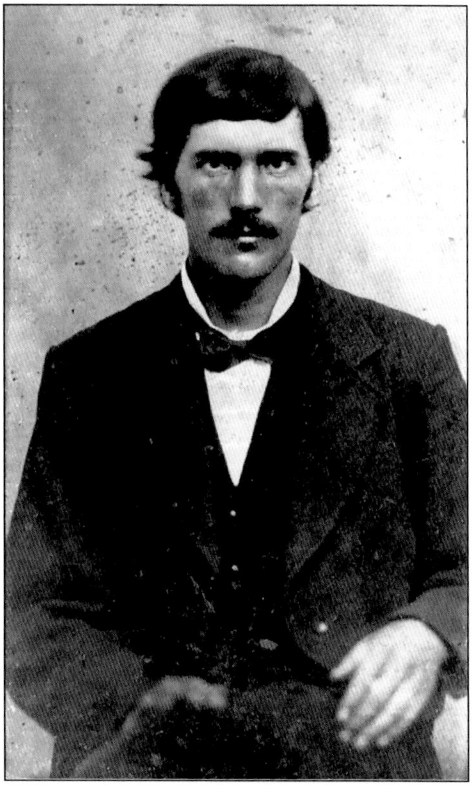

An Early Ancestor of the Ashe County Colvards. Pictured *c.* 1885 is Christopher Columbus Colvard, the son of William Neal and Sallie Bower Colvard and a resident of the Orion Community.

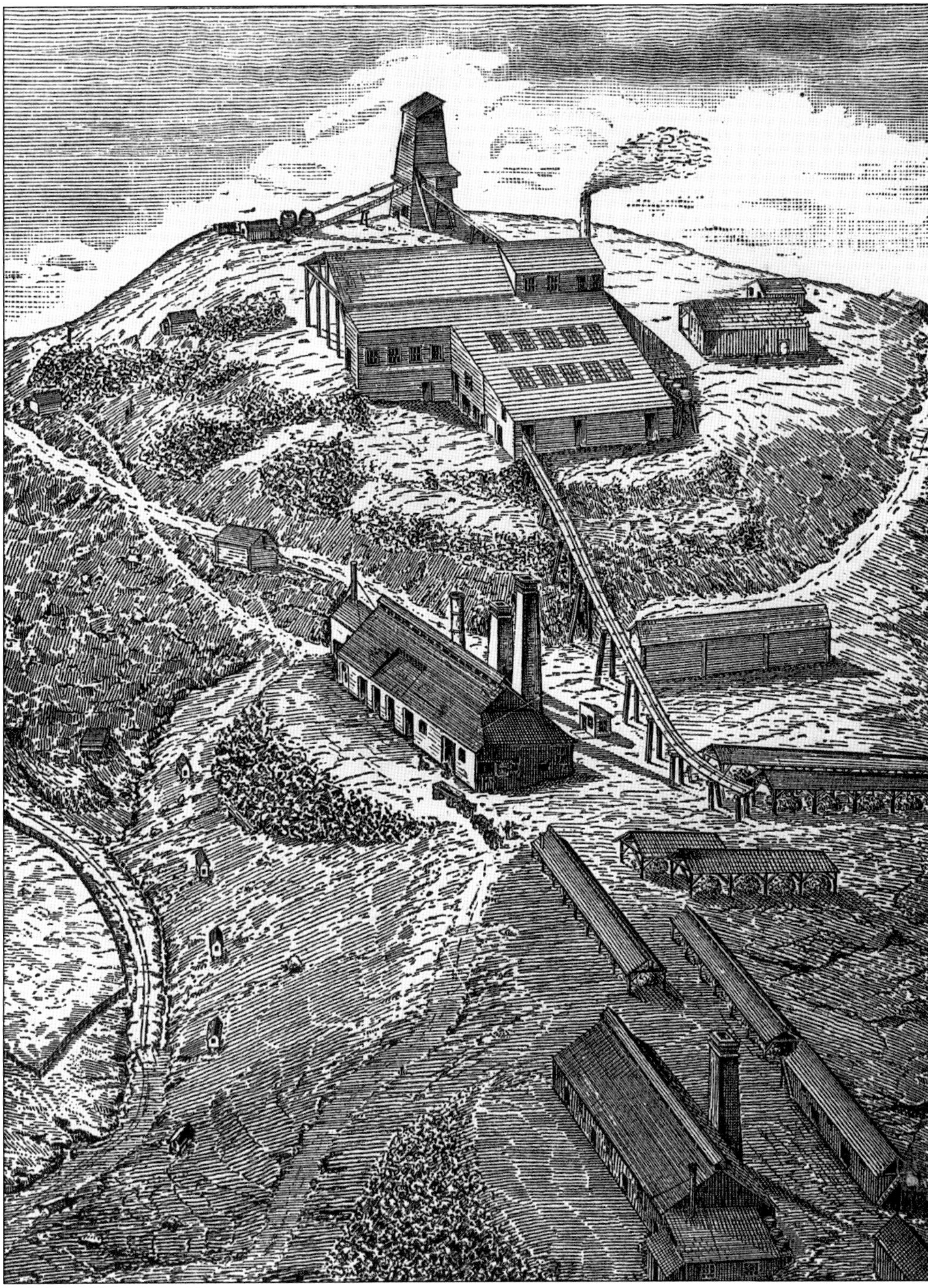

AN IMPORTANT EARLY ASHE COUNTY INDUSTRY. For about 10 years, Ore Knob was the leading copper producer in the United States. This drawing of the Ore Knob Copper Mine dates back to 1880. The mine was owned by the former Buckhannon Company of Virginia. Around 1870, the facilities and approximately 500 surrounding acres were purchased by S.S. and J.E. Clayton. By the late 1880s, high labor and transportation costs caused the owners to close the mine. It reopened later but closed its doors for good in 1962.

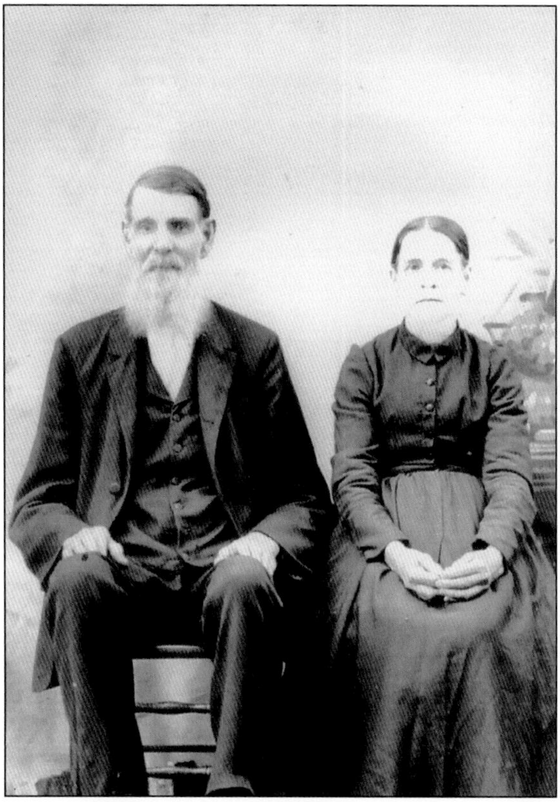

FREDERICK AND JULIA FAW SEVERT, C. 1900. Frederick (Fed) was a Civil War veteran, serving in McRaes N.C. Cavalry, CSA. Julia was a direct descendant of Squire and Sarah Boone, parents of Daniel Boone. Together they raised a family of 15 children in the Frank Dillard Road area.

SETTLERS ON THE SOUTH FORK OF THE NEW RIVER. Pictured at the John V. Miller home c. 1910 are, from left to right, John Miller, son Jesse Miller, wife Candis Severt Miller, and their other three unidentified children. Their home in the Boggs Community, was built in the 1860s, near the site where President Clinton spoke when he came to inaugurate the Heritage River program.

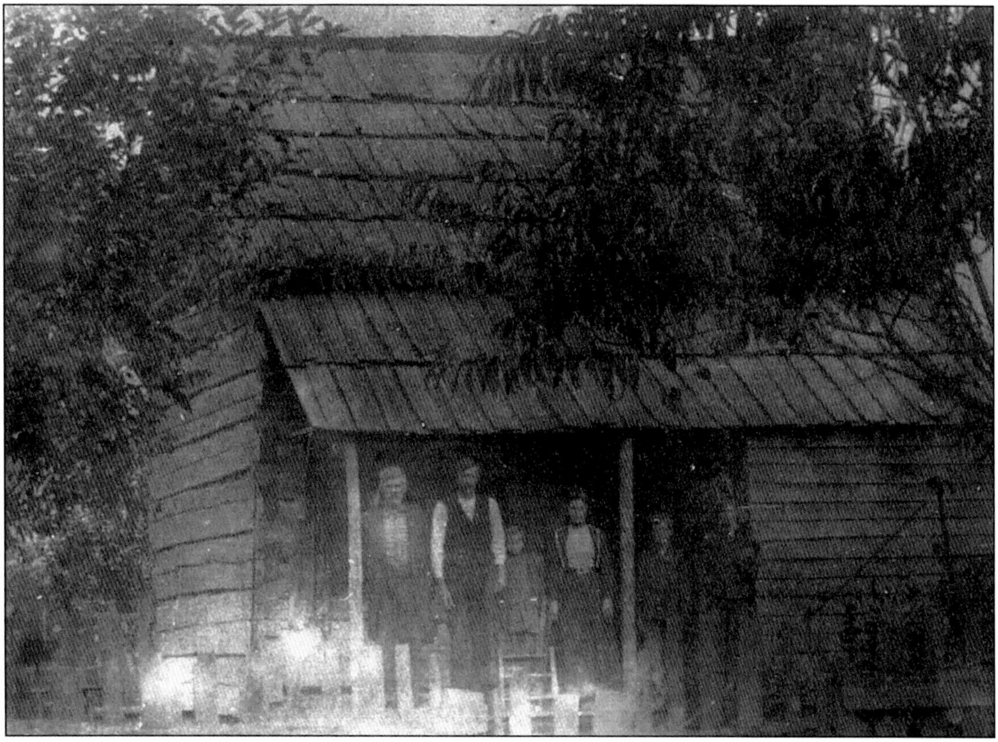

Dressed for an Occasion, c. 1919. Pictured from left to right are the following: (seated) Zora Williams Colvard, Reeves Goodman, and Della Duncan Stanley; (standing) Quincey Duncan, Boyd Richardson, Harold Don Williams, and Annie Vannoy Lemly.

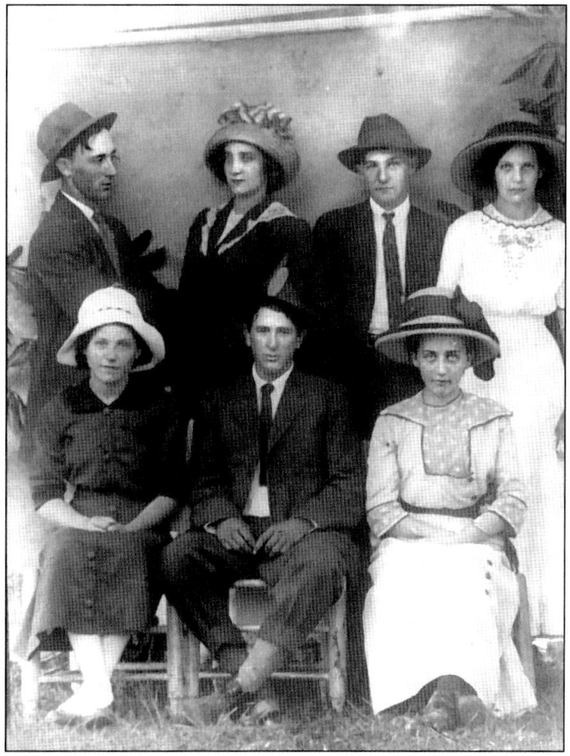

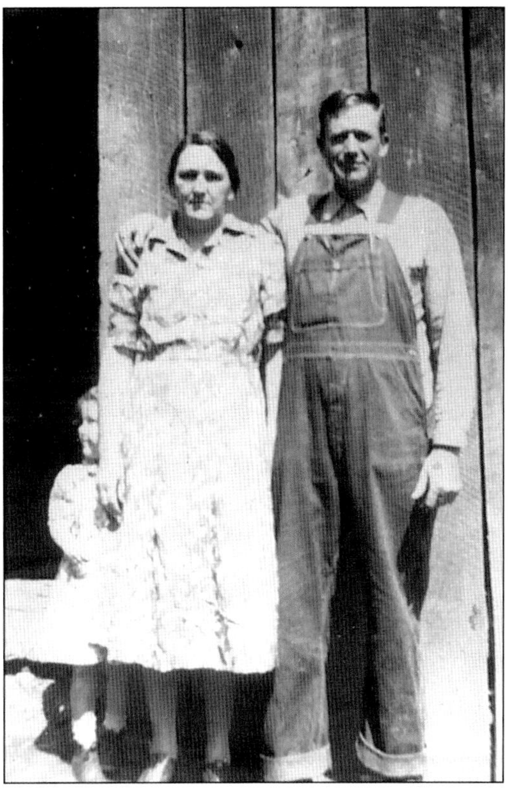

Mary Lou Miller—Camera Shy. Her mother and father, Letha Dillard and Dan Miller, raised a large farm family near the Boggs Community.

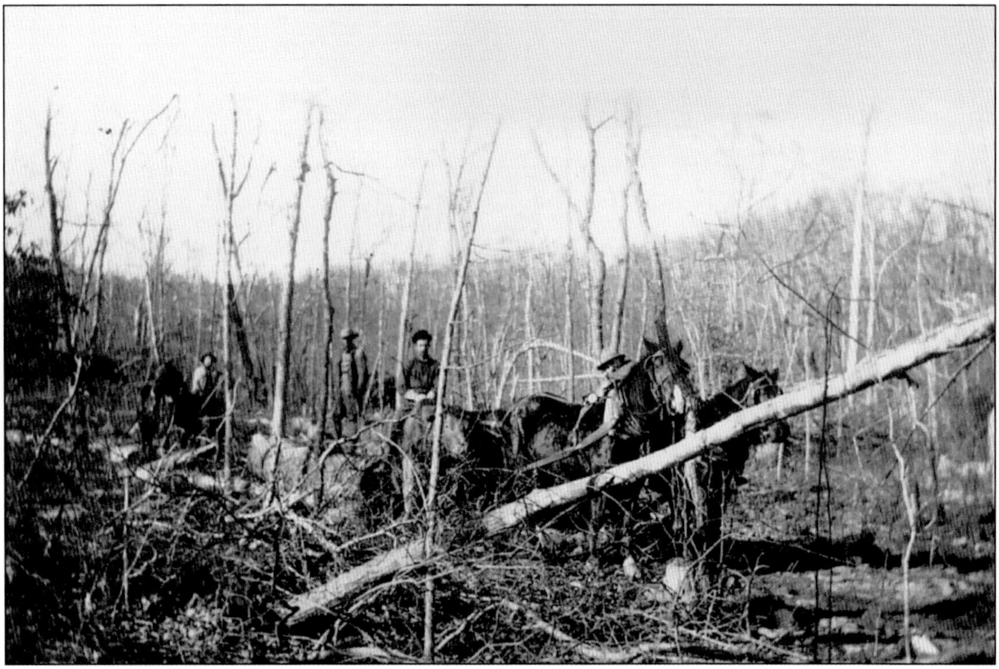

LOGGING—ALWAYS A MAJOR INDUSTRY. Brothers Fred and Glenn Colvard are logging in this *c.* 1922 photo. They made cross ties and switch ties from hardwood lumber to support the Virginia Creeper railroad.

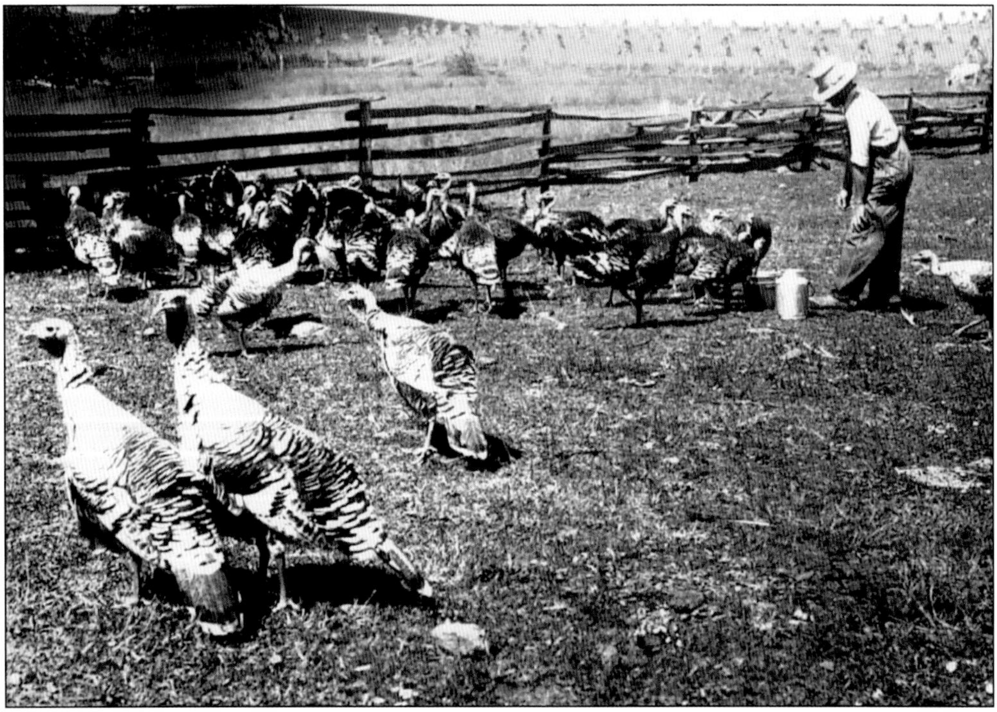

THE TURKEY INDUSTRY. Fred Colvard is pictured above with a flock of turkeys on his farm in the Orion Community, *c.* 1931. Ashe County's turkey industry predated the chicken boom.

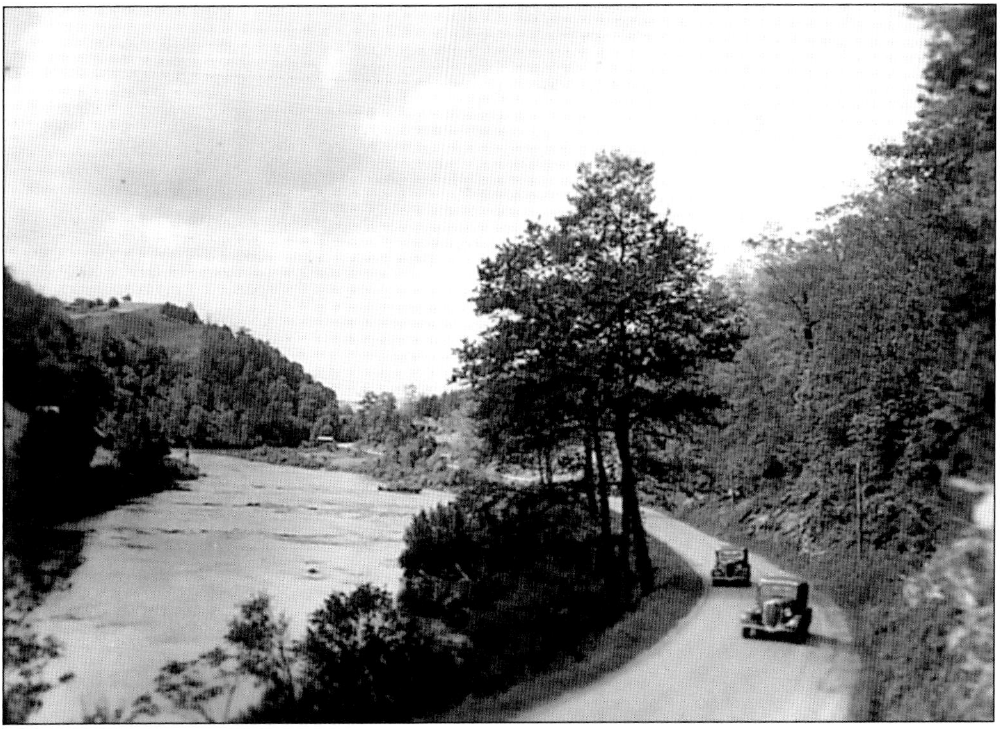

THE NEW RIVER AND HIGHWAY 16, C. 1934. The road to Glendale Springs followed the river as it does today.

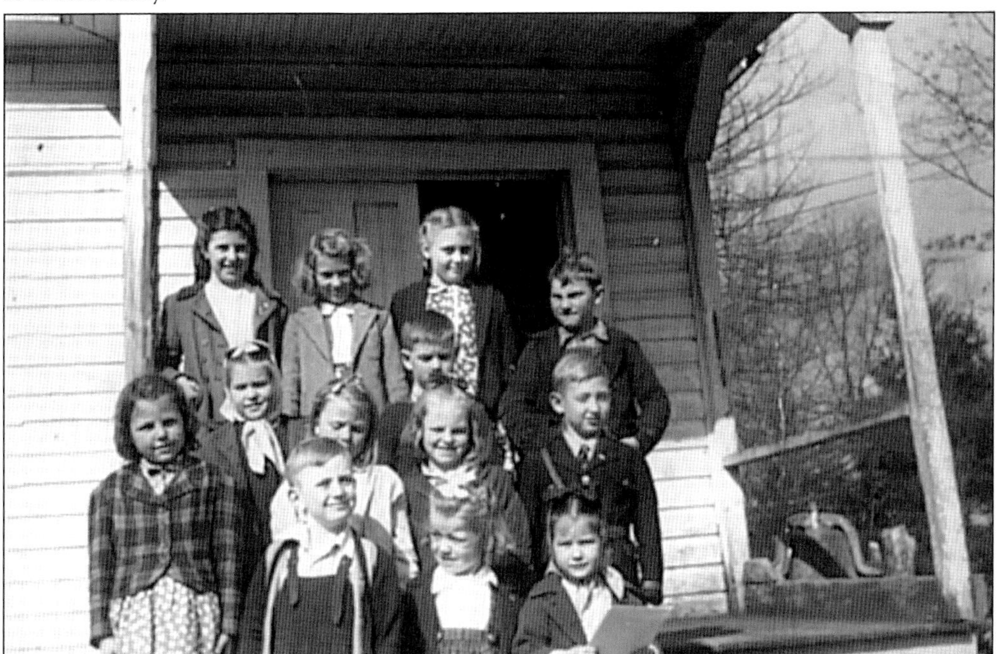

A CLASS OF THE GLENDALE SPRINGS PRESBYTERIAN CHURCH. Included in this *c.* 1944 photograph are Mrs. Delmer Ross's Beginners' Class and Mrs. J.W. Luke's Primary Class. The children raised chickens to make money for their Sunday school projects.

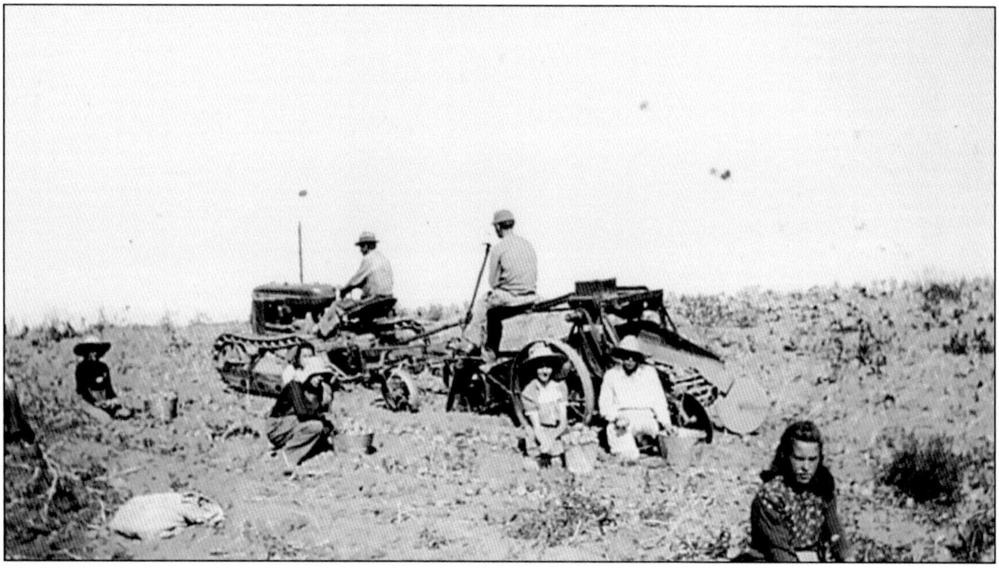

Two Ways to Dig Potatoes. Diggers in the Colvard potato fields of East Jefferson, c. 1940, used both hand-digging and an early example of mechanized potato digging. "Sequoia" potatoes were developed on Colvard Farms and won national fame.

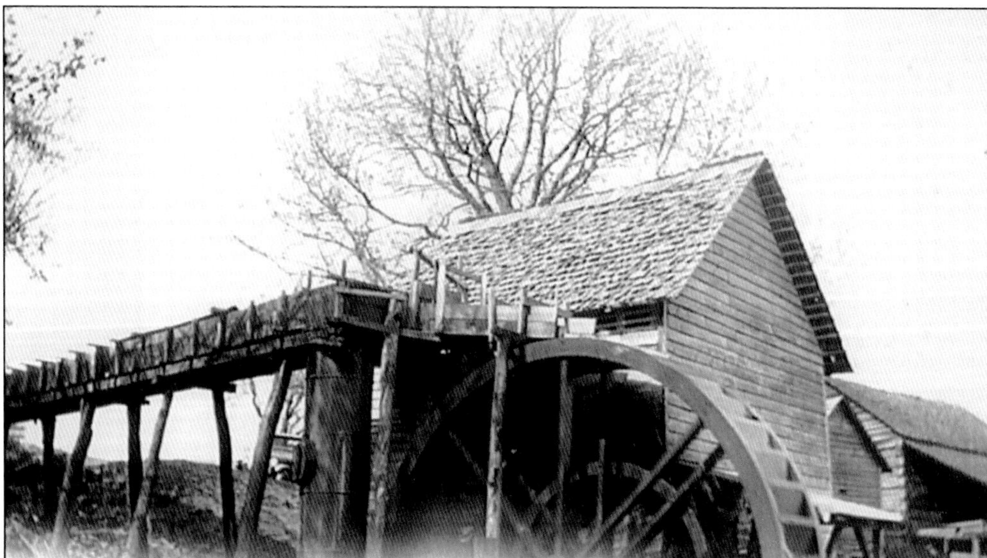

The Lynch Colvard Grist Mill, c. 1945. The lack of proper transportation routes led to the creation of gristmills along creeks. This one was originally the Absalom Bower mill on Naked Creek in the Orion community.

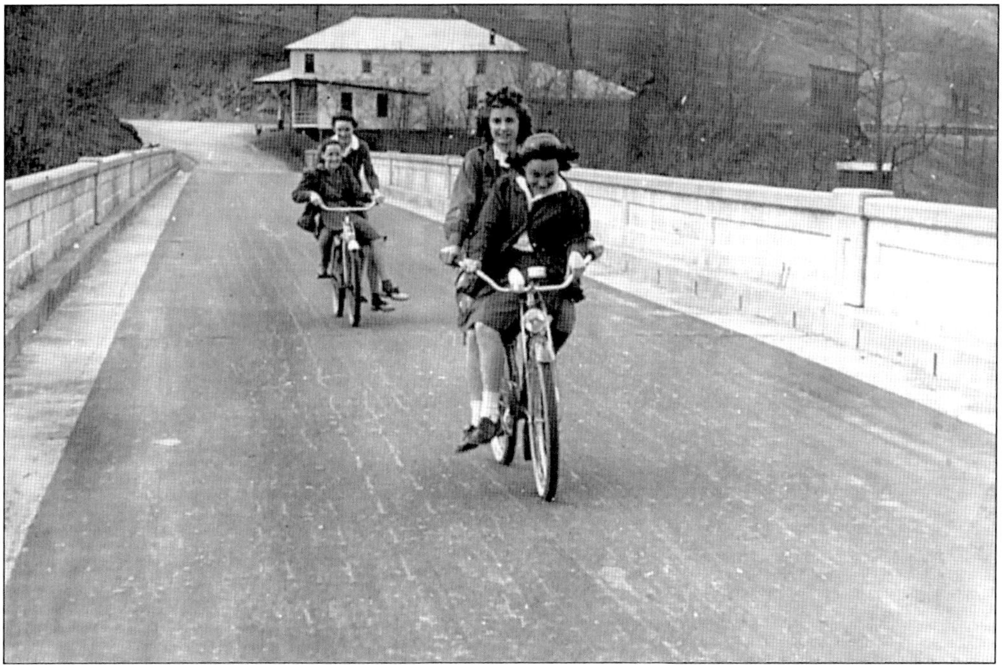

CYCLING OVER THE SOUTH FORK OF THE NEW RIVER, C. 1945. Phyllis Nuckolls is pedaling the lead bicycle. The picture includes Zenna Mae Jones, Clide M. Jones, and Irene Hall. The building in the background is now the New River Outfitters and General Store.

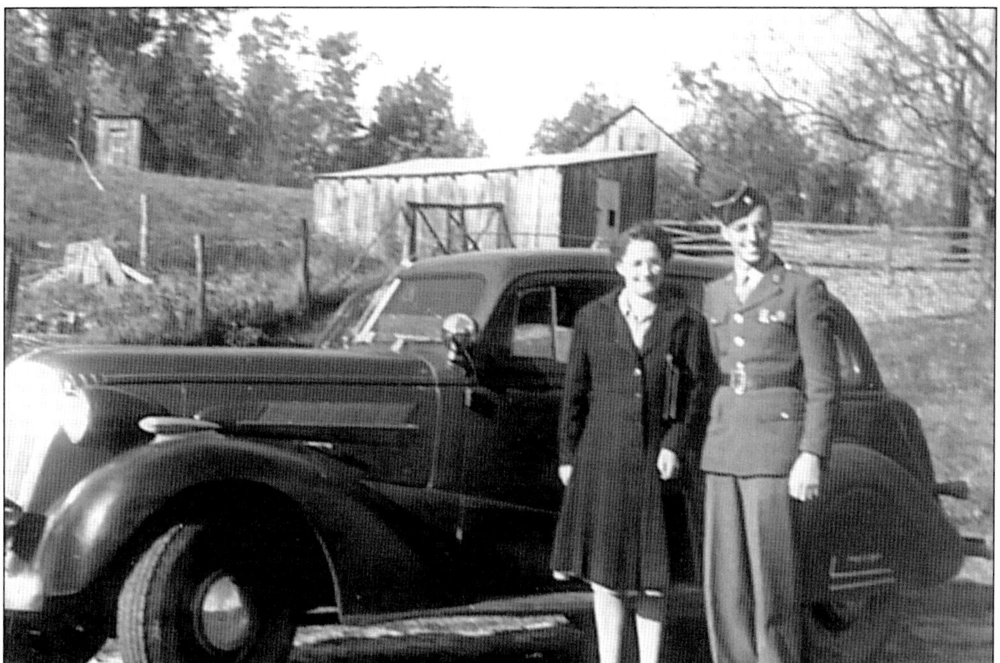

A PROUD MOTHER AND HER SOLDIER SON, C. 1944. Maggie Hill Nuckolls and son, Zane Grey Nuckolls, pose for a picture while he is home on leave.

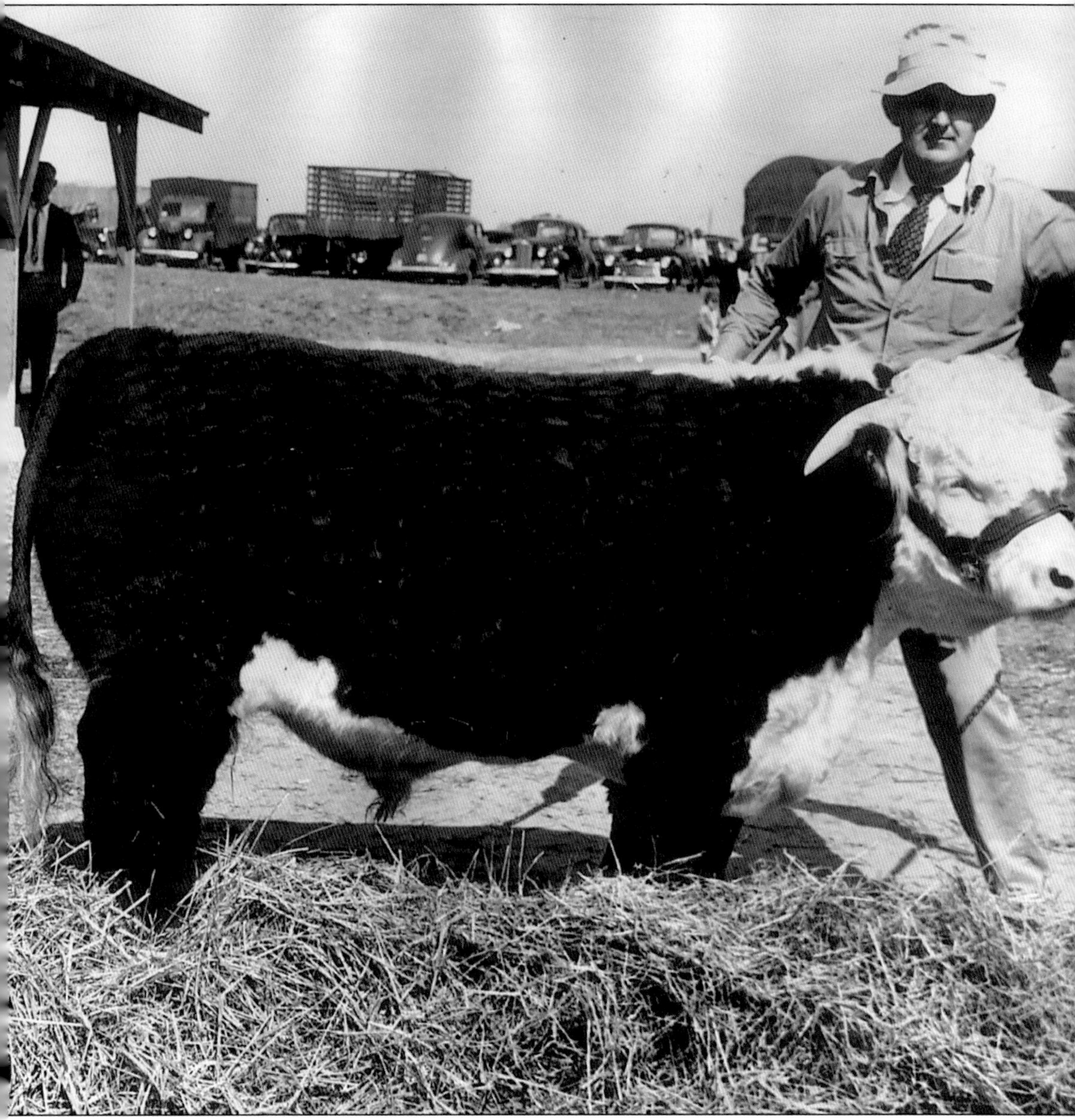

A GRAND CHAMPION. This prize-winning Hereford bull was raised in Laurel Springs on the Doughton Meadows Farm. This 16-month-old Hereford breeder, Meadows Domino 66, won every class he was shown in except one. He was named the grand champion of the NC State Fair and was sold for $10,000. Jim Graham, the superintendent of beef stock at the state fair, is holding the tether in this c. 1949 photo.

MARY LOU COLVARD. Mary Lou is pictured in 1957 in her garden in the Orion Community. The daughter of Virginia Witherspoon Colvard, she was the organist at the Orion Methodist Church for many years.

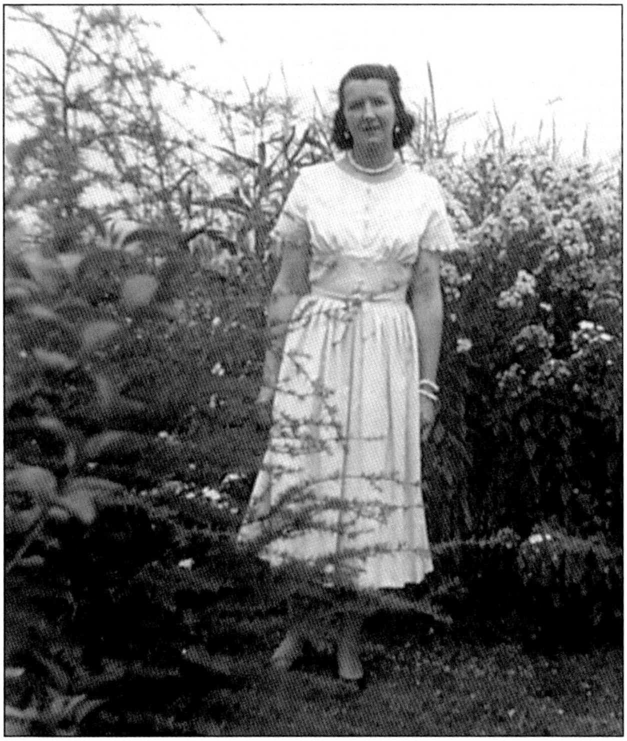

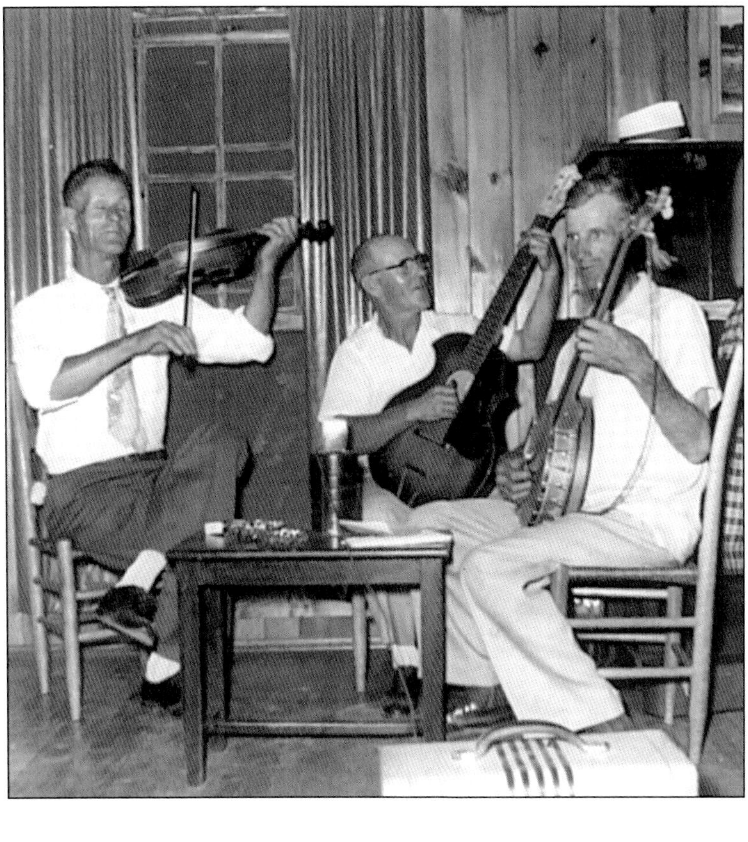

THE HENPECKED HUSBANDS BAND OF SCOTTVILLE. Pictured from left to right are Bill Williams, Charlie Coy, and W.G. Nuckolls, c. 1958.

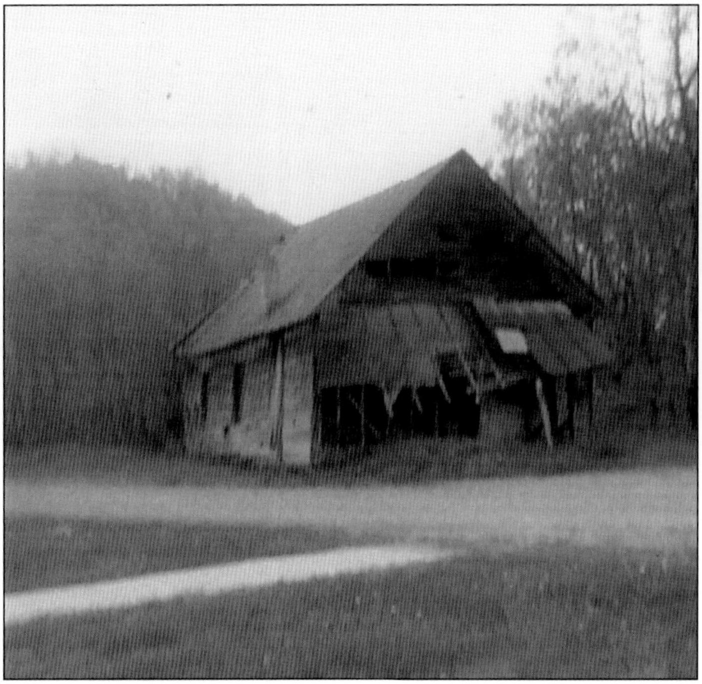

BOGGS SCHOOL. Formerly an important building in the Boggs Community, this old school house, pictured *c.* 1962, closed in the 1940s. During the 19th and early 20th centuries, each community had its own school building.

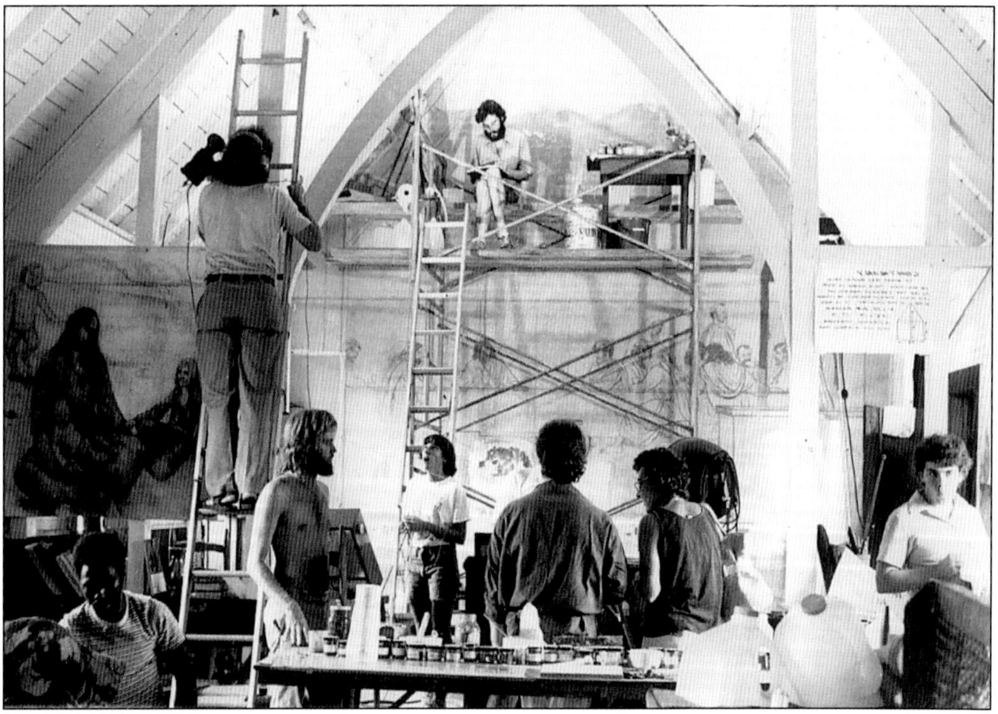

ART IN GLENDALE SPRINGS. While painting *The Last Supper* in 1980, Ben Long sits at the top of the scaffold. He painted four frescoes in two Episcopal churches in Ashe County. The "cartoon" of the fresco is visible on the wall. The young people are some of the students who spent the summer in Ashe County studying the art of fresco painting under the tutelage of artist Ben Long.